INTOXICATED

ANIMA Critical Race Studies Otherwise
A series edited by Mel Y. Chen, Ezekiel J. Dixon-Román, and Jasbir K. Puar

INTOXICATED   RACE, DISABILITY, AND CHEMICAL INTIMACY ACROSS EMPIRE

MEL Y. CHEN

Duke University Press   *Durham and London*   2023

© 2023 Duke University Press
All rights reserved
Printed in the United States of America on acid-free paper ∞
Designed by Courtney Leigh Richardson
Typeset in Portrait by Westchester Publishing Services

Library of Congress Cataloging-in-Publication Data
Names: Chen, Mel Y., [date] author.
Title: Intoxicated : race, disability, and chemical intimacy across empire / Mel Y. Chen.
Other titles: ANIMA (Duke University Press)
Description: Durham : Duke University Press, 2023. | Series: Anima: critical race studies otherwise | Includes bibliographical references and index.
Identifiers: LCCN 2023013436 (print)
LCCN 2023013437 (ebook)
ISBN 9781478025320 (paperback)
ISBN 9781478020561 (hardcover)
ISBN 9781478027447 (ebook)
Subjects: LCSH: Disability studies. | Queer theory. | BISAC: SOCIAL SCIENCE / Ethnic Studies / American / General | SOCIAL SCIENCE / LGBTQ Studies / General
Classification: LCC HV1568.2 .C446 2023 (print) | LCC HV1568.2 (ebook) |
DDC 362.4—dc23/eng/20230901
LC record available at https://lccn.loc.gov/2023013436
LC ebook record available at https://lccn.loc.gov/2023013437

Cover art: Fiona Foley, *Black Opium*, 2006, photo of video in "Bliss" room. Photo: Mel Y. Chen.

For Julia, my person

CONTENTS

Acknowledgments ix

INTRODUCTION 1
Intoxications, Intimacies, and Interformations

1 SLOW CONSTITUTION 18
Down Syndrome and the Logic of Development

2 AGITATION AS A CHEMICAL WAY OF BEING 62

3 UNLEARNING 100
Intoxicated Method

AFTERWARDS 142
Telling the End Not to Wait

Notes 165
Bibliography 177
Index 187

ACKNOWLEDGMENTS

All those I am forgetting, because I hope you know, and I still forget.

So many to name, in order without logic, and with a sense of gratitude for their holding: Courtney Berger, the best editor I can imagine, the enthusiastic visionary Ken Wissoker, and the rest of Duke University Press—the board, the staff, and all those helping these books emerge. Thank you! Anne-lise Francois, Natalia Brizuela, Karen Nakamura, Cori Hayden, Michelle Murphy, Maxe Crandall, Diana Cage, River Barad, Zamira Ha, Nova Ha-Choy, Eli Clare, Sue Schweik, Sunaura Taylor, Georgina Kleege, Alanna Thain and Nik Forrest, Erin Manning. Salar Mameni. Roshanak Kheshti. Amber Straus for the chicken soup. My incredible students, all. My colleagues at UC Berkeley in Gender and Women's Studies who make the academic life feel rightly tuned: Paola Bacchetta, Courtney Desiree Morris, Patrice Douglass, Barbara Barnes, Eric Stanley, Minoo Moallem, Laura Nelson, Leslie Salzinger, Elora Shehabuddin. One who has changed my thinking being in ways I am still finding out: Trinh T. Minh-ha. Judith Butler. Althea Grannum-Cummings, Sandra Richmond, Lani Hunt. Macarena Gomez-Barris. Vivian Huang. Ianna Hawkins Owen. Dana Luciano. Eben Kirksey. Jack Halberstam. Lawrence Cohen. Sharad Chari, Karl Britto, Nadia Ellis. Nathan Snaza. Julietta Singh. Riley Snorton. Hentyle Yapp. Former students more recent: Natalia Duong, Brandon Callender, Julia Havard, Caleb Luna, Kia Middleton, Takeo Rivera, Shakthi Nataraj, Mihiri Tillakaratne, Thea Gold, Amy Fujiwara Shen, Katrina Dodson, Ivan Ramos, Sean McKeithan, Alexa Punnamkhuzyil. Charlotte Prodger, Kira Hall, Aimee Bahng, Ari Heinrich, Huma Dar, Kiran Asher, Eli Nelson, Banu Subramaniam, Sushmita Chatterjee, Jan Grue, Eva Hayward, Aimee Bahng, Lisa Lowe, Julia Watts Belser, Marcia Ochoa, Susan Stryker, Hsuan Hsu, Cynthia Wu, River Barad, Erin Manning, Nejat Kedir, Haden Smiley, Mana Hayakawa,

Sanzari Aranyak, Anicka Yi, Ari Heinrich, Ahmed Ragab, Martin Manalansan, Lochlann Jain, A. K. Burns, Jake Kosek, Jerry Zee, Noenoe Silva, Jonathan Goldberg-Hiller, Alisa Bierria, Juliann Anesi, Lana Lin, T. T. Takemoto, Amy Sueyoshi, Nirmala Erevelles, Vanessa Agard-Jones, Carolyn Dinshaw, Carla Freccero, James Kyung-jin Lee, and Jill Casid. Mimi Khúc. Jina Kim. Sami Schalk. Kyla Tompkins. Susan Chen. Jih-Fei Cheng. Jian Chen. Lauren Kaminsky. Zakiyyah Iman Jackson. Candice Lin for sharing ratty brilliance: I get to write about your work now. Jasbir K. Puar, with whom I'm so fortunate to have worked and thought with all these years as coeditors of *Anima*, and Ezekiel Dixon-Roman, our new and wonderful coeditor. Williams College Art History and Women's Gender and Sexuality Studies, where I served as Clark Professor and where Marc Gottlieb, Robert Wiesenberger, and Emmelyn Butterfield-Rosen made ways better and Vivian Huang and Ianna Hawkins Owen brought queer home. My gracious hosts and students at Harvard's Studies of Women, Gender, and Sexuality, where I served as Matthiessen Visiting Professor of Gender and Sexuality for a resident six weeks before the pandemic hit and where Amy Parker was a thoughtful and kind manager.

All those audiences who shared important insights over the years and who had the kindness to invite me.

Bibimbap, my daughter, a cat who years ago taught me to eat with others again and who peed on both my first conference jacket and the keyboard I used to write my first book. My mother, Ruth, with an unstoppable mind and craft of words and just core drive; "Plants want to live," she said, and she knows. My father, Michael, whose tender and pure heart and curiosity about the world makes his stunning erudition a feature of his modesty. Friend. My brother Derek, who shares in everything and is open to all of it, with whom I have come through grief. Julia Bryan-Wilson has fed me, with words and delicious things, and has also touched me daily with her extraordinary commitment to finding and making worlds together while loving me fiercely; and I've learned immeasurably from her trenchant and informed and also real talk approaches to art. And her, now my, family—Trent, Seth, Lucia, Rosy, D'Arcy, Becca, Susan, Carroll. Kyla Schuller, who reintroduced me to toad in a way that I never anticipated. Broad, gray Warty and inch puck orange Elmer, glorious toads from our yard and from the Michigan lakeshore. A. B. Huber, who knows how to keep me feeling alive. Endjah, having experienced with me sustaining revelations of the Queer Women of Color Media Arts Project (itself wondrously back in my life, helmed by Madeleine Lim and Kebo Drew), held on with some fundamental trust as I struggled through illness and alienation: they assured me when I emerged, "Mel was just down the street." Devi Peacock came in like they'd always been there, reminding me how I could draw new lines around and through my and our worlds. And also Cassandra Falby, Ajuan Mance, Yeva Johnson, Maura King, Indigo Som: QTPOC4SHO on you go and thank you for chortling me and also holding each other through this pandemic. Chantelle van Heerden and Julia Bryan-Wilson helped to break my blocks by promising to "look at it," and even outside of their immense feedback, ushered this book out of an unreachable para-time; and they were followed up in the close reading by dear friends and immense thinkers Chad Shomura and Tim Choy. I am also grateful to Eben Kirksey and an anonymous reader for their own pivotal feedback on the full manuscript. Pamela Lee and Geoff Kaplan for food, laughing, crying, and taking care. Karin Martin and Amy Yunis for being our COVID movie night—couldn't have done it without you—and for ongoing meaningful friendship at the core. Margaret Benson-Thompson carved out space and urging together: "Maybe it'll happen this decade—but it doesn't have to happen at the end of it!" Mikey stepped into the blanket crostata just as I finished wrapping it for him, and offered his chin to tuck it under: he knew this completed me. Fiona Foley told me all about the tawny frogmouth family perched above her house, pointing to the branches where they had been, and that held me as much as the scene of her prodigious book research sprawled on the interior table. And Margo Rivera-Weiss drew with me in Oakland taquerias and cafes, making a home that still grows, and yet they are already gone—but I'll see you on the dim sum cart, my dear friend. "Crip Jean," meaning Alison Kafer, Eunjung Kim, and Julie Minich, my collaborators and friends who found ourselves writing the introduction to *Crip Genealogies* in the middle of the pandemic, and going every which way together. Alison, you have held me with forms of deep recognition and acceptance that I have not known otherwise. Gil Hochberg, family. In all of this unparalleled resonating, my beloveds make everything make sense when it makes no sense (and needs to), and thus have brought me from the heaviest brink countless times. Thank you for helping me to live right and to hold to and grow on that life like the thing that it is, and not the thing it's supposed to be. To think, and also to not think. We're a mess, a beautiful mess.

INTRODUCTION INTOXICATIONS, INTIMACIES, AND INTERFORMATIONS

This is a strange book; welcome. Please know, at the outset, that I wrote this book for several reasons, only some of them rational. Perhaps bearing the intractable burden of a second book,[1] it is written with both openness and fracture, moments of novel legibility even as the text reaches for different registers, tries to set different prints. I still follow what seems inevitably to be a characteristic mode of transdisciplinary scholarship with a dance between density and touch.

Intoxicated attends to the fibrillations of what we might call an affective nexus between race and disability—not as they are, or should have been, but as they seem to become. And they do become; even if racial or disabled *identity* can be experienced as permanent or immutable, scholars in both major specialties know the immense complexity in their lives as notions. Neither is given, not even when historically situated; rather, each is unstable, protean;

each is also given extraordinary potency. Is the race/disability nexus I attend to a peculiar one? Perhaps, given the spatiotemporal paths I choose to traverse here, which I visit more than a hundred years ago but are still ever-present in England, Australia, and beyond, and given that the global enactment of the nineteenth-century British commonwealth was itself peculiar. The archival cases that I bring forward here—particularly from a mainstream biopolitical imagination of contemporary life—might also appear fairly peculiar when examined in queer, disability, and critical race modes of thinking.

At some signal moments in the book, I turn to the nineteenth century as a way to make sense of contemporary entanglements of intoxication, race, disability, and sexuality—what I am calling "chemical intimacy"—for it is in the nineteenth century that many of the dramas seen today were formatively staged and given a kind of patterned shape. In two of the historical precedents considered in this book—the case of "mongoloid idiocy" introduced in 1866 in England and the Aboriginals Protection and Restriction of the Sale of Opium Act from 1897 in Queensland, Australia—one can perceive the presence of quantified and qualified raciality. In the first, proto-Asian and white raciality as viewed through European scientific categorization appear together in an intellectually disabled person. In the second are fairly insistent deployments of Chinese and Aboriginal-Torres Strait Islander as well as white raciality primarily in relation to questions of racial integrity through sexual reproduction. If racial essences or materials are present, raciality consists in how the encounter between racial beings is given *reconstituting* meaning, and what additional potency is lent by the *consequential* (non-incidental) presence of intoxication in both scenes.

The need to investigate ongoing interactions between race and disability cannot be overstated, as scholarly work and many recent activist movements—disability justice and the Movement for Black Lives among them—have helped to make clear. Environmental justice movements of all kinds have, furthermore, made the point that racialized and Indigenous peoples are overwhelmingly made to absorb environmental harms (and their associated disabilities, to the extent that they rise to thresholds and priorities of identification), often over generations. And if the occupation of a racially gendered position is enough to discredit someone intellectually, then the dyad between race and disability is well entrenched indeed. But exactly how is it that some forms of disability themselves bear distinctly racial histories? I wouldn't allow that one just falls out of the other, as many still claim about race—that race is simply derivative of class, or that one is simply a nuance of another.[2] Nor would I insist on the uselessness of one or another term, as if disability were simply "white" or race were simply, at this point, institutional; I continue to hear versions of both. Rather, I accept that race and disability live with deep mutual entanglement; and I have also spent too long in these weeds to call any of this obvious or formulaic. There is, and was, far too much traffic, too much mysterious exchange.

This book adds itself to these voices plumbing the entanglement, with a plea that—owing to its mode of knowledge making—perhaps you may see fit to take note of resonances rather than seek out thorough coverage, resonances in surprising places. This is a book that disavows the consolidated areal metaphor of coverage, of thorough aboutness—another form of cripping in a place where transdisciplinary objects already push exhaustive diligence out of practical reach.[3] One aboutness that has surprised me, however, is the insistent presence of the university: in many ways this book concerns itself with the politics of knowledge in the academy. Perhaps in response, I'm letting go here of a thoroughly, neatly tight grasp on a form of scholarship that grates hard on its material, too hard anymore. Instead, that will come and go with the moment; read what you like; take in the proximities that you seek. Included in what I am letting go is a sense of thoroughness or readerly currency in citational practice, and I write this with some apprehension; to speak to this question directly, even if reparative citation refuses to accumulate canonical intellectual property, it still attempts to give rightful credit to names and traditions. But non-thoroughness isn't only a directed political curation of the type that Katherine McKittrick would dub citational "erasure" (following Sara Ahmed's announced programmatic refusal to cite white men), nor is it, in McKittrick's further historicizing of Ahmed's intervention, a longer-established, clear-visioned black studies praxis or method "that helps us, collectively, understand and navigate and perhaps undo the wrongness of the world . . . not about who belongs and who does not belong in the index or the endnotes; rather, it is how we, collectively, are working against racial apartheid and different kinds and types of violence."[4] The wish is there to build citational company in shared reparative spirit; neurodivergence however queers even anti-imperial citation, because accretive iteration itself runs out of time, giving way to agitated reading, slow thinking, agitated writing, slow reading, agitated thinking, slow writing. And sometimes the fog doesn't clear.[5]

There is one *seemingly* unlikely place where the nexus between race and disability vibrates, has vibrated, quite resoundingly, and yet is perhaps one of the most transparent participants in becoming, for it represents nothing but change. Change that tips into damage, or threatens abandonment, spiritual escape, or even revolution, or all three. That place is toxicity—or intoxication. Both toxicity and intoxication hover around disability (as intoxicated incapacity or depressed capacity, for example); and because of the chemical intimacies attached to race, they also hover around that. If you join me for these archival explorations, you will witness intoxication's explosive role in two scenes that became immensely relevant for the disability-race nexus, and in very different ways. The telling that is most attendant to history's abuses is that oppressive policy and settler colonial imagination made it a likelihood that Indigenous land and the surrounds of many racial others would be most exposed to toxic chemicals.

And this is true. I also had some different questions. I wanted to know how the inedible soup of illusion and design sloshed and cavorted into beloved beings, altering their lives and deaths forever. I wanted to describe beyond doubt the doubling effect in which chemical abuses were followed by discrediting of the beings so affected. You can call that racism, settler colonialism, and it is; but it also has more to teach me. I delved into a nineteenth-century historical archive (which appears in chapter 1), that of John Langdon Down, because I finally had to face it, after years of disbelief, that someone could gamble, and so ostentatiously, to make connections that had no business being made. Later I realized how ordinary and in-line his scholarly gesture was, and how ordinary it might still seem today, but with a few tweaks. And I thought about the making of connections that had no business being made and wondered about that; that's when I decided to look at Down's archive more closely. Which connections had no business being made? It was no longer an example of "look how bad it got," but of "think twice, it's right here next to us."

But all the above still discusses intoxication like it's only a violent reflex of pollution, coming on like a wave from elsewhere. I also wonder about what it brings in spite of itself, and how it has been welcomed, even desired. In other words, I want to consider here intoxication's own capabilities—the ways it seems to enable taking leave of a flattening, even murderous present, to a temporal and sensory otherwise, to a place of tolerability. Is there a way in which it is matched, even suited, to the resonant natures of race: that racial beings often feel so much more spectacular than, so much more than, what is alleged?

Intoxications

Besides the fraught and mobile *toxic* in *intoxicated*, my subtitle highlights the terms *chemical* and *intimacy*. This introduction would be the place where one might define them. Yet I have always resented definitions. They distort, they territorialize, and they feel compulsory, particularly to someone who couldn't easily feel their way to the center of a word. My training as a cognitive linguist—which I sought in part because of the elusive mystery that language represented, and the promise of what I took as word puzzles—has lent "professional" heft to my suspicion that definitions are too prescriptive, not allowing for the semantic play and richness of, say, metonymies, subordinated or peculiar meaning; who's to say that that over there is not more important? Sometimes, but only sometimes, "subordinated metonymies" are also the affirmation of subordinated knowledges. At other times they mark the possibility of an experiment of contiguity without propriety. My investment as a teacher and scholar has been to decenter approaches to learning that take some simplified definition as a fulcrum, because it then delimits what can happen. A book's introduction is usually the location where an author's terms are provisionally sketched, but true to form I begin *Intoxicated* obliquely. Besides representing a kind of chemical intimacy, toxicity subtends the entire project, and it is explicitly consequential for each of the historical touchstones studied in this book, including how they are approached.

If we were to try to reflect on means by which things come to operate, then toxicity behaves like an affect, an affect from which both toxin and intoxication can also be derived. But why not turn to primary references from medicine or science? Firstly, medicine or science cannot be primary arbiters in this book, even if they inevitably participate in my thinking. Both domains—diverse and contradictory as each is—suffer from heavy capitalization and the burden of interest. To take one example that has stayed with me all these years, Michelle Murphy made clear in their book on sick building syndrome that early versions of toxic thresholds in the regulation of chemicals in the United States were defined only with regard to one type of ill for human being—cancer—and even then, with the caveat that such definitions must not interrupt the flow of the chemical industry.[6] Such invested policy suggests that both the designated-toxic and the designated-nontoxic cannot help but be equally implicated in chemicality. How we then define where chemicality begins and ends becomes not a question of quantification, threshold, scientific trace, or material history alone. This is important, because some of the scenes in this book are about domains that have been securely established as a chemical absence, or seem not to be concerned with chemicals at all. While I am more interested in the management of matter that could become lively, whether living or not, I remain drawn to scenes in which chemicality could be not only a racial allegation but a constitutional appliance.

Whatever scientific definitions of toxicity I am sympathetic to are outrun by what I would argue are the forces of communal emotion, government, and economic policy; as a comparator from this contemporary moment, consider the invested, quite incompatible definitions for the COVID-19 virus (*not quite a toxin, behaves like a toxin, behaves like an affect*): the scientific community's or epidemiologist's rendering of the coronavirus, versus the right-wing imagination of a hostile bioterrorism from Chinese people (the "China virus"). Affect is agnostic with regard to the material bindings of its operands, which is precisely what makes affect a punt for some thinkers but useful here for the surprises it reveals. Toxicity generally is taken as a severe affect, one that frequently threatens death. But in the United States, intoxication, differently, seems to carry a milder aspect. Whereas the term *toxicity* advertises severity and the threat of permanence, the term *intoxication* suggests inconsequentiality, everyday tolerability and easy recoverability, and carries sensibilities of freedom, gentle excess, or moderation—with the exception that *legal* intoxication might yield blunted responsibility for severe harms caused by the intoxicated.

But one of the most harmful aspects of oversight is to consider toxicity as a unipolar phenomenon—almost as if to follow its cue of exception—rather than as something rampantly interwoven with other phenomena. In this book I map some of the ways that toxicity, disability, and race live—and have lived—together, in rich exchange, in what could be considered an affective approach to select scenes of chemicality, the toxic spectacular along with the toxic ordinary going back to the turn of the twentieth century. The forms of coexistence, communion, and multipronged governance mapped here illustrate the hostile and sometimes beautiful confusion happening all at once, and reveal forms of becoming that do not hew to fantasied integrities achievable only in sites of advantage. That is, the colonialities that are sometimes identified as so neat as to be simply diagnostic are just one of many points of failure.

In some ways this book extends the argument that a state archive and its controlling fantasy are superseded, challenged, by its referents, living or dead. I take the argument further to profile means of art and worldmaking that occur within and nearby the educational sphere; that include and even embrace forms of intoxication that not only debunk traditional forms of order, but also allow the seeking of forms of collective indistinction, restfulness in non-masterful partiality, vibrations of different, truer coherence.

Toxicity also takes on a particular vibrancy in relation to debility, a term whose relevance to this project has been made profoundly available by Jasbir K. Puar.[7] I find that disability and debility remain in vivid exchange, exchange that is more complex than polarity or binarity, and that care about the conditions of their interaction is important. If disability has a significant adherence to administrative being, then debility tells of the conditions of, or forewarning, disablement (that may never be recognized as such), including statistical materializations that are beholden to necropolitical arrangements. Debility is the secret behind the cultivated fantasy of the autonomous imperial, neoliberal body that falls all too neatly into place for well-ensconced structural conditions best positioned to take advantage of legal measures like the American Disabilities Act.

This book's approach to toxicity, understood in its capacious, expanded sense as a form of troubled, changing, or compelling intimacy, allows the exploration of repulsive political affects and dynamics wrought through a fantasy of chemical exchange. In this approach, substances—even nonmaterial but deeply consequential entities such as the bodies of finance capital—are carriers of political meaning and, in their effectivity and rationalization, and their shared occupation of medicalized discourse, lend themselves to embodied logics, sharing more rather than less with what are understood as "actual" toxins. Furthermore, distinctions between "intoxication" and "toxicity" reveal themselves to be non-neutral differences that articulate through affects and temporalities.

Intimacies

Much like any form of influence, perhaps, toxicity rearranges matter—at least as far as whatever is deemed "intoxicated" may be concerned, meaning that it also rearranges the world. It can kill a body, or affect a group. It also has the potential to modify feeling itself, whether in terms of emotion, or its broader analogue, affect. The sense of ensemble can shift, altering bonds, even the nature of kin itself, including how kinning itself is done. It is important to note that although a threat or alteration (indeed, queering) of reproductivity is the most obvious aspect of sexuality to attend questions of toxicity (such as species or human familial survival in a polluted environment), there are many other factors relating to the movement of a group through time and its means of being affected; associated questions of inheritance, transfer, and gender also become exposed to queer possibility. Furthermore, the intimacies—the active proximities and resonant alignments wrought by "toxic substances" that are brought in line with bodily sites and systems—are many; but they extend well beyond the individuated body, particularly when they become a matter of governance, a management of chemicality that works across communities, across populations.

Some kinds of affections linger; they can become habitual, too. I have written about intoxication before. The concluding two chapters of my first book, *Animacies*, explored the affective worlds linking pollutants, including those categorized as toxins under certain conditions (lead, mercury), and their dangerously proximate (nominally) human bodies further marked by conditions of relative vulnerability to forms of structural and other violence.[8] There, while traveling the affective depths of the administration of lead, I began to appreciate not only the truly prodigious contemporary reach of intoxication logics, but also their concentration around—and underneath—the modern categories of race and disability, each of which has taken on an administrative function in addition to its layered hauntings. It was not enough to take each as an ostensible integrity upon itself, however, because they have long been intertwined, interconstituted, partly through the destructive tools of colonialism: in particular, the securing of administrative benefit through the fictitious measurement and also spiritual indictment of capacity to secure what could then be presented as a purportedly immanent achievement of the circumscribed human—the governor, the propertied, the worthy.[9]

In the time since I concluded that research, I developed an even greater sense of the importance of the transnational, in all its senses, to a historically textured apprehension of race or disability. Coming to terms with the fabric of the transnational lives of race, time, and disability meant locating some moments in which race and disability's historical mutual imbrications were traceable in their generativity, especially where the status of one or another as an administrative category was still inchoate. It remains important, certainly, not to reanimate race as a unified abstraction without living specificity, without living meaning, unless it had consequence precisely as such an abstraction.

Why does intoxication often lurk in scenes where race and disability come together? Because, first and foremost, it is a means of "constitution by policy," not only an attempted disablement of a population but a tamping down of what is imagined to be a "cleanly" cognitive mode of resistance by legal or other means of distinction. But also: Because it is taken as spiritual, metaphysically liberating, even cosmic; because it involves the disordering of things, sometimes by blurring, sometimes by rendering spectacular; because it is worldmaking, and world collapsing.

As I argue, intoxication could never be taken as innocuous from the point of view of governing. In turn of the twentieth-century Australia, Aboriginals' "protection" from opium's ills, for the Queensland legislators, was but a posture for the implementation of drastic punitive and radical forms of economic expropriation, containment, and gendered and sexual control. Disability, in its turn, appears not only as a threatened result of racial mixing (as deficiency or the weakening of white stock) but also in other modes of constitution that are particular to the intoxicatory scenes of each of the archival nineteenth-century cases in this book. Note: I call these "archival" only because they were partly touchable through archives.

In particular, there is something about opium's temporal characteristics as a drug (and in its particular formulations in England, as well as in Queensland) that interacted in strange and compelling ways with the temporal characteristics of the *images* of slowness, proto-disabilities in the form of intellectual delay and Indigenous workers' purported "malingering," that were arguably undergoing description in London and Queensland, respectively. And it becomes clear, too, that race and disability in their eclectic configurations could not be considered as segregated integrities, but as interacting participants *within* the shifting integrities understood to be provisionally human individuals or people of some kind, subject to overlapping, if not identical, regimes of judgment and manipulation.

In chapter 1, "Slow Constitution: Down Syndrome and the Logic of Development," I begin by tracing the antecedents of slowness in theories of race as well as disability. Moving to my first archival study, the case of mongoloid idiocy (Down syndrome), I extend the focus on constitution to consider what I call racial tuning and chemical suitability, and understand environmental injustice (and environmental privilege) in terms of "constitution by policy." One condition for this suitability in Down's case might well have had to do with the disseminating knowledge, including sensory knowledge, of opium's effects in China—and in Chinatowns in London. The constitution by environmental substances, or environmentalization, can be found in the popular contemporary depictions of slow-moving zombies and their attachment to signifiers of urban decay, as well as capital indebtedness. Slowness is indeed an artifice of capitalist modernity's and neoliberalism's self-imagination: with the delineation of speed and efficiency come the identification of what they would overcome or outdo. But the resistances to such speeding orders are complicated and often compromising. If academic labor has been subjected to increased speeds (and it has, differently across the categories of employ), attempts to modulate such forces are found in attempts to outline gently resistant (yet still neoliberally aligned) and individually "sustainable" practices like those found in a recent book entitled *Slow Professor*.[10] Much as these moments of coming-to allow for improved forms of self-care, this management approach skims the surface of speed's global casualties.

But slowness is also an imputed characteristic of intellectual disability, which is all too often unjustly projected as productive time's other; and slowness furthermore is a feature of reclaimed, anticapitalist crip time: Retorts the person with muscle weakness or brain fog, "I'll finish it when I finish it." And again, slowness is a feature of the global imagination of the relative development of nation-states, which has a legacy relationship to colonial economies. These are not unrelated: consider the long-burnished destructive fictions that continue today, of the indolent, languorous, unproductive racialized worker from southern climes; or that of the mechanically repetitive, asocial, subhuman Asian that has been produced from the point of view of US illusions of labor. Racism often has a polarizing temporality, and in this chapter I discuss the insistent *decelerations* of racialized chemical intimacies.

In chapter 2, "Agitation as a Chemical Way of Being," I lay out agitation's primacy in such seemingly alienated domains as Western biomedicine, education, and political agency and expression. I explore agitation's underexplored valence as a chemically intimate or multiply intoxicated way of being, and move to entitle the racialized gestural lives of disabled, including environmentally harmed, people, as legitimately political acts alongside the choreographed gestures of muscular, avidly nondisabled protest. I briefly revisit the scene of opium in China, historicizing beyond and after the nationalist actions of Lin Tse Hsu, to break out the diverse roles it played in bodily politics and regime change. Then, against the temptation I have laid out previously to revalorize agitation as having potential for resistive, rather than delegitimated, being, I turn to explore the possibilities (and abuses) of white agitation, in particular the forms of white violence and spatial aggressions made so apparent in scenes of police violence and the January 6, 2021, occupation of the US Capitol. I conclude with a turn to "nonhuman" agitation, that of ash, in a commissioned work of Badtjala artist Fiona Foley that is installed at the Brisbane Magistrates Court in Queensland, Australia.

Chapter 3, "Unlearning: Intoxicated Method," continues with Foley's work, while first considering the question of differential being and emergent agitation in the university. Foley's *Black Opium* installation in the Queensland State Library stages a site of learning kin to, but precisely not located in, the university proper. I continue with an attention to the intense bodyminded choreographies of the university where it comes to its unreal demands on cognition, juxtaposing it with the everydayness of brain fog. Michelle Murphy, in "Alterlife and Decolonial Chemical Relations," writes, particularly in mind of Indigenous life: "Studying alterlife requires bursting open categories of organism, individual, and body to acknowledge a shared, entangling, and extensive condition of being with capitalism and its racist colonial manifestations."[11] Inspired by Murphy's injunction to do better than recycling and thus reinstituting damage in chemical study, I attempt to profile and honor Foley's lead rather than following the extractive script, mindful of my own ongoing accountabilities.

I close with a turn to intoxicated method as a justified mode of (dis)engagement; it is a mode of unlearning in part precisely through the ways it allows metaphysical suspension or worldmaking already established. This is not so much a question of drug voluntarism, though it could be, as it is a form of "(in)toxic(ated) historical presentism." In a time of pandemic and wildfires, it is not only the ash shearing out of place; climate change is throwing spaces and places asunder in ways that outscale the habitual temporalities of the manageable for a critical majority. One of the consequences is the divide between private and public in relation to the management of viral and ash particles, and its inutility outside of the schemes of the propertied. I extend some of these thoughts in my brief "Afterwards: Telling the End Not to Wait," on "edge times" and the climate experiment that draws all in its clasp. I consider a queer-crip imaginary as proffered (in my reading, opportunistically) by artist Mai-Thu Perret, in a 2007 work titled *Underground*, rich with ambivalences (as to value) and an explicit discussion of (un)learning. I conclude with a meditation on the underground, affirming and perhaps foregrounding the role of racialized debility-disability in furnishing what Kandice Chuh has called "illiberal, uncommon sensibilities."[12]

Here I feel the need to add a further caution to my approach to both race and disability, marked as troubled terms for me, terms not only historically dynamic but also worth reworking. Beyond sociology, where the term *racialization* refers to the ascription of racial characteristics to a group not otherwise known as such, it is now fairly common interdisciplinarily to use this term to express the ways in which a structure has become, in some way, internally organized, informed, by race or racial difference. But what does it really mean for one notion to inform another—or, taking a different manipulation, to comprise it? Ever attentive to language and its sly relation to materiality, in this book I choose to take race and disability as "notions," not concepts or categories or words, because they no longer feel like any of the latter; they are ideational *and* lexical but not exclusively so, because they cannot map without materiality and they are certainly not separable from it.

A "notion," drawing on feminized and craft associations, can refer to a token commodity (a usage that originated chiefly in the United States in the nineteenth century in the craft arts and that, according to the *Oxford English Dictionary*, referred to: "Small wares, esp. cheap, useful articles. Now chiefly: spec. haberdashery; buttons, hooks, ribbon, thread, etc."), whose minor existence has nevertheless an effervescence of meaning, a creative potential that may or may not be fulfilled, an effervescence whose effect may come from the very opacity and temporality of its constitution.[13] It may sound deeply inadequate for me to state that on their own, notions, particularly the racial and disability notions under formation in the nineteenth century, are fairly meaningless (small wares, "cheap") unless assembled, creatively, with other pieces. This means they cannot stand alone, they cannot be comprehensive, and are dependent. Notions best approximate, to me, race and disability, and are what, through either solidity or intangible evanescence, we engage at our own risk. In her excellent book *Fantasies of Identification*, Ellen Samuels called the nineteenth-century appropriation of early biological characterizations "fantasies of identification," which, she wrote, were "far less concerned with individual identity than with placing that individual within an identifiable group."[14]

Chapters 1 and 2 are organized around states (and archives) that showcase some of the purportedly negative consequences of disabling intoxication, ones that I instead re-narrate as generative facets of racialized chemical intimacy: slowness and agitation. Chapter 3 examines what can be done with the epistemological uncertainties that arise from the clash between unevenly secured civic being and the ongoing material experiments of modernity, what I call unlearning, itself an inherently experimental, anticipatory, and unknowing mode.

Interformations

To end with "unlearning" is not only to valorize and commend the challenging intricacies and promises of agitative art and being with the inherent creativeness of racialized disability, or crip of color being, or the textual forms of undisciplined, transdisciplinary conjuncture and conjecture. I am an academic—and, like many of my colleagues, also neurodivergent, even if I have an unstable relationship with the linguistic signification of this term.[15] Ending with unlearning is also to insist on the seemingly contradictory reason I have so far remained *in* the academy: to help or at least give permission to my students to unlearn the modes of the university that make sensations or assertions of present-day colonialities feel forbidden, that deny colonized or mad positionalities entirely, or shape beings in ways that make them unrecognizable to themselves and their loved ones; to allow for all the ways of being cognitive and also noncognitive, affective, passionate, offscale, and lively, that are disallowed in these stringently classed and racialized intellectual bodily cultures; to allow for necessary work to thrive. Where life has felt possible in the university—and it has, in spite of itself, by virtue of those who also live here—I want for it to feel livable, and to make it more livable still. For that to happen, whether or not knowledge accumulates, unlearning must continue.

My hope in this book is not only to complement a broad revisitation of two archival nineteenth-century moments—moments that retain some awful presence in their legacy, as Fiona Foley, one of the artists whose work has been pivotal to my thinking, makes clear with her work—but also to, along the way, point to the famously protean materialities of a race and disability that in no way could be isolated from one another in the nineteenth century, and arguably still cannot be today, as Moya Bailey and Izetta Mobley outline from a Black feminist perspective.[16] To that end, *Intoxicated* extends the lessons of what might have been called "moments of interformation" toward more contemporary registers, thinking about the ways agitation finds racial and disabled articulation under consideration of environmental harm, white aggression, political resistance, and ordinariness, and about the overlapping intoxicatory unravelings, or unlearnings, of the strictures fomented under the names of race and disability.

In examining legacy effects of historic traces around race and disability, I feel respectful kinship with Chris Bell, including his edited volume *Blackness and Disability*, Alondra Nelson, Leroy Moore, Ellen Samuels, Nirmala Erevelles, Jasbir Puar, Sami Schalk, Moya Bailey, and Therí Alyce Pickens, and many, many other people from whom I continue to learn, among them my editorial co-conspirators in *Crip Genealogies*, as well as the authors within that volume.[17] It feels critically important, also, to follow the impulse we followed in *Crip Genealogies* to look beyond works on "disability" toward works that may not self-announce as being "about" disability in critical ethnic studies, critical race work, Black studies, Asian American studies, Latinx studies, Indigenous studies, and more. Many historical works, of course, do not find easy placement in modern disciplinary and content-field-based nominations. To overlook these works is a practice of injustice, and my intention has been to work across and in relation as best as I am capable and as I learn.

At the same time, it requires more—the hard work of forms of alliance—to reach beyond a field that recommends you stay within its clear boundaries, and to reach in a gesture that may carry the condescension of false inclusion or overwrite. This is not to say, on the other hand, that I have been easily claimed by disability studies, for I suspect some of what I do is dyspeptic to the field. I have longed especially for more kin to think about the troubles and intersections of Asian being and becoming in relation to disability (thanking Cynthia

Wu, James Kyung-jin Lee, Lydia Brown, Eunjung Kim, Natalia Duong, Michelle Huang, Jina Kim, Mimi Khúc, Chad Shomura, Leslie Bow, and many, many more). Even Asian being that also isn't Asian, as we will see: Wu writes, "The challenge for scholars as this line of inquiry moves forward, especially in the field of Asian American studies, is to explore how these interpretive lenses can be repurposed to go beyond—but not transcend—a predictable archive."[18] This book is my effort to continue to think alongside Asianness as a non-isolate and as something that notionally and materially is deeply entangled with other forms of being, and other positionalities, in ways that are both beautiful and devastating.

What are called "race" and "disability" are notions that sum—into labile, responsive form—massive distributions of being, sensation, and matter, distributions with interested histories. Affect studies suggests that if the calculus of race and disability often seems simple or formulaic in terms of legislation, labor practices, or public policy, what it reveals under examination, even within these domains, are deeply contingent, highly specific formulations that only come to seem entrenched and repetitive. It is true not only of race, but of disability, that the scopes of their deployment are endlessly flexible and appropriative. I have thus felt compelled to think in relation to both notions ever since sensing the vastness of their complicity with the mechanisms of capitalism and, by association, education, which inevitably articulates (even if complexly) into majoritarian society and its embroilments.

And yet: At the present moment, both race and disability seem to risk, especially in the fixing language of diversity, being institutionalized as orthogonal in nature to one another rather than co-constitutive. This has resulted in feckless and further harmful administrative "solutions" to diversity problems of insisting, on the one hand, as many US universities have over the last couple of devastating years, that a reckoning about Black lives is possible while looking askance at a history of medical and environmental injustice, or asserting that disability in all its variations during the COVID-19 pandemic could be handled—handily—by turning to the American Disabilities Act, which was never supposed to be anything more than a legal device to encourage or advance compliance. And it is a great disservice to take disability as one and the same with damage, or as a nonintersectional monolith, alien from other more familiar measures, an invocation that I also regularly see. And so, rather than a strikingly unipolar compliance, which in many cases serves as a last resort, I am deeply interested in intimate alliance and its many forms; a willingness to hold many factors while they remain supple, dynamic, and in constant change in relation to one another. My ultimate wish is that of common thriving.

In this spirit, attention not only to the form of knowledge making as method, but also to the *presentation* of knowledge, is important for the writing of this book. Who will read it? How will they want, or need, or wish, to encounter it? How will the forms of address work, as they are perceived? If universal accessibility remains an elusive goal, particularly due to conflicting access needs, what choices does one make? Are there ways to offer choices even in a book that is purportedly linear, in at least a core sense?

Many years ago, when I was midway in my writing of my dissertation, a young colleague asked me, "So what is your argument?" and I promptly found myself both speechless and ashamed. I think that I gently negated the idea that I had one, amid neuroqueer confusion, racial diffidence; I now wonder that someone cared to have the work encapsulated in a sentence or two. She went on to ask, "Well, what is your discipline?" and to my again mumbled description of linguistics and queer studies, she then retorted, "Everyone has a discipline." I remain surprised that one could be certain that things work this way. Even if I got lost in periphrasis, the overarching feeling was that in my mind there was *so much going on*, as well as, of course, a worry about its contents, that perhaps there was nothing of worth there. Is this just neuroqueerness? Brain fog? Interdisciplinarity? Transdisciplinarity? Field specificity is a disciplined want. Looking back, I think rather that on top of what might be called a generalized brain fog, I also had *many* arguments by virtue of the intellectual bridging I was trying to do between fields, and by virtue of not ruling out relevances—and that also meant that disciplinarily I could feel that I had *none*. What a strange load to sit with. Throughout this book, I detail and think from moments in which method is not only confounded, but changed by unexpected circumstance.

I have been struck by this interminable battle in someone who is a seasoned interdisciplinarian, between thinking I have "something," but in such multiplicity that it could be untrainable, and "nothing," not for lack of ideas, but because it feels so diffuse. Kind of like brain fog. But better. Or not better, as the book will eventually claim. This "something or nothing"—this treatment of ideas, or arguments, as fleetingly shaped masses—is not terribly different, as it turns out, from past and present experiences of genderedness, or intersectionally ample being, at the very least when I have tried to understand myself against a national culture or bureaucratic backdrop (not a recommended daily assay for people like us, even if it is required), or, most poignantly, the strictures around a kind of aestheticized minimalism even within intersectional or otherwise sympathetic domains among academic intellectuals. This means that unless you can motivate the inclusion of a particular factor for your argument, it isn't "necessary" to write about, it sits out of place. This happened in relation to queerness for a student for whom I participated in a defense recently: despite the passionate inclusion of queerness in the student's presented method, its necessity was questioned by a colleague otherwise sympathetic to queer studies. This paring down, this praxis of minimalist cropping, is an enormous loss, even if I don't know how to solve it.

The investment in the delivery of a condensed argument—with all respect to arguments and their potency—continues to toss opportunities onto my path. Almost twenty years after the disciplinary/disciplining question, an audience member at Wesleyan commented on a talk I was giving (entitled, in fact, "Something about Nothing"), on trans pronouns and the multilingual stresses, liberties, and assaults of pronominal "it," that they "weren't convinced." I promptly replied with a smile, "I'm not trying to convince you of anything!" and simply stated that I was there to allow for certain new forms of thinking to take place. I leave the rendering as argument to you. Some things haven't changed; I continue to resist what I experience as an often extractive rendering of knowledge making—is "the argument" really all you want, and is it enough?—preferring to rest in the possibilities of worldmaking, of feeling the touch between things, the new, odd, unfamiliar movements that become possible in the encounter. For a given reader, this may resolve into a satisfying form of operationalizable interdisciplinarity, or it may not; perhaps the promise I sense in studying the relationship between race and disability—one of the most vulnerable interchanges at the university—is precisely not in remaking an institution (or buttressing its institutionality), but in the possibility of its unlearning how to be one.[19] The stretch and movement between things, premised on change and even nonidentity, is what makes vivid and, indeed, lasting alliance possible. It turns out that "everybody has a discipline" is not the attitude of most intellectuals and thinkers—just of some well trained in the academy who are so invested in a familiar distribution that it becomes natural for them.

This is not to say that the "redistributive" method that appears from time to time (not always!) in this book—"redistributive" being a play between propriety and property—that I've dug even more into after *Animacies*, works for everyone. For me there is a certain opaque transparency to aligning this method with slipperier objects and operations. Throughout this book there is a valorization of blurring, for reasons that will become apparent, and blurring is meant to enter the subjectivity of the pages. The sense of transparency comes from the feeling that there is an odd, ulterior familiarity in the redistributive modes of writing and thinking, and that one might succeed in naming some of that familiarity's sources, or some of its good company, in the living methods of others. Transparency is equally part of why I am no longer able—despite being a very private person—to restrict certain living vocabularies of importance to me, like transness, from being available wherever I go; it is part of disclosure, and it is part of what some of my people call "dirty laundry." Using that transparency in or alongside scholarship, however, is opaque still to me. That is, I try my best to effect resonances as described, but am also at the moment incapable of giving a fuller description of how it is meant to work. Perhaps, too, that is part of unlearning. My humble attempt at it, at least.

Beneath everything in these pages, in the voice I present here and its unuttered underground, is an orientation to being that is an ethics, deeply informed by the ones who have come my way and proposed shapes for my inchoate sensibilities. I hope this book honors them as they would like. Only some of them will take interest in the words or images that fill this book, but others might sniff it, or flip it, or bite it, or mash it, and I look forward to that.

This book is about how things take shape, and how they don't.

1

SLOW CONSTITUTION DOWN SYNDROME AND THE
LOGIC OF DEVELOPMENT

In the 1860s an English clinician named John Langdon Down, during his time as medical superintendent at the Earlswood Asylum in Redhill, Surrey, seemed to find a compelling pattern in the phenomena he observed in a number of his young, white, intellectually disabled patients. He summed up his findings in a brief published paper in 1866, dubbing this set of patterns with the remarkable terms *mongoloidism* and *mongoloid idiocy*. Researchers believe he was identifying what is today known as Down syndrome.[1]

This chapter will be framed, and primarily concerned with, this transformative moment at which certain novel diagnostic capacities—along with certain suturings—emerged. The first half of the chapter will closely consider Down's research setting, concerns, and conclusions. Given that I am concerned with the patternings within Down's deployments of race, disability, and sexuality, much more focused attention is required to draw out these dimensions, and also to weigh their specific, if implied, modes of relation. Most remarkable, in fact, are the intoxicatory underpinnings of this case, as well as the historical reach or legacy of antecedent images of slowness that, I argue, themselves came to take on—with the help of Down and other racial-disabled conceptual concentrations and affects—a racial aspect.

Let me start this story by tracing my own journey into the tangled histories of Down, opium, and racialized chemical intimacies. It begins with a blur: For many years I'd known of an English physician's crafty associating of racial ideas with disabilities. I was quite stunned to understand that he not only thought this possible, but was interested in mapping one-to-one relationships between races and disabilities (each of which by that time had the seeming ontological solidity to enable him to perform such a mapping). But I had avoided the investigation. For one thing, what seemed a florid liberty taken with so many lives felt too painful to countenance. Rather, my *own* countenance shrank at the possibility of facing/looking—perhaps in part because Down's diagnostics included the racial evaluation of facial characteristics. What is called research, I have learned in these many years of engagement, involves facing not just the possibility of a radical, self-righteous or demoralizing clash between one's self-imagining and the territorially pungent, freestyle imaginings from elsewhere, but also a *tender* encounter within which only one vulnerability might be transparently felt—one's own. In all, Down's project sounded beyond zany: like many racial or disabled fictions, it functioned as a stalwartly minimalistic formula of association or assignment of deficit, appealing to the magic of toxic simplicity. Why should anyone trained otherwise give time to that? What would be a defensible interest in Down's archive?

The main reason I eventually found it possible to respond came from the sense that Down's legacy still demanded study. I had the nagging feeling that it had fed, if not spawned, disturbances in many proximate terrains around both race and disability, some of which lived on in people close to me. This was something I'd grown up with: if race was a beast of visuality, then East Asian looks slid all too easily toward Down syndrome, and the opposite was true of the "looks" of Down syndrome (and here we can also note majoritarian disability's own tendency toward the visual). What exactly were the offenses of such association? And what to do with these profound misattributions? After all, the widespread official replacement of the term *mongoloidism* with *Down syndrome*—a device by which particularization to a specialist's name would seem to remove the sting of constitutional attribution to a whole people—did little more than scratch the surface of the structures that had given the former term any meaning. Perhaps that is why the terminological replacement was not thorough, and *mongoloid* remained—not only in lay usage, but even, it seems, in clinical practice.[2]

In any case, the day came when the case fell to a tolerable scale for my investigations. It was the result of an ongoing calculus of my own tolerance of the toxic: that something become small enough to perspectivize (I think I had to recognize the sheer modesty—inadequacy—of the effort itself), and that it also be broadly consequential enough to justify my sustained exploration.

If we consider science to be one feedback loop between the realm of research and its social, cultural, and political uptake, the function of the scientific uptake of "recapitulation" had as much to do with legitimizing colonialisms and other imperialisms as it had to do with an experimental curiosity and a ranging set of questions about difference, variation, evolution, and humanity. In this sense, British clinician John Langdon Down might be claimed to be a central, not derivative, figure in the history of race and disability science, motivated by a local (if, for purposes of the production of knowledge, fairly avaricious) curiosity in his patients.

In July 2015, I traveled by subway, intercity rail, and bus from my temporary lodgings in London to visit three archives pertaining to Down's nineteenth-century medical practice: the Surrey History Centre in Woking; the London Metropolitan Archives; and the Langdon Down Centre in Teddington (Earlswood Asylum, where he made his findings and from which he forged a reputation, no longer exists as such; the site has been developed into apartments). The Langdon Down Centre is the former site of Normansfield Asylum, one of the hospitals Down served as medical superintendent after his time at Earlswood. The Centre today houses a true panoply: selected clinical archives of John Langdon Down, the Down's Syndrome Association, the Normansfield Theatre (an active performance venue), and the Langdon Down Museum of Learning Disability.[3]

Do some impressions still echo in your vivid memory? Do you wonder what they are meant to do, in your scholarship, in your life? Here is one of mine. I was treated hospitably during my visit to the Centre, which I'd presented as an archival portion of my more general research on the "history of disability and race." At one point during the introduction to the Normansfield archives at the Centre, perhaps after my re-presentation of the above reasons for being there, came an awkward pause: because race had entered the room, my host, locking eyes with me, quickly got out of the way: "The reference to Mongolism was a mistake, of course, people didn't know better at the time." This seemed somewhat in apology but also, I must conclude, an exculpating insistence on the positive legacy of Down. I may have acknowledged with a courteous (robotic?) nod, but my thoughts immediately after was "if I weren't Asian . . ." and "Must I acknowledge?" Whatever it was seemed to suffice, but I now ask: What handshake had we shaken, what contract had been signed? And what immediacy bound contemporary Asianness to Mongolism to "race" such that that comment was sensible at all? The archivist went on to show me the museum and the beautifully painted Normansfield Theatre. The Theatre plays a key role in the Centre, highlighting Down's then-unusual genre of compassionate care, which included his and Mrs. Down's commitment to enriching the cultural life of their resident patients. Intended or not, the sequencing of the visit augments the chances of securing an exculpatory impression.

I report this verbal apprehension with the archivist, arranged in space and time, because it is *method*, a method of encounter. It framed my visit from the outset, prefaced any encounters with the archives; such exchanges play a role in the doing of research and also what research emerges after it. I also couldn't write anything else first. To record the framing encounter only for the purpose of concealing this initial apprehension later, making way for the writing of the legitimate research, is no longer acceptable to my own sense of daily method or the kind of research I yearn to enable for myself and others. To save it only for whispers behind the scenes with selected companions whose interest is obviously shared, is a survival strategy that may be necessary for many in positions of relative vulnerability, but one that I can no longer sustain myself. This is the difference between editing and editing out.

In fact, I am haunted by this particular genre of locking of eyes from certain white scholars, particularly given that during periods of my life it has been difficult to make eye contact even without such conditions. And I am not steeled enough that I needn't recover from such encounters, in part because of this sticky issue of fluctuating scale (again, the territoriality of the encounter). Were I to say, *I don't agree to the simple hedging you offer*, or *That doesn't really take care of it though*, or, *Well, no, it wasn't a mistake at all, was it?*, I wonder what would become of my following requests for more information. If anyone has been so numbed by the bureaucracy of disability access compliance to think it is a question of mechanics, it's worth remembering that access of any kind— including to archives—is also about negotiation; it certainly isn't given. Evidence the hundreds of thousands of Native remains held by university archives and tribal members' known difficulties gaining access or procuring appropriate and respectful methods of stewardship.[4] Access is always politicized.

Something similar happened after a conference in Potchefstroom, South Africa, on queer visualities. After my talk, drawn from this book manuscript and quite uncompromising about race, a middle-aged South African white woman came up to me during the break, again with some discomfort, and said to me in a quiet voice, "But do you think that it could really all be just about *compassion?*" Initially thrown, I was quickly suffused with a kind of nausea; I broke the gaze and got out of there. The completist use of compassion in her plea reminded me of its apparent significance for Down's claim to giving dignity to his patients. But it feels complicated. Her locking of eyes, in her case a bit pleading, a bit moist, tells of an informal but all the more gripping contract, built perhaps over centuries, hinting in this case at the scene of the weirdly coeval queer East Asian American scholar (rather than, say, South Asian South African scholar) who has opined about race to a (in this case, lesbian) white South African auditor. Clearly a notion that needs complement, in this case the critical and more primary element of (white?) compassion, which was in fact what I think she was asking for or even promulgating *from me*. The affordances of a witness.

The idea of compassion as she offered it presents as a clunky device for the softening or even erasure of racial domination. Notwithstanding the complex and potentially irresolvable transnational juncture of our scholarly, social, and geopolitical locatedness, it is not all or even mostly mine to forgive, however. And the reality is that the Centre archivist's willful gaze *succeeded* my own turning toward the archives, after a long time of my determinedly facing away: it's as if the reframing compassion can appear when or where it is needed. Some of these moments feel so queasy and out of time that they threaten being beyond inquiry, beyond mention. But I wonder, too, if these are the expected agitations that emerge, naturally, from the act of calling up, reviving, something so very ghostly and strange. So please don't take this as a grievance; I don't intend it as such. True, I'd rather not meet such gazes, or be asked to consider compassion as if it is either something I owe or something that hadn't occurred to me. Instead, I register these events here as insistent gestures of attempted framing, or reframing, that do participate in my own process of grief and the sense of communal losses across generations in the research: grief and loss that enter and become, have rights to, method.

I return to (the rest of) the archives. The setting for Down's clinical research was a state system of "lunatic" asylums that had swelled after 1845's Lunacy Acts, particularly throughout the English and Welsh counties. Each county was required to house and treat "pauper lunatics," people deemed to fit a fairly broad definition that ran between disability and debility. Indeed, it is clear that some of the reasons people were admitted could be linked to some of the ills of malnourishment, lack of social supports, environmental risk, and insufficient shelter; the institutionalization of the struggling poor for corrective purposes creates a strange cyclicity between poverty and punitive or controlling approaches for what then become entrenched as constitutional flaws. This cycle is not so strange upon reflection. According to Helen Gristwood, in another asylum north of London known as Colney Hatch, 25 percent of women there had worked in match factories, where they were likely to be harmed by white phosphorus.[5]

From 1855 to 1868, Down was the managing physician at Earlswood. There, a number of young English patients with identifiable and yet unmapped disabilities presented him with a striking explanatory opportunity for his studies of idiocy, which attracted widespread interest from scholars and experts and would play a central role in eugenics in the United States and the UK. For diagnosticians, "idiocy" was understood as the lowest, least curable rank, to be distinguished from "imbecility," which was just below "moronic." Each level of reputed intelligence was characterized by an equivalent age range of normative child intelligence, regardless of the age of the person diagnosed. In patient ledgers used by Down's clinic staff at the time, a line was dedicated to identifying intelligence measures. Down drew on Johann Friedrich Blumenbach's dominant division of the world's human races into five essential groups, including the Mongol, the Malay, the Ethiopian, the Caucasian, and the Native American, and also on ideas of racial temporalization contemporary to that time.[6]

I wonder if you are beginning to glaze over at this point, to recoil, or to drop this book; indeed, precisely here might be the ideal scholarly place to drill down, and to quote exhaustively from Down's article and subject it to traditional analysis. My academic training treats such argumentative form as requisite, even obligatory. But I had to ask what it meant to recycle the fairly predictable, Blumenbachian material undergirding Down; for instance, there exists a strangely florid, even poetically compelling text by Blumenbach on racial appearance. I do not include the extended passage here.

The key scene: Down's paper remarked that a number of his Earlswood and visiting patients could be understood as *"one of the great divisions of the human race other than the class from which they have sprung,"* hinting at a kind of itemizing substantiation of disabled being.[7] This is a claim to categorial substantiation, by the way, that occurs just four years earlier than the date Foucault (retrospectively) hypothesized as having constituted the beginning of the life of the category of the homosexual (1870). In a logic that today seems striking, his young, presumably white research subjects—I did not find any who were not apparently white—who were distinguished by not only cognitive but also phenotypical characteristics such as an epicanthic fold—must have reverted, atavistically (through, in the common terms Down used, "degeneration"), to an earlier, now stagnant, racial stage, which he described as Mongolian, or alternatively as Mongoloid idiot or imbecile, fully counting as 10 percent of the population of people he described as idiots.[8] In what seems a fell swoop, due to Down's well-received work *Mongoloid* thus became an operative term to describe people with what is today known as Down syndrome. Down believed he could identify atavistic eruptions of earlier racial (Mongoloid) characteristics in the otherwise European descended child. In the famous 1866 short paper announcing his findings, he wrote straightforwardly and yet swept over exception, writing that his patients' Mongol identity meant that "when placed side by side, it is difficult to believe that the specimens compared are not children of the same parents."[9]

Here it is important to note that Down viewed the phenotype as *more* selective than race: that all these children's images are such that they must be *of the same parents* rather than *of the same race*. With this brief aside, Down suggests something of a queer reproduction of this congenital condition. Alternatively, we could say that he imagined nonwhite parentage as having itself a queer *density*. There is a durable ambivalence here, precisely because race, sexuality, and disability are placed in untraceable relation—diachronically with regard to the process of deliberation, and synchronically with regard to what is doing what to what.

More generally, the norm being expressed here is the use of a nonwhite race as a zone of deferral and marking, which accounts for the other kind of difference (as they interarticulate). To follow my interest in not only intoxication and its effects, but also its governmentality, I learned a further detail: Down used opium to sedate some of his patients in his English clinic. In fact, several forms of chemical restraint, having replaced the more visibly severe forms of mechanical restraint in the early nineteenth century, were quite widespread throughout the century in the asylums, and shifted by the turn of the twentieth century to much more conservative use. Considered critically, this sedation could have been deployed for many reasons: in the schema of standard treatment of a condition, the displacement of mechanical toward chemical restraint; a practical ambiguity around conditions calling for pain relief, as in laudanum; and in a more critical sense, the controlled synchronizing of an institutionalized population, or a temporal calibration of developmentally delayed patients understood to be in some sense outside of time.[10]

I now return to a detailed treatment of Down's invocation of the precursor to modern-day Down syndrome. As I mentioned at the opening of this chapter, while Down's Mongoloid figure received the lasting attention, in the larger scheme Down was interested in assimilating various kinds of intellectual disability to racial types, with the idea that all of the non-Caucasian races, which were inevitably doomed to relative slowing vis-à-vis Anglo-European whites in the human history of evolution, lent a white child's delay a particular character ("a classification of the feeble-minded, by arranging them around various ethnic standards"—Blumenbach's typology).

Here it is worth remembering development's longer temporal trajectory, its implicit evolutionary chronology. For Down, it was the stagnated Mongol race of faded glory (but, interestingly, glory nonetheless, perhaps making it synchronically *worthy enough* to enter these white bodies as a dilatory pollutant) that atavistically erupted in the bodies of white children, a raciality whose implicit and yet constitutive presence was sufficient to explain their developmental disability. Here, the white Mongol, Down's most famous "ethnically classified idiot," was identifiable by a combination of phenotype and conduct, to be distinguished from the real Mongol. The peculiar hybridity and transmaterial characterization suggests that it might be too simplistic to describe this form of intellectual disability as simply racialized: the piling-on and arrangement of racial categorization, temporal persistence, heredity, and synchronic incapacity were at once arbitrary and consistent, precise and sweeping.

Down's apologists, even those who concede that he took part in what has turned out to be a massive enterprise of scientific racism, mention that these ideas were not entirely of his making; they often note, as if in contrast, that he had great enthusiasm for the care of these young patients. (Recall the archivist at the Langdon Down Centre who showed me the dramatic theater that existed for the cultural enrichment of Down's patients.) Transracial and transabled benevolence and sentimentality, like what Down arguably showed, have a long and terrible history in colonial practice. Yet despite the appeal of wishing away such projects and their proponents, modern-day moral judgments of historical figures who were fully ensconced in the rapacious spirit of colonialism continue to be open to debate.

It may be surprising that Down's closing words, which he described as being of great "philosophical" interest, expressed his hope that a human *unity* could be asserted—precisely in light of the fact that race seemed to be so mobile, moving from body to body in ways that soundly rejected the idea of fixed racial, directly heritable divisions of humanity. Perhaps what may be learned here is that race's mobility—at least for Down, who was far from a unique fantasist—is precisely a (newly opened) question of temporality and transfer, of which linear transgenerational heredity by way of heterosexual sexuality is a narrow example.

While some interpreters of Down syndrome explained atavistic mongoloidism by a long-view image of seemingly earlier interbreeding, by Down's own account such atavisms could appear *within a single generation*, not necessarily by the fault of the mother; this was what was contained in his notion of the congenital. The thinking about heredity, atavism, race, and incapacity was still much in formation in the nineteenth century, but Down's indeterminate theorizing could be understood as germane to (even if it only happens to resemble) contemporary formulations of queer theory, which themselves benefit from the field left open by more specified intertwinings of normative medicalization, sex, race, and kinship. Disability studies scholar Chris Borthwick, in "Racism, IQ, and Down's Syndrome," wrote of the destructive value of insults attached to misrepresentations:

> The analogy between "mongolian idiots" and Mongolians was insulting to Mongolians, and contributed to their dismissive treatment by Westerners in the colonial era. Analogies, however, point in two directions. If it was insulting to compare Mongolians to people with impaired functioning, it was also insulting to compare people with a disability to the Victorian stereotype of an uncreative, limited, passive race that had ceased its development before the British. Both groups were seen as developmentally delayed.[11]

With similar confidence, Daniel Kevles, in "Mongolian Imbecility: Race and Its Rejection in the Understanding of a Mental Disease," concludes that "the detection of [Down syndrome's] cause in chromosomal accidents finished off its vestigial association with racist atavism."[12] Later, I ask whether this misapprehension in fact endures.

Down was professionally embedded in a series of meaning-lending discourses, from which his evident drive to make more meaning, particularly that which would garner him scientific credit and a new disease characterization, is not surprising. I would, however, caution against stopping at moral judgment and/or strictly nominal abandonment, such as in only changing a name. Borthwick exemplifies this approach.[13] He discards the old "characterisation of people with intellectual impairment as equivalent both to children and to people of different races as 'worthless'"; he likens it to the troubling contemporary work of Herrnstein and Murray's *The Bell Curve*, which adhered to similar ideas of innate racial difference in intelligence.[14]

Down's massively influential racialized approach to the study of developmental disabilities, as compacted in the neat phrase "mongoloid idiocy," has persisted. The World Health Organization standardized the use of the term

Down syndrome in 1965, after a plea from the Mongolian People's Republic, which was then a socialist state about to forge a significant Cold War alignment with the Soviet Union against China. Yet outside of clinical use, the term *mongoloid* and its linguistic kin continue to be used in various versions around the world. Furthermore, mongolism was but one nomination to partake of racialized and temporalized developmental logics that remain robust today.

Constituting Slowness

Some reflection reveals that race and disability both feel intimately entangled with slowness. For one stable basis, we can thank, in some uncannily fundamental way, the alignment, in the maturation of the modern colonial era, of the distant colony and the center with the imposition of *delay* in relationship to the present, a relationship that was deepened by the economic imperialisms that themselves came to carry the illusion of a capitalistic neutrality, even while the orders of labor in the United States have a racialized history due precisely to the inextricable participation of colonial attributes. As a first and ungeneralizable instance, the existential denials of chattel slavery were woven into the building of capitalism in the United States. In general, there seems no other way to understand the temporal schema in the United Nations rankings of developed countries, its seven major geographic regions, and their alignment with the UN's Human Development Index.

Development is one of modernity's key signifiers. It is a richly multifaceted word and a generative packaging of time, as in the category of "developmental disability" within which Down syndrome belongs. It is better to say that it is a set of near-homonyms that refer to human individual growth, on the one hand, and economic fate, on the other, both meanings in turn referring to the notion of progression toward a seemingly desirable end. They can lead to contrastive visions—for instance, the idea of disability as the wrong kind of phasal development (which, owing to the politics of reproduction surrounding it, including but not limited to eugenics, is also sexualized and racialized); and, from the perspective of early psychoanalysis, homosexuality as the stagnation of sexual development.

Positive notions of development are haunted by notions of their failure—misdevelopment, undeveloped, regression.[15] One trope of cultural studies and critical theory is the idea that a proper system is buttressed by the surrounding of a favored entity by its negated others, so that temporal others (such as the so-called regressives, third-worlds, and misdeveloped) are what subtend and make possible the distinction of modernity's exemplars. Economists of neoliberalism might say that entitlements—say, in developing economies or in the bodies that inhabit them—are not equally earned. I want to bring all these senses to bear here in my attempt to argue for a continued exploration of the relations, identities, textures, and affects that flesh out what is easily contained within the categories of disability and nondisability (for instance); it is the exchange between the two that tells a very interesting history.

The racialized colonial order thus doubles into what Trinh T. Minh-ha calls the "third world in the first world," assigning to racialized geographies both latency (or latent capacity) and poverty (as arrested, incapacitated, nondevelopment).[16] This sweeping global trope is in part what informed Edward Said's attribution of orientalism to the work of the imagination; and it further entrenches incapacitation by fixing possible trajectories into their own (potentially unreachable) timeline. For such a reach, the consequential, and selffulfilling, imposition of temporality is positively cosmic in its reach: It even follows the discourses of space exploration. As Johannes Fabian wrote in one of the most important analytical indictments of a discipline's temporal practices, anthropology's "denial of [temporal] coevalness" to its Others "ultimately is expressive of a cosmological myth of frightening magnitude and persistency."[17]

It should not be surprising, therefore, that any contemporary image of slowness, seemingly mundane but also descriptively elusive, may well derive some of its character *from* racial and disabled notions, notions that find apt complement here. This is not the same as claiming that slowness derives out of them exclusively, as if through calculation. Indeed, race and disability inform one another, are effectively interconstituted; around these, like a moon, temporal slowness circles, offering a pale and creeping cast.

If slowness shifts among a feeling, an image, a quantification, or a quality, then perhaps one way to develop a feeling for slowness's historical character is to pursue a journey of sensation, vibration, and archive along its traces. Within the systems of marking and arrangement that go by names of race and disability, I'm particularly interested in their participation—not just as recipients of meaning, but as contributors—in the rich and disparate, incohesive set of familiarities that both feel like, and get nominated as, slowness.

In order to examine the complexity of these terms in relation to constitutional being, this next section explores the idea of "slow" populations in development, the idea of a material(ist) constitution of a living being, the fit or aptness of environmental biochemistries broadly construed, and, finally, the germinal interarticulation of race and disability—an ensemble that continues to commutatively enflesh each of these notions in their turn. The idea of the notion that I raised in the Introduction thus becomes the stage for such interconstituted entities and for the dynamics, such as the attractions and impositions of chemistries to bodies, by which they are made. This is assuredly an awkward attempt to shift the habitual staging just enough so that the very formation of such categories as race can be objectified and, putting to rest the old concreteness (by which race is incalculable in new materialisms and other implicitly generalist—and yet undoubtedly Euro-American-white—frameworks), a proto racial materiality can be given more attention once again. I am particularly interested in getting at the specific chemical-material consequences—and renewability—of the fungibilities of racial bodies.

My approach to these questions is centered on a set of trajectories, judgments, and materialities that converged around and within the event that led to the specific naming by Down. But there arises a question of method: Given the availability of divergent contemporary frameworks, how, precisely, should one narrate the commingling and interarticulation of race, disability, and chemistry in the bodies of Down's patients? By means of a mechanistic retrospective calculus of the likely consequences of scientific racism? In terms of a Deleuzian theory of affect? By means of ad hoc diagnosis? In terms of Down's own craft in the interest of a signal contribution to theories of idiocy? Or, perhaps, all of the above?

I am interested here in the materialist proposition embedded in the notion of "constitution," an assemblage-like term referring to the composition or makeup of a human or nonhuman entity, and a term also used in a lay sense to refer to fortitude or inherent capacity. Constitution, for instance, aided colonists in understanding what modifications were needed for British forces working in the inhospitable tropics or climates, as Mark Harrison examines.[18] Constitution was naturalized for Down in his claim that regression increased for his mongoloid patients during the winter months: Down writes, "Their mental and physical capabilities are, in fact, *directly* as the temperature," and, as I argue, continues to inform the rules of interaction and interpenetration for bodies and their sticky contexts, albeit critically understood differently for different bodies and different contexts.[19]

With the notion of constitution I am aiming for a broadened framework for understanding the role that the extra-human element in the interarticulation of race and disability plays in leveraging different kinds of human integrity, and the blurry making of embodiment in ways that may have started from scientific illusion but, in ramified policy, were dug into bodies. In developing a notion of constitution that is species- and animate-neutral, I am attempting, however crudely, to allow for a flexible approach to transgenerational peoplehood, respecting Indigenous genealogies as well as the Western new materialist idea that a sum—of the body and a chemical substance or the body and definitionally exogenous substance—can be, whether a right or wrong thing, the scene of a certain integrity and potency, however tenuous or temporary.

The white supremacist racial fictions—about cognitive disability, morality, and pace of living that frame some racial groups as slower than others—suggest a compact expression of temporality, race, and chemistry: of constitutional congealing. Both within and away from the United States, the temporalized characterizations of delay have been freely applied to Indigenous peoples and peoples of the Global South, as well as racialized immigrants less securely anchored to recognizable infrastructures of modernity. For instance, the association of certain racial characteristics with cognitive deficiency continues insidiously in the United States and elsewhere, both below and above the surface. Furthermore, we face a vast continued reach of eugenics history and thinking in contemporary technologies of enhancement and reproduction. I only wonder at the degree to which "constitution" may have forgotten its chemicality.

Referring to the earlier discussion on disability studies scholarship about John Langdon Down, both Borthwick's and Kevles's confident denials, for all their illustrative power, make deeper, *proto-material traffic* between Mongolian raciality and Down syndrome seem unthinkable. They effectively deny the pervasive fixity of what Denise Ferreira da Silva has diagnosed as a foundational social scientific rendering of race. Far from defending Down, I would nevertheless like to push further than Borthwick and Kevles to ask what more might be understood from the inheritances of Down's and similar deliberations in the present day, before one is ready to dismiss these "archaic," "obsolete," racial-disabled imaginations in favor of a substitutive, indexed, and purely referential modernity, in which the only realm in which one thing can also be another, say, is the realm of the contemporary digital. (Da Silva might additionally claim that where this modernity manages to disavow race, it continues to conceal the imbrication of a persistently racial economy.)[20] For even Borthwick notes that the underlying image of the "ladder of development remains influential, and the conception of disability groups as quasi-races is still a powerful ordering force."[21] Notably, Licia Carlson's *Faces of Intellectual Disability* substantially examines species discourse in relation to the representation of intellectual disability, implicating race; however, the case of Down syndrome is only lightly explored in this regard.[22] Imaginations presented as archaic seem to me to be alive and well today.

In particular, with regard to mongoloidism and its possible contemporary reflexes, I do suspect that something has survived of intuitive racialities by which Asians are understood as lacking in capacity (to the extent this could be a legacy of earlier stagnation discourse, and I think it is). Indeed, East Asians, who continue to be understood as possessing less body hair and more facial flatness, marked in relation to a presumably white standard, may be depicted as "neotenous," more "like" white children, say, before the white children grow to develop more mature features. Adult men have been advised to eat less soy to prevent neoteny and depressed reproductive capacity, what so easily becomes in a Western context a form of queered Asian virility.

The overlaps between race and disability are not restricted to regions of interior constitution, for phenotypic identification continues to have its hold on such overlays. In *The Shape of the Eye*, author and poet George Estreich, writing a memoir tied to the life of his daughter, who has Down syndrome, and whose biological mother is a Japanese war survivor, precisely refuses to let go of this mutuality.[23] Does his infant daughter look "Asian," as some acquaintances commented, because she has Down syndrome or because she has a Japanese biological grand/parent?

A critical reading suggests that a lack of capacity is attached to the model minority Asian figure of today; one need only recall the sticky impressions of permanent exoticization and of the bungling immigrant stranger, the one slow to catch on, that also accompanies "even" model minority figures. Indeed, this very stickiness threatens to make the impression that the examples appearing here are merely caricatural. Hence, my final example, which involves both interior and phenotypic constitution: In 2004, William Hung, an engineering undergraduate at Berkeley, performed Ricky Martin's "She Bangs" for an *American Idol* talent show audition that did not advance him. As I recall it, the collective effect of the distribution of this viral audition clip was an energetic, and vast, laugh—less so the groan commonly owed to a poor performance that lacked, say, the transformative heft of camp.

About a decade later, in the style of "where are they now," a contemporary photo of Hung returned to the Perez Hilton celebrity gossip site. I see "Remember Me?" or "What Happened To?" moments as a way, in the temporal politics of recall, to make something both iterative (maybe even chronic) and belated at the same time. The condition of their presence is a look back, so I see resonance with the citation of objects of so-called ethnic history. In the updated photo of Hung, someone seemed to have used a picture annotation tool to crudely scribble "Remember Me?" and added white liquid dribbling from his mouth.

I'll break here to say that to my surprise and chagrin I got voluminous pushback from my copyeditor on my drafted writing about Hung. They were concerned whether I had the legal or moral right to write in that way (originally using awkward phrases like "laughingstock anti-fame") about a living person who might resent being reminded of a traumatic moment in their "personal" life, and suggested that I choose a different example or turn it into a hypothetical one. On the one hand, I appreciated this series of inquiries, for admittedly Hung had for the decade since my introduction of his case into my work become more of a fixture than a living being. But I also found it strange for the copyeditor to have singled him out as someone who might need legal or moral protection from me, as I write about how the public record instantiated the race/disability nexus outlined in this book. After all, we are in a time when queer social media analysis about multipronged reiterations of past or present social harms is today so widespread as to be unremarkable (in the common trope of TikTok: "This is what happened. Let's talk about it"). Nevertheless, the copyeditor's remarkable concern—taken at face value as such—was an opportunity to reflect on the impact of my writing, and so I gratefully took it. I newly worried about harming Hung with my book, which both felt ridiculous—is he going to read or hear about an academic revisitation and if he does, will he be inescapably retraumatized, rather than, say, given an opportunity to reimagine the mechanisms of that harm?, and also felt sincere—I am uninterested in inciting hurt if I can help it.

I realized too that the copyeditor's cautionary warning resembled a particular ethical wedge newly at play in recent years and reaching a height at the time of writing this book, a wedge about which I openly feel some distress. There have been increasingly widespread moments in which a citation of harm, according to the complaint, releases harmful content and thereby reiterates that harm. An earlier antecedent might be Andrea Dworkin's argument that pornography harms women by staging their sexual exploitation.[24] Contemporarily there have appeared an array of controversies in universities in which students report feeling (re)traumatized by pedagogical stagings of harm intended for analysis; or by the use of images historically produced within a group now experiencing injury from that same image.[25]

Ultimately, as is apparent, I chose to keep the example. I named Hung, but, mindful of the copyeditor's and others' sensitivity, I also aimed to highlight both my sympathy and the ways in which early reality shows exposed their subjects to unanticipated forms of online abuse. However, let us be clear that any act of pointing out resemblances to disability is not in itself something I, as a disability theorist, will assume is harmful on its face, for that is to collude with the abjection of disability; the same goes for queerness or animality. What you read here is the result of critical tonal changes and text perspectivization more to my own reflections rather than an abstract all-knowing subjectivity.

In Perez Hilton's revival of the figure of William Hung, comments on the website below the annotated photo referenced above showed a continuing familiarity with disability-racial tropes. Among them is what appeared to be a sincere question: simply, "Isn't he mentally [R-word]?" Another reads: "His 'fame' stems from his goofy appearance. If he looked less like a [R-word], he would never be thought of again. My BF and I think he has downs, anyone else???"[26] One of the reasons this caricature of Hung shot to notoriety, in my view, is that he contained in one figure both the exemplary engineering student at Berkeley and, shimmering underneath, the phenotyped caricature who had developmental delay or at least—I want to note—a form of social incapacitation.

Any Asian American might have a parallel story to tell; I certainly have plenty of my own. In a Midwest high school, I gained the notice of a popular and good-looking classmate who approached me with a compliment about a skill I'd demonstrated. Flummoxed, I stared at him, and a stream of mumbles left my throat. Something like "oh real fum fum fum." He narrowed his eyes, shook his head, and walked away. It was at that moment of failed heterosexual and interracial procedurality that I determined that I must thenceforth teach myself the social skills I so desperately needed for whatever semblance of citizenship I could attain—or toil in oblivion.

This is a generic story that anyone who was once an awkward teen could tell. It is also part of a history in which so many of us in the Asian diaspora strove for a kind of exhibited competence, one that had a relationship to ableism but was also deeply underwritten by racial expectation, both ours and others'. Am I glad a model minority slot existed in which to direct my self-civilizing efforts, consorting with ableism and disability ("social"? "physical"?) at once? I have absolutely been formed in part by this struggle, and yet I mourn the mildness I left, mourn the speech my parents gave me, wonder what freedoms a relaxation of these trained muscles might yield back.

Hung embodied anxiety about Asian-American status by paradoxically keeping both mongoloidism/disability and model minority status in tension. Hung's queerness, his seeming heterosexual incapacity, was part of the joke: Just having sexuality has long been seen as an achievement of relationality for an East Asian (American) individual. So we can call that infantilization and neoteny—the milk; but we can also talk about the sexual queerness of Asian males—the cum. In either case, disability is not far from the surface.

The case of William Hung demonstrates that one of the correlates of the racial description of disability, such as mongoloidism, is that disability continues to lurk in the description of races and may lurk in the defining theme of race itself, race as a colonial trope of incapacity. Rife contemporary examples of racist labeling of nondisabled East Asian individuals and collectives, like Hung, as "mongoloid" not only mark the potent legacy of Down, but also speak to the sticking power and attraction of the embodied metaphor as well as of the collapsing of developmental time. Thus, what is called the racist enjoyment of gawky or lumbrous "Asian" failure, such as has been narrated of Hung, may obliquely have to do with a double presentation of social disability in the form of nerdiness, as well as a hardly suppressed image of Down syndrome.

For the above reasons I am hesitant to strive for a confident difference (outside of a firm rejection of their collapse by ignorant forms of power) between the race and disability of the once Mongol, now Asian figures—and of course these two are also not simplistically related genealogically; the links between these are messy, vertical and lateral, and also queer.

Absent Opiates, Opiate Constitution

I turn now directly to the constitutional question of material biochemistries and intoxication, namely, for Down, the (non)participation of opium in the complex of race and disability. But I first pause here to spend some time on the question of toxicity. First, it is important to clarify that, if we a priori concur that opium is a categorically bad substance and that all research judgments of human actions should follow from it, we may lose something in the analysis. I am less advocating for value neutrality within research than for analytically breaking up a terrain in which toxins, particularly within biomedical perspectives, would seem templatically and exclusively to cause damage. The full range of contemporary opium derivatives—opiates—straddles the biopolitical divide between legitimized medical management and criminalized use, a divide that reflects in significant part the competing interests of major stakeholders in health care industries, prison industrial complexes, and welfare states, to take just a few; furthermore, the very history of opium use is diverse.

I further wonder what it would mean to also say that opium has its own *inhuman* temporality when acting (biochemically, or by some other conception) within human bodies. Opiate inhuman temporality, certainly, being the condition of biochemical transformation "in" a human, but also involuting human temporalities and percepts and other indexical orientations, and decentering a normative embodied temporality. Considering the affectivity of various substances, in and through the bodies of their hosts, while applying a critically disabled perspective on the demand to satisfy health and performance norms, opens some new possibilities of thinking about governance, welfare, medicine, and self-determination.

What I hope to have briefly shown above is the range of hidden potentials that continue to reside in medicalized concepts due to colonial logics of development, time, sexuality, and race that reach substantively into the contemporary period. A discursive and medical history of toxicity is beyond the scope of this chapter; my goal instead is to exemplify the rich interanimations of toxins and toxicities, the repulsive dynamics of racism, and temporalized modes of control (chronicities), whether in the clinic or in the traffic of contentious transnationality. In all examples, it is a *production* of the toxic, whether or not specific chemicals are invoked, that bears imagining in the whole; to only manage toxins as biochemical processes might be to unwittingly collude with the dynamics that produced them.

The line between toxicity and intoxication not only should be addressed and rethought; in particular, I suggest that intoxication—rather than toxicity's absence in the form of nontoxic—be considered the unmarked (as in the ambient or default) variety of the living, in a way that aligns however oddly with what is called neurodiversity in contemporary revisions of disability. To presume intoxication, rather than nontoxicity, is to adopt an environmentalist presumption that not all can be known about the more or less universally shared condition of living with—and by—contaminants; to reject clear divisions between body and mind; and to forego the tempting categorization of purity for subjects deemed healthful or exempt from the classification of severity.

This revision has consequences both for the body norm of classed and racialized bodily purity and for pharmaceutical tuning in the interest of capitalistic productivity, which works as a companion to intoxication within zones of privilege. In a general sense we might see at play in the scenes above an assemblage of racial notions, temporalities, and biochemical constituents that I understand together as racial tuning.

"Has the Nurse Dosed the Child with Opium?"

Toxins—or poisons—have a rich and mixed history. They can be curative, as in vaccines, through an invocation of the dangerous element; they are injurious to the health-desiring or health-exemplifying individual; and they are biopolitically brought to bear on certain populations considered constitutionally deserving of them. It is relevant to consider temporal resonances between certain bodies and the medicalized or medicalized coercions upon those bodies: for instance, the queered reproductivity of disabled, racialized, and/or Indigenous people who are sterilized in the name of (others') eugenic betterment; the containment of alcoholisms and other substance attachments as part of impoverished lifeworlds whose source is governmental, racist, and settler-colonialist rather than merely explainable by a "constitutionally deserving gene" understood in terms of, say, alcoholic proclivity among Native Americans.

The possibility of a genetic explanation yielded decades of disproportionate genetic research on American Indian groups in ignorance of other critically important factors that ultimately rejected genetic dominance—it is essentially one constitutional move (genetic inherency) over another constitutional move (guided intoxication). Popular understanding continues to support this belief.[27] The complicated dynamics of the increasing dominance of genetic models for medicine as well as for issues such as Indigenous sovereignty continue to be explored by a number of scholars in science studies, such as Kim TallBear.[28]

Advocates of prenatal testing will often privilege the fantasy of a nondisabled future by implicitly or explicitly positioning disability as the sloughed-off dredges of a perfect nondisabled future world, as Alison Kafer and other disability theorists of "futures" have argued.[29] Advances in technology are often explicitly tied to the elimination of a bodily or intellectual difference that is templatically understood as undesirable. Recently, a "more accurate," "more reliable" test for Down syndrome has emerged.[30] Its politics of life and death and comparative value, understood through the mobile language of risk, were contradictory at first glance, then easily mappable from the point of view of critical disability. For this test, the possibility to abort an undesired fetus due to a reliable positive test result for Down syndrome for "high-risk" mothers was an advantage over other supposedly inferior tests that had greater risk of miscarriage—that is, one wouldn't want to abort a fetus that might have been "healthy"). However, Eben Kirksey notes that amniocentesis is still used to confirm suspicion of Down syndrome, demonstrating that risk is understood selectively.[31]

That futurity also bears the weight of postraciality, which we can identify in visions of the technophilic future that have been critiqued in Afrofuturist scholarship as being implicitly about the cleansing of marked raciality. Along with the burgeoning of sensing methods, as the detection of toxicity (as aerial pollution, as bodily intruder) becomes distributed in a number of senses—across a populace and government (through neoliberalization), and through time and space—what narratives of danger, expulsion, fatalism are built and what desires are they connected to? Ultimately, what kinds of racialized, sexualized, temporalized acting citizens do these make, and what are or will be their investments in a fantasied future populace that looks and acts a specific way (and not in other ways)?

The Down case particularly helps to illustrate the importance of suitability: What kinds of co-constitution are harmonious, and by what process is that harmony enacted? The single most key aspect of Down's diagnostic process may in fact have been the use of opium. As I mentioned earlier, Down's clinic did what was not particularly unusual for clinics at the time: it sedated many patients with opium. And yet, for a successful diagnosis of mongoloid idiocy, according to Down, that opium should *not* be present.

That is, Down, insistent that the focus of discovery is that which is congenital—not that which has arrived after birth—stated that the present aberrant constitution must be distinguished from a series of explanatory conditions that must be ruled out, the first being the question: "Has the nurse dosed the child with opium?" Rather than attributing toxic cause in this case, Down held that opium had to be absent for the diagnosis to thrive. (Later, he asked: "Can it be that when away from the family attendant the calomel powders [known as mercury chloride] were judiciously prescribed?")[32] Diagnostically, then, Down's criteria for identifying this form of mongoloid idiocy, or indeed any form of "congenital mental lesions," were not just phenotypic but also environmental ("whether the supposed defect dates from any cause subsequent to the birth or not").[33]

Thus, for purposes of diagnosis, Down admitted that intoxication by the drug needed first to be *ruled out*, given that, in some fairly obvious way, its effects must have mimicked the condition itself. Hence, there existed, at least for Down, a suitability of opium (or opium intoxication) to Down syndrome, and of Down syndrome to opium—and, perhaps, of opium to delay, or slowness, itself—proximate constituents that the diagnostic process must then segregate in order to find the real thing.

This *likeness* of idiocy to opium intoxication suggests that opium intoxication could not be quite the same as the mental or intellectual impairment of these youth, and yet it was *close enough to need to be distinguished*, raising questions of where to locate the intoxication or impairment, where to identify the source of slowness. The likeness also suggests a kind of material alliance between the distortionary achievements of intoxicants, such as opium and mercury chloride, and the differences in measures like examined cognition, looks, or temporality, borne by the bodies and minds of children who are understood as being congenitally affected. Material alliance could also name the comparable emplacements of certain substances whose chemical relation (as determined by a chemist or biologist)—a similarity of molecular structure, say—might be fully outdone by their shared administration within the practices of a clinic, a system of governance, or a zone of colonial discard and promulgated exposure. Their arbitrary non-arbitrariness makes them occupy common political positions in ongoing encounters of substance and action.

Simultaneously, in line with evolutionary theories of that time, the Mongol within the youth simply sufficed to stand in for the developmental delay; no other explanation was necessary. Thus, what would it mean, in spite of the widespread use of opium at the time, for these particular youth to be understood to be *constitutionally deserving of that opium*? What does it mean to think about developmental time, global economic time, and delay together, as Down did, and in particular about the commingling of racial delay with developmental disability to the point that the two cannot be separated? And to ask questions about what the legacies are here, to take this kind of thinking as not exceptional even in the present? This is ultimately to think not only about what opium intoxication means, but simultaneously about how race and disablement are defined in the face of that intoxication.

Transmaterial similitude is a tricky beast. What *is* opium, after all? In terms of chemical elements, or mediums, or modes of detection, each of these characterizations falsely seems to contain what is always larger than its material or perceptual identity. At the level of method, I suspect we are too often led to think that common reference to "a chemical" allows for phenomenological, or even experiential, similitude when very little works in relation to the narrow scope of elemental or molecular designations. Rather, the kind of likeness detailed by Down is, I would rather say, quite a nonevent in that it represents the common genres of the materialization of race or disability. Not just then, but today; they are simply distributed differently. Notions feel more uneven, less regulated, and hence more honest. They are neither exclusively ideational nor lexical; they cannot map without materiality and are not separable from it.

Opium's Asian Conspirators

In the light of such intoxication and the temptation to normalize its politics, it is worth recalling the political and material landscape of imperial transactions that spawned the push of opium deep into China in the early half of the nineteenth century by way of the British colonial deployment of trade in India. Indeed, following opium around its enactments in and transactions beyond the British Empire yields important counterpoints to the expected narrativization of poisons and governance, some of which will be addressed in chapter 2. Opium had already been in use for centuries, and in China its use was consolidated in relation to a number of dynamic factors. Because much of the opium was exported by way of the (British-owned) East India Company's Indian sites to China under Queen Victoria's rule, a push toward free trade—free for some, at least—rendered the Bengali sites exclusive to British traders from 1834.

What made the Mongolian figure a ready fount for Down's imagination of minded, developmental pathology? Was it neatly explainable by means of what might have been a ubiquitous Blumenbachian reference to a physical resemblance? Though the question remains unanswerable because it was never possible to enter Down's sensory mind, as much as he may have made some diagnostic logics available through his writings, I have to wonder whether the image of the "stagnated Mongol" might have been sensorily *embellished*, for Down, by the drag of opium and its Chinese involvement, whether in the racialization of the opium dens and the white experiences of opium that populated London's Chinatown by the mid-nineteenth century, or in the reports of Chinese addiction in China. If this works as I wonder, then chemical suitability, in this case, becomes a vehicle for further material carriage.

Given the mixed ills and pleasures of opium, the uses both manageable and addictive, it is important to register forms of competing discourse in their diversity. I confess to all too often responding to the local at the expense of the transnational—in part due to compact US-based frameworks that simplify the rich exchanges that are constantly at work. The cost of this standardized orientation is massive, since one thing that is lost is precisely the blur—the dizzying perspective that attends the transnational scene, not just at the colonial centers with their preordained and obscurantist logics but the irresolvable uncertainty that demands further inquiry and methodological humility.

Less than thirty years before Down's publication, Chinese Qing Dynasty commissioner Lin Tse-Hsu, who set off the series of Opium Wars, wrote a famous "Letter of Advice to Queen Victoria" in 1839, a letter that revealed signs of exasperation. He decried the ruinous effects of British opium in China and the barbarity, capital profit, and criminality associated with it as one turn in an extended encounter that eventually resulted in the Opium Wars. What was the effect of opium on China's international station, and what connections can be made to the travel of Chinese ideas about toxicity? Earlier I asked, "What is opium?" In his letter to Queen Victoria, Lin was specific in describing opium as a kind of poison:

> We find your country is sixty or seventy thousand li from China. Yet there are barbarian ships that strive to come here for trade for the purpose of making a great profit . . . all taken from the rightful share of China. By what right do they then in return use the poisonous drug to injure the Chinese people? Even though the barbarians may not necessarily intend

to do us harm, yet in coveting profit to an extreme, they have no regard for injuring others. Let us ask, where is your conscience? I have heard that the smoking of opium is very strictly forbidden by your country; that is because the harm caused by opium is clearly understood. Since it is not permitted to do harm to your own country, then even less should you let it be passed on to the harm of other countries—how much less to China! Of all that China exports to foreign countries, there is not a single thing which is not beneficial to people.... On the other hand, articles coming from the outside to China can only be used as toys. We can take them or get along without them.... How can you bear to go further, selling products injurious to others in order to fulfill your insatiable desire?

We have further learned that in London, the capital of your honorable rule, and in Scotland, Ireland, and other places, originally no opium has been produced. Only in several places of India under your control such as Bengal, Madras, Bombay, Patna, Benares, and Malwa has opium been planted from hill to hill, and ponds have been opened for its manufacture. For months and years work is continued in order to accumulate the poison. The obnoxious odor ascends, irritating heaven and frightening the spirits.

... The fact is that the wicked barbarians beguile the Chinese people into a death trap.[34]

Lin called opium a poisonous drug (and a harmful thing) and explicitly connected its use to barbarism (and arguably its developmental backwardness—he was not uninterested in hierarchy) to England. The allegation that England let domestically forbidden substances such as opium "be passed on to the harm of other countries" such as India and China calls to mind the contemporary corporate dynamic of environmental externalization as a deflective form of cost management—most notably, however, in the use of India's territories for hyperproduction. By noting England's barbaric interest in both profit and poisoning, Lin drew attention to England's interest in harming places and bodies other than those it called its own. In a reversal of a common racial allegation, Lin seems to suggest that the opium addiction pulls English barbarians' "beguiling" of the Chinese into an intoxicating alliance with the addictive effects of the drug itself: to drag Chinese people toward "a death trap." Lin accentuated the divides between national and transnational policy, partly as a way to dramatize what he saw as the relative spiritual generosity of China's beneficial commodities and its trade practices.

While Lin Tse-Hsu believed opium was illegal in England, at this time it was not yet used recreationally in England. But recall that opium *was* conventionally used for the medical sedation or treatment of Down's institutionally housed clinical patients—a kind of chronicity, Elizabeth Freeman's term citing agnosis rather than prognosis, what she describes as a phasal, iterative existence leading to neither cure nor death, and not based upon a building up of wholeness for the preferred biopolitical subject.[35] Freeman is interested in chronicity as a way of occupying time, but I'd like to think about it primarily as an occasion for thinking simultaneously about the temporalities of disability and debility imposed from without. In the case of opium, chronicity becomes the global and local reach of a toxin used to effect a kind of chronic suppression in two places at once, in two populations that are deemed radically geographically separate but also, perhaps, constitutionally congenial, metonymically congealing like with like.

Lin's association of barbarism with England, not China, reminds scholars of the necessarily overlapping, perhaps even competing, temporalities or progressions by which racially and imperially positioned people considered each other. For some scholars, white Western supremacy's conceptual victory is a complete sweep that has the effect of occluding other imperialisms such as China's. In this case, by noting England's barbaric interest in both profit and poisoning, Lin drew attention to England's interest in doing harm to other places, in stark contrast to China's alleged innocence. Lin accentuated the divides between national and transnational policy, partly as a way to dramatize what he wanted to represent as the relative spiritual generosity of China's beneficial commodities and its trade practices.

Perhaps you sense my struggle in the fairly analytic words above. It is a bit about a personal struggle of accountability to a family genealogy that predisposes one toward attachment. I had known about Lin Tse-Hsu all my life. He was a source of family pride: he was our ancestor who fought off the British, destroying the ships' stores off the Southern China coast in his anticolonial determination! How odd to recognize only now that the anti-British-importation Tea Party resonates. The Tea Party, like Lin Tse-Hsu's story, may serve as anticolonial in relation to the British, but it disregards settler colonial and interior forms of management, such as the degree to which the story of the Opium Wars might eventually serve what would be eventual Han nationalist sentiment and indeed planned settlement throughout China.

In this account India remains, and will remain, in partial shadow, and it does not suffice for me simply to mention that within Bengal, traditions of opium use existed for centuries before opium's explosive emergence in networks of transnational capitalism fueled by colonial arrangement. The allegation that the British simply imposed opium, and Chinese and Indians submitted to it, is flattening, and indeed, Zheng Yangwen's meticulous study of the "social life" of opium in China makes it laughable.

Instead, Zheng shows how opium use in China of course followed its *own* eras, from an early period of tribute usage among elites to its spread among the poor through cross-class urban forms of entertainment such as sex in urban centers. The emergence of what would eventually be roaring operations of smuggling and governmental suppression was fueled in the late eighteenth century by the British East India Company's attempt to control ever greater forms of capital, what Lin Tse-Hsu called the Queen's insatiable desire. And between the first Opium War and the second, missionaries not only became more active in the battle against opium but, as Zheng claims, actually took over the moral narrative about opium, changing how it was received outside its borders. Opium had been cultivated all over China, and in India, and for some time. The acceleration of usage that led to Lin Tse-Hsu's confiscation of opium shipments turned out to be linked to a failure to contain opium within the wealthy classes, preventing its entry into realms of "distaste." Most importantly, opium was "not only a [immensely diversified] cash crop, but a political crop."[36] That is, opium literally funded political shifts, including the Communist Revolution under Mao—and here it is worth returning to the question of what the opium wars may have contributed to Han ethnic retrenchment and settlement within China.

Where does opium begin, and where does it end? What are the legitimate ways to understand its temporalizing reach, whether in political dissent, onto Chinese, British, and Indian bodies, and via condensed images of diaspora? It would be dishonest to spin the simplest tale linking opium's aphrodisiac or lambent qualities to political slowness. Yet desire, and the commodification of it, played an enormous role in China's political history.

Constitution by Policy

The above analysis must be completed by another observation: the sense that opium in sedative form had a directly *institutional* function, rendering likely resistant subjects more docile. Such containment strategies condensed the effects of animacy, and of deanimation, by drawing ever more tightly together the downward web of race, evolution, and sentience, so that a "Mongoloid" body could simply be understood to be self-explanatory, self-perpetuating, and magically self-generating because it was not conceivable otherwise.

This kind of condensation of animacy, a kind of "making constitution," can be amply identified in contemporary cases, the most visible of which at this moment is the association between poor children and high traces of lead in the water supply in the city of Flint in the US state of Michigan, where it was revealed that community concern in Flint about contaminants in a re-sourced water supply had been ignored at many levels of government. The revelation that it was primarily poor Black children whose lives (and whose minds, in view of the consensus that brain damage is viewed as the greatest threat from lead toxicity) were at stake, entered national political expressions of sympathy and community outrage at levels that seemed sensitized to (and to some degree responsive to) reverberations from recent years of Black Lives Matter activism.

Environmental justice work has long pointed to a dehumanization of certain communities that insidiously assists such long-standing abuses and asymmetries of care. On top of what are already institutionalized networks of privilege and neglect, access and closure, Blackness has not simply or only been treated as radically other, as suggested by some racial ontologies, but has a positionality too easily crafted *within* animacy hierarchies: de-sentient, de-evolved, and poorly judging subjects, subjects whose subjectivity is alienable or insufficient. Tellingly and hauntingly, in light of the consumptive theatricality made of Black deaths today, Saidiya Hartman writes, in reference to John Rankin's florid restaging in 1837 of what he saw as the theatrical evils of slavery:

> Can the white witness of the spectacle of black suffering affirm the materiality of black sentience only by feeling for himself? Does this not only exacerbate the idea that black sentience is inconceivable and unimaginable but, in the very ease of possessing the abased and enslaved body, ultimately elide an understanding and acknowledgment of the slave's pain? ... Does this not reinforce the very "thingly" quality of the captive by reducing the body to evidence in the very effort to establish the humanity of the enslaved?[37]

Hartman incisively attends to the performative making-evidence of the Black body in ways that she doubts could have remedying effects for knowledge. This needed questioning has consequences for method as well as for ontology, obliging caution, too, for diagnostic, even purportedly anti-racist, deployments of constitution as a notion: that is, constitution should neither self-replicate nor further entrench the beings it would contain. From a different angle, Eve Tuck regards the rehearsal of frameworks depicting harm as damage-based research and calls for Native communities to turn away from feeling that such research is a necessary evil that still furnishes access to rare resources.[38] The importance of ontology (which Tuck described as another word for colonialism), to the extent it is engaged, is such that the depth of racism cannot be adequately apprehended if it is narrated as the momentary abandonment or neglect of otherwise full and rights-bearing subjects.[39] Such is the transhistorical ontologization of race, deeply materially embedded, and motivated in clusters of meaning and materializing vectors in such a way that it seems to work both backward and forward in time. For all these reasons, it is not only important to be attentive to empire's recurring, and racialized, fear of the interpenetration of chemicals and minds, but there are further cautions about consequential fixities resulting from research. Such fixities or representations not only further disadvantage communities but threaten their further materialization by an image that powerfully abrades against acts of self-determination.

Toxic Assets

Not all (slow) constitutions are wrought by the clinical imagination of a model individual human body, replicated across a class. Sometimes constitutional affects can come from illusions of capital itself, as I briefly illustrated in the Introduction. I turn now to offer an extended historical example of a nexus of toxicity-disability-race that foreshadows the agitated beings of chapter 2, with a focus on finance capital.

For all the abstraction of contemporary economics, the US financial crisis of 2007 (and ensuing moments of danger, such as the near-collapse of small banks such as Silicon Valley Bank in 2023) put into relief finance capital's reliance on imputations of "health" and "toxicity." This seemingly metaphorical overlay and the dynamics it afforded were more than fanciful—their ramifications were materially consequential. Within that global crisis, it is striking that the term *toxic assets* was commonly applied to deregulated and dehistoricized mortgage products that, in their unmanageable volumes, insecurely guaranteed massive amounts of debt and were hence afforded primary blame for the crash. As a registration of the dominance of abstract free-trade entities over the geography of national borders, the crisis articulated transnationally.

Historically, the term *toxic asset* began as a financial term referring to an asset with a market value far below its book value, making it unsellable. In practice, such assets needed to be written off the books as soon as possible, because their values declined so precipitously that a corporation might not recover its "health." Capitalism's ironies, the opposing interests of its parties, enflesh a seeming conflict within the term; specifically: How does the toxic asset, this contradictory blend of positivity (asset) and negativity (toxic), come to flag the means for a local *recapacitation* of a financial "body" whose concomitant *debilitation* of other "bodies" is erased by the naturalization of finance capital? I will address this dynamic in the pages to follow.

By the intentional use of the terms *body* and *capacity*, I mean to generously expand the stage for an approach that will link actual and figural connections among individual human bodies (the common stage actor of medical scenarios, the "patient") and larger, often corporatized, abstract bodies whose effective materiality ironizes even the word *corporatize* as well as the idea that literal bodies must be medically central. The use of terms such as *health* was remarkably present in discussions of the economic crash. I am interested in what I suggest is an integral fabric of racialization within dominant disability and illness narrations and accounts, even within scenes seemingly remote from the clinic. As is true of racialization in general, effects are never merely figurative; they are materially consequential.

Along the lines of the naturalizing work done by the imputation of "health," and its concomitant systems models, I note as well the importance of homeostasis within finance capital. Nation-states and corporate entities seated in the Global North have grandly benefited from a trusted homeostasis of an international financial body within which the United States understands itself as fundamentally active. This is a seeming homeostasis built upon the naturalization of the free movement of capital and, correspondingly, the tricks of the World Trade Organization (WTO) and the North American Free Trade Agreement (NAFTA) policies and rationalizing frameworks that make that movement invisible. These meta-corporate, meta-national organizations incur their own swaths of debility through combinations of juridical challenges to environmental, labor, and public health protections; the assembly of transnational industrial dependencies under corporate direction; and the usual accumulation of profit/impoverishment. This accumulation can be understood as a dynamically linked dyad of capacity/debility.

Here I refer to Jasbir K. Puar's development of the idea of "debility," which she opposes to "disability." If disability is a more atomizable list of conditions viewed as specific to the individual body, most compatible with Euro American identity-based rights formulations, then debility points to a broader, biopolitical mapping of both actual and fictionalized capacities and debilities that are lent to statistics and that can be shared by populations.[40] Debility meaningfully functions as a way to begin to understand the grave transnational consequences of actions that can ironically be wedded, for Puar, to neoliberalized nationalisms going by the names of gay rights or disability rights.

One reason debility takes an important patterning in this book is that "disability" is treated partly as a matter of administration and governance, and in fact as a somewhat rare achievement; like many other categories designated for legal protection, it has many undersides (for instance, the erasure of hate speech on the basis of race and sex sits beneath the positive legal claim on just one of these). When "a" disability reaches the status of a legal category, it does so in the context of a legal protection that is shaped from within, not from outside of, majoritarian legal schemes, under norms of coherence, and is therefore exposed to the provisions of legal legitimation, rather than being based on, for instance, the rendering of intersectional justice. Whereas debility could be considered an extant reality of capitalist modernity today, only some of the conditions for and consequences of debility meet the conditions of recognition and interest to be considered as administrative disability. This complex relationship between debility and disability might be considered in synchronic analogy to what my archival cases outline: (moments of) the diachronous development of administrative categories of disability out of otherwise inchoate (to alienated systems of legitimation and value, at least) living conditions.

Whereas finance capital has long been naturalized as a core system not only transnationally but also within the United States, it has come to seem remarkably "unnatural," particularly under the cold light of representations by Occupy visionaries of 2011, and as I write in 2023 the major risk to the system posed by widespread small bank failures has the same effect. Under such destabilizations, its proper affects as well as its implicit investments come into relief. And it is useful to note that part of the United States' extended economic event of 2007–12 was blamed on a flush, like a bad algae bloom, of toxic assets linked to the real estate market, perhaps further informed by environmental images of fetid, blooming ills. From the point of view of the system, toxic assets—besides their identity as disconnected in actual value from their book value and thus unsellable—are financial entities that are products of uncertain and untraceable genealogy, thus in some sense queer and racially unmoored.

This is a reminder of the implicit presence of sexuality in calculations of reproductive value, in this case in the proprieties of the reproduction of capital weighed against one another. Perhaps in part because of the ranging queerness of unlinked assets, and certainly because such assets function contagiously by being resolutely negating—better get it out of your system or you might die—

the vital logics of finance capital demand that they must be sequestered if at all possible. From the point of view of individuals, the loans were rickety byproducts of a multi-administration effort to encourage broad-spectrum homeownership while delivering unequal costs of this implementation: a racialized and classed distribution of safer to less-secure loans was administered such that, once packaged and once collectively failing, the less-secure loans became macrotoxins in the larger system.

The financial language includes the idea that balance sheets can become "impaired," banks can pass stress tests and then be deemed "healthy." Even the toxic assets themselves are alternatively called "impaired assets" and, being illiquid, are deemed mobility-impaired, against which one can meaningfully juxtapose the willed free movement of capital. Already we have a concern about contradictions between the imagined neoliberal national body, against which toxic financial products threaten ill health, and the metonymic subpopulation of the toxic that must be alienated from the accepted flow of capital for that nation's own security. These persons become the background spectators of a system that resolutely wishes to overlook them while reaping the windfall of their expropriated assets. At the same time, under the rubric of crisis, corporations retreat and retool, creating new classes of unemployed and unemployable. In the financial world, the classed/raced people exposed to the bad loans disproportionately then come to represent, stand in for, the toxic asset. They are glossed by Laura Kang's invocation of the "racialized figure of undeserving and undisciplined 'subprime' borrowers in the U.S. housing market."[41] And yet the importance of their "health," financial or otherwise, was negligible in relation to that of the institutions, which were restored with "stress tests" and redoing the books.

In 2013 it was reasoned that Spain should get European help to quarantine toxic assets by removing them from banks' balance sheets. (Note that the term *quarantine* had a very active medical valence for human bodies in the COVID-19 pandemic that began around the start of 2020, but instead of calling that use "literal" versus the treatment of toxic assets as "metaphorical," I am much more interested in the affective deployments common to these cases.) Note the language used by Spanish budget minister Cristobal Montoro: "A first very important policy is to clean up the banking system . . . we need to segregate from those balance sheets the assets that are damaged by the crisis."[42] If the language repeatedly invoked to define the fearful attitude toward these toxic assets is that of "dirt" and "contagion," we might also consider the semantics of laundering, in this case the rewhitening of property as finance capital. The European Union's governing logic of how to handle its trouble countries mirrors US decisions about its own banks. Transnational capital is a debility/capacity machine at work. Its central dynamic is arguably retoxification (through capital accumulation, as well as industrial externalization in the form of chemical imposition) and detoxification (the withdrawal from designated "risk"), always with the racialized poor to be repeatedly flayed by its actions.

The next section may feel an abrupt shift from transnational capital to a repeating theme in popular culture. Yet the logic of indebtedness connects them and, furthermore, continues the narrative of the exaggerated re-homing of financial risk from corporations to human bodies. And it makes further sense of a humming nexus of race and disability that normally goes undetected. I further demonstrate the deployment of environmentalization as a partner to intoxication, and the blur between contamination and contraction, infection and illness, disability and debility.

Environmentalization: Zombies among Us

The past fifteen years have been marked by an upsurge of interest in the zombie figure. US popular culture has embraced all form of monstrosity, but particularly zombies: zombie hordes of diverse characters, mobilities, and provenances shambling, snarling, whimpering, and running, through mainstream films, TV shows, novels, and video games.[43] Arguably, anticapitalist demonstrations related to global economic crises and retrenchments from 2007's Occupy movement may have been a moment of the zombie's eruption into the light. While some probing performance studies analyses map the reflections of economic zombification onto Occupy-based theatrical performances, I want to look more closely at the contemporary zombie's realization in terms of the differences made evident by transnational queer and disability perspectives.[44] It is important to reject the seeming transparency, or inevitability, of the more common economic analysis—one in which zombie capitalism not only produces but also predetermines the cultural, indeed embodied, shape of the biopolitical figure of the eternal, undead laborer who exists under desubjectifying conditions. Identifying the presumptive debility within that predetermination marks disabled difference within and of the zombie horde, while extending the questions in this chapter about the variants of slowness.

There is debate about which of the many monster films of the 1930s to 1960s was the greatest popularizer of zombies. George Romero's 1968 *Night of the Living Dead* is recognized as having implicitly domesticated zombies, which up until then had been explicitly linked to exogenous Vodou. In their many popular forms today, it might be too optimistic to claim a faithful derivation from West African or Caribbean Vodou traditions, in which a zombie is understood as an animated corpse, except perhaps that they, even when whitewashed, racialize a Black-brown undead and can potentially be inflected—as they were for some Haitian slaves—by the threat of a commission to eternal labor. Tavia Nyong'o once named the zombie figure's enduring Blackness, rather than, as can often happen, generalizing the historic zombi-slave to a present-day postracial horde of the disaffected. Colonial processes of generalization, fetishization, and appropriation blur the indebtedness and genealogical relation of contemporary zombie "voodoo" figures to what has been commonly credited as their progenitor, Haitian Vodou zombis. These processes align with the spiritual exoticism and orientalism common to the American West. Given the tremendous variety of zombie forms, characteristics, and appearances today, it feels less beneficial to try to draw a reliable genealogical map among them than to identify what *kinds* of zombie have been instrumentalized for what apparent kinds of purposes.[45]

Without diminishing this important marking of race, I nevertheless wish to shift away from the more general conclusions that are facilitated by an implicit equation and automatic negation of both desubjectification and disability, and toward the *quality* of ability/disability emphasized therein. In my view such an observation can be productively in conversation with the implicit Blackness—or, to consider the complexly racialized textures of contemporary labor, the nonwhiteness—of the eternally laboring figure. I wish in particular to consider larger discourses involving the relationships between shifted capacity, the will toward a certain kind of life, and (economic) productivity and participation.[46] In the background sit several readings of the popular zombie figure: as a convenient foil for the undead laboring or economically poor hordes of late capitalism (differently from some Occupy representations in which zombies represented rapacious capitalists in whiteface), as one that shambles to a temporality akin to slow death, and as a marker for one end of humanity's parsing through the undiluted register of life.

Eating as Viral Reproduction

In investigating the strange politics among zombie vitality, disability, and death, a key question remains: if the zombies of popular culture wish to eat, then what kinds of eating do they engage in? How do queer forms of ingestion, digestion, excretion, and reproduction intersect with zombie ways? Some zombies, particularly the infectious variety, eat in a manner of sorts. They move their jaws, they clamp, bite, and chew, although not for self-sustenance but to reproduce—yet here, not even to reproduce themselves, but to reproduce a *quality*: that strange drive toward lifely/deathly perpetuation. Rather than this being performed through the individuated casting of a set of rituals by a Vodou practitioner, many contemporary zombies may themselves perform this reproduction in a viral fashion, so that the parasitic substance itself operates as directive toward their behavior and desires (as in rabies, for instance). They cannot digest what they eat, for their own viscera are often disordered or nonoperational (they neither urinate nor defecate); and their apprehension by the uninfected or uninjured involves a mixture of fear and disgust. This ostensibly postracialized caricature of zombies of popular culture thus queerly reproduces horizontally through a combination of viral contamination and eating, a contradictory bodily logic that confounds even the identitarian valences of communicability: in a strange temporality, the object that is eaten becomes simultaneously dead and undead, itself and not itself.

The mouth, still key for biting and infection even while the digestive tract (viscera) no longer operates; the brain, still key to the perpetual animation of the zombie even if (or precisely because) it is, for all practical purposes, disabled. In myriad visual instantiations of zombie figures, such as the TV series *The Walking Dead* (which has been quite faithful in its visual schematics to the comics of the same title),[47] exposed viscera—viscera functioning otherwise—seem to signal a region between disability and death. It is this in-between region from which neoliberal characterizations of disability have been arguably drawn; indeed, Not Dead Yet, a disability rights organization that acts against the facilitation of euthanasia on the basis of ostensibly unlivable disability or pain, has named itself as a precise registration of this dangerously ambivalent region.[48] Such a fixture on the viral communicability of zombieness, furthermore, draws on and benefits from two extant tendencies: one, the ever-growing pantheon of diseases imagined to be rapidly communicable across borders of all kinds; and two, the obscuring of neoliberal global economics' role in zombification by misrepresenting movements of capitalist depredation as lateral or rhizomatic (for instance, that disability could reproduce disability by association, rather than capitalism producing disability in a more vertical sense). Indeed, dead/undead begins to sound very familiar in relation to the practical suspension of disability between capacitation and debility within the US context and elsewhere. Puar's examination of the disability/debility dynamic within Western colonial paradigms captures this shadowy disability well: by exceptionalizing disability (enumerable, perceptible, and bureaucratically amenable disabilities), it is then possible for capitalist and colonial (patriarchal, racist) states to evacuate the vast realm of debility.

Elspeth Probyn, framing her wide-ranging queer exploration of food with an appeal to the body, offers apt contrastive guidance for reading food in zombies. She writes:

> Eating both confirms what and who we are, to ourselves and to others, and can reveal new ways of thinking about those relations. To take the most basic of facts: food goes in, and then, broken down, it comes out of the body, and every time this happens our bodies are affected. While in the usual course of things we may not dwell upon this process, that basic ingestion forces us to think of our bodies as complex assemblages connected to a wide range of other assemblages. In eating, the diverse nature of where and how different parts of our selves attach to different aspects of the social comes to the fore and becomes the stuff of reflection.[49]

What happens, then, when food does not go in but instead just flaps around, exiting a holey corpse-spot as soon as it seems to enter? Less literally: Are these only fictive bodies that struggle with "the most basic of facts"—eating without ingesting and while exposing, in some sense, their own failing viscera? Disability scholars, particularly those using the form of narrating and analyzing disabled experiences, have had plenty to say, in rejoinder, about journeys through visceral uniqueness and its staging within and outside of disability community ("different aspects of the social"). While it may seem understandable to resist associating a spectacularized, shambling zombie, which may need some assistance to achieve its goals, to a human being's ordinary need for a personal assistant for eating, movement, or excretion, I equally wonder about the oddity of *not* recognizing the evident presence of disability among the zombies. I say this not to assert a unified identity category, or to demand that disability colonize every space of corporeal difference, but to see what becomes analytically possible if we recognize disability's structural relevance to precisely those kinds of corporeal difference that come prepackaged, safely of a different world. The gesturally and pragmatically spectacular stumble, or shamble, and digestive dysfunction, scream disability and yet are illegible as such because such evidences are naturalized to the fiction of the racialized horde, where disability cannot exist but debility flourishes.

Such recognition is uneven at best, but it has been around, with mixed results. Wade Davis's *The Serpent and the Rainbow*, having presented itself as a narrative account of Davis's study of Haitian Vodou zombi rituals while a graduate student in ethnobotany, serves as a notorious backdrop for any study of zombies as it has been critiqued and ethically opposed by multiple sources.[50]

Davis's main source of funding was a pair of scientists who were eager to identify what they believed was a single plant source that would produce the stupor and near-death state characteristic of the known zombie cases in Haiti; they had the eventual goal of generating new pharmaceutical knowledge.

Even though Davis introduces his book under a sympathetic guise of writing openly about the devastating role of colonialism and the slave trade in the life of Haiti and its citizens, the book is also framed un-self-consciously with its own rapacious and extractive interest in seeking out useful biological material. The book quickly resolves into its own humanist anthropology in which Davis realizes that a single isolated chemical action—the biochemical toxicity of tetradotoxin—cannot be self-standing, but instead serves as a material basis for "magic" and other immaterial Vodou cultural processes. Writhing beneath the lurid, novelistic detective story of Davis's search remained the figure of the ethnobotanical gold, the specific toxin that would be discovered to effect—albeit in concert with the magical beliefs and cultural materializations of the Haitians—the illness, the metabolic slowdown, and the zombie trance that enabled a body to be revived from its recent grave to be committed to labor. However, such disability was not always temporary: Davis noted that not all of the reanimated he learned about had recovered enough to become usable for labor. According to his sources, some who were revived appeared to have cognitive and motor disabilities that had not been there before. Davis's understanding was that they were not able to be fully and successfully revived, and that damage had been done somewhere in the process. A biomedically influenced account, unsurprisingly, must register disability insofar as its goal is to measure the variable effects of a biologically suppressive toxin on human bodies.

Debility and Debt in Zombie Economics

Here, recognizing the radical insufficiency of the biomedical approach to disability in zombification, I continue to think about disability in the context of capitalism, continuing the discussion of toxic assets above. Within systems of transnational capitalism, the transnational labor both within and beyond the borders of the United States, attuned to the priorities of Western-owned capital by which free trade is unilaterally envisioned, is systemically subject to deprivations imposed on laborers and residents, only some of which lead directly to changes that are commonly legible as disability.

In this scheme, the poor and working class become the background spectators of a system that resolutely overlooks them while assuming the not-insubstantial windfall of their expropriated assets. At the same time, under the rubric of crisis, corporations retreat and retool, creating new classes of unemployed and unemployable. This consolidates a transfer of risk. Given economies in which the vast majority of disabled people are already categorized and managed as nonproductive, and the ways Lauren Berlant has identified in which those economies answer underprivileged American aspirations toward the good life with the stunningly blithe biopolitical result of something they label as slow death or lateral rather than forward movement, the reach of debility here alone is quite astounding.[51] Disability and poverty increasingly touch one another, and biopolitically they are rendered proximate.

According to the late anthropologist David Graeber, the world today shows a legible division between creditors and debtors, legible because the indebted generally constitute formerly colonized countries that have been made subject to arbitrary debt amounts (as when, importantly, Haiti after its successful uprising was made indebted to France) and/or interest rates that are impossible to satisfy.[52] Ultimately there is a system of the chronically indebted (so-called Third World countries or former colonies) and the apparently exceptionally indebted (such as Germany or the United States, despite the fact that the United States is in fact a debtor nation), but hardly incapacitated, that works both internationally as well as intranationally, and this system is linked with what Graeber calls a moral economy of debt. That economy of debt is also racial, and not only transnationally: Denise Ferreira da Silva's *Unpayable Debt* traces the colonial provenances, including the fungibilities begat by the economic systems of slavery, upon which ostensibly universalist discourses continue to depend.[53]

The bad debtors are not only morally unredeemable, because they brought this upon themselves and thus not deserving of forgiveness; they also are in a relationship of indefinite obligation. Thus, these formal relations of debt come hand in hand with moralities and affects. As Puar writes, "If signification and representation (what things mean) are no longer the only primary realm of the political, then bodily processes (how things feel) must be irreducibly central to any notion of the political."[54] Given the rapidly canceling operations of impending homelessness and the failure of social supports to meet even their sharply reduced mandates, in the lives of individuals chronic indebtedness risks an accelerated temporality of death.

Incipient Awareness of Disability: Radiant Slowness

Keeping in the background this relation of chronically indebted subject to debility, I move now to talk about the peculiar disabling of zombies in popular visual and gaming cultures. Popular zombies are so translucently modeled on disability—indeed, racialized disability—and audiences are so familiar with them, that there is a rehearsal of cognitive and physical disability in their specific movements, their cognitive fog, their labile moods, their missing limbs; spectators and game players enjoy rehearsing the mind-numbing ritual of exorcising—that is, running away from, or violently attacking—those disabled bodies in order to maintain the security, strength, and noncontamination of their own.

Such audiences curiously perceive and fail to recognize the ways in which such zombies map onto disability. At the height of popular zombie entertainment, several ironic websites today appeared, dedicated to "disability rights" in the name of these cognitively impaired, physically impaired zombies whose personhood is allegedly nowhere recognized in the American Disabilities Act. One of these was zombierights.org (now defunct), which had the ostensible goal of selling a book called *The Zombie Survival Guide*. The site stated: "They are and should be called the living impaired. As such they should be eligible for government care during these trying times. Zombies find it hard to maintain work due to their condition and require special care.... Accept them into society. They are people too. Remind them of this fact every time you see one lurching down the street, or hiding in a dark alley." Note the coincidence of disability and class in this example.

Max Brooks, the author of *Zombie Survival Guide* as well as the best-selling *World War Z*, demonstrates that he is fully aware of the status of zombies as thought-provokingly "disabled" subjects, just not living ones, or not quite persons, who temptingly invite discourses of pity and empathy.[55] Such gestures to disability represent an "emergent use of disability" that registers its integration into a zone of recognized rights-bearing subjects even as the zombies themselves are only barely recognizable as embodiments of that disability. We might identify not only an index of global capitalism's investment in eternal labor, but also, more specifically, a push-pull between rights claims and exclusions of tentative subjects played out through postracial raciality and post-disabled disability in the figure of the contemporary zombie.

Another example is the website zombierightscampaign.org, which has a section called "The Lurch for the Cure." And we must note here the repetition and significance of lurching, which we can only understand as the expression of zombie undeadness or proximity to death; that understanding is built on already having an implicit recognition of the biopolitical devaluation of people with cerebral palsy and the more general linking of brain injury and motor control. This link between lurching and zombies does not go unrecognized among people with cerebral palsy. Isaac Stein, for instance, in the *Disability Studies Quarterly* connects his more palsied movements to a heightened zombielike appearance.[56] What does it mean, then, that the lurch has become such a resilient, signal quality of the undead? Another website, CURE: Citizens for Undead Rights and Equality, has an FAQ for the unsupportive human: "Zombies are not always able to choose to change their behaviors, but adult human beings have the intelligence and ability to choose between behaviors that hurt others and behaviors that do not hurt others. When given the choice, it makes sense to choose compassion."[57] Under neoliberalism, compassion is an affective obligation, much like hope, that comes without transcorporeal or transidentitarian investments in justice.

The ostensible owner of the website Zombrex turns out after several clicks to be the video game maker Capcom, which continues to make millions on its zombie-shooting games (*Dead Rising* and *Dead Rising 2*) with multiracial human casts that are staged invariably in devitalized, dilapidated urban zones. So compassion—that word again—is fine, but you should kill the zombies, as they should be eliminated in the final accounting. This disability-savvy Internet Capcom gaming twist is made even more elaborate when we recognize that the number of game-playing disabled people is not insignificant; as one disabled gamer has written, the experimental worlds provided within these games allow for fantastical avatars of all kinds of abilities, as well as alternative possibilities for social life.

One final twist is that in these cultural productions, cure seems always to be an ill-fated wish of the naive, as one can see in season two of the *Walking Dead* TV series, so much of whose zombie overwhelm scenes take place in places of infrastructural abandonment (prisons, open yards, alleys, occupied buildings, roadways)—spaces that again racialize and class zombie being. But I take the presented naiveté of cure not as the thoughtful adoption of an ambivalence about cure by disabled people in a regime of medicalized health that devalues disability, but instead as an expression of the neoliberal pessimism about the difficulty of integrating the already disabled or debilitated (except for the white monied disabled men repeatedly represented in mainstream films). As Eunjung Kim writes, "For many, cure demands that we suspend our living in the present and instead wait for a future without disabilities and illnesses, urging us to not live in the present... the promised transformation through cure is enticing enough to make losses and hastened death acceptable, even expected."[58] Zombies matter not because they are, to use Jack Halberstam's term, a silly archive,[59] not because they are pop culture, but because they are pedagogical: they are vitalized precisely by way of haptic networks that teach (troubling things about) the contaminating sensations of disability, raciality, gender, and sexuality. The pedagogies are themselves quite stable, not easily dislodged. Years later, I have not forgotten one mother's response to a presentation I made from this work. The entertainment value of zombies in this contemporary sphere of television and gaming means that they come with an understanding that they are fun to think with. In an amiable protest against my allegation about zombies' incipient disability, toxicity/virality, and racialization, such that the rehearsal of their killing leaves me with many painful questions, that mother came up to me only to say: "Well, my son really enjoys it. Sometimes young people just want to shoot and have fun!"[60]

In light of the political limits of disability nationalisms and selective recapacitations that Robert McRuer and Jasbir Puar have in their turn articulated, it seems to me that these zombie figures, these virally intoxicated entities that have become dangerous to a privileged few lifely subjects, could usefully help to accentuate or dramatize the well-deserved question marks that dominant spheres must entertain about integrity and identity in a posthumanizing biopolitics. Recognizing debility, the ongoing proximity of certain populations to chronic indebtedness, might be a way for a transnationalizing disability studies to be able to cite the valuation—the rejection of negation—of disability (which otherwise might tend toward a narrowed American identity politics and toward a disability nationalism) as an enactment of affinity, and the possibility of harm, in the same breath.

Against Health: "There Is No Waste"

I end this section with a gesture to a different zombie, Xombi, a DC Comics character created in 1994 by David Rozum. According to the narrative, a Korean American scientist named David Kim was developing a nanotechnology virus, and through a course of dangerous events had to be injected with the virus in order to save his life. When his body was populated with the nanotechnology and he was revived, he became Xombi. He did not suffer any particular loss of capacity, except for a strange fixing, a bodily permanence with details: In the first issue of the revived series in 2004, an early panel shows Xombi in the middle of grabbing two beer bottles, reflecting on his bodily efficiency. A thought box reads: "Chet [his best friend] just finished his third beer and he's been to the bathroom just as many times. I've had five and I'll never have to urinate. Ever. I can even drink five more and be just as sober as I was before I started my first beer." A second thought box, to the right of the first, reads: "My body is super efficient now. Everything can be processed, even stuff that was never meant to be food. There is no waste."[61]

For all his continuing rational, cognitively elaborated powers through his xombiness, I am most interested in Xombi's peculiar configuration of embodiment, one positioned between the wasteless, changeless undead, invulnerable to (further) intoxication, in which everything can be perfectly processed or everything can't at all be processed (presumably there is no waste in either case; for the latter I am thinking of the eviscerated zombies that shamble through the *Walking Dead*). I wonder what might be promised by the hint of melancholy accompanying this declaration; in the previous frame Xombi has named the loss of his pre-Xombified, more aged self, as well as the loss of his assistant and friend whose life became the cost of his own revitalization.

"There is no waste" compels a different series of associations: the presence of waste—of excess, of proliferations beyond those that are heterosexually mandated—for me is coextensive with the spirited presence of queerness (one willfully racialized as nonwhite) and with a resistant troubling of the mercilessly raw cuts of late capitalism that can make labor, comfort, or wealth seem but a distant dream. The antipsychotic drug Abilify, understood as providing a *restoration* of capacity by way of chemical modulation, is not for these who are marked by terminal waste; and biomedicine's deep capitalization only widens gaps of interest and exploitation, such as might be said of Wade Davis's motive for traveling to Haiti in the first place.

I am also reminded of disability's sometimes reluctant, sometimes gleeful (crip) hold on nonproductivity—its definition under capitalism is nearly synonymous with antiproductivity—and the gorgeous things that can occasionally happen within a life lived against the grain of colonized time.[62] If remembering the raciality of today's zombies remains important, at the same time I also love not knowing where these bottled-up (constipated), eviscerated (scarred), munchy (sampling, nibbling, grazing) shamblers (motor impaired) are headed, what energies motor their bodies, and how they'll get there. As evidently disabled avatars, not just resolutely healthful subjects of economic devastation, they are much more like ourselves and our companions in life than most of us have allowed ourselves to admit. If it's been hard for any of us to find the right way, then I submit they've got to be on to something. Pooping is reproductivity; no waste is queerness, and it is also stagnancy: there is no poop is constipation, but "there is no waste" is also some other kind of life. "Some other kind of life": some other kind of human, some other kind of species, some other chain of reproductivity, some other genre of living.

Slow Time

The Arabic name for poppy is abu an-num (ابو النوم), "father of sleep"; Linnaeus gave the poppy plant the name *papaver somniferum* (sleep + bring) in 1753. These namings constitute a recognition of the poppy's extant history of *altering* uses, animate contact between human and plant, already for millennia. Even though sleep is not identical to slowness, the term *somniferum* might provide a link to intoxicatory renderings as dynamic in sentience. It otherwise seems certain that there have long been common ways in which to consider opium as in fact a slow plant, though the definition of slowness is infinitely variable; the intoxications of a slow plant (or, at some point, drug) had the effect of slowing perceptual time for its user, and perhaps also for its external witnesses. Furthermore, moving beyond the dyadic mode of medicinal delivery—that of modern doctor to patient, or of specialized healer or shaman—what ways exist to consider the use of opium as *self*-tuning in some cases? When was opium necessary to get through the conditions of a barely tolerable present?

And are there ways to understand the stretch and tug between the present tense of the verb *slow*, of biopolitical and biochemical actancy, and the adjective *slow* or the past participle *slowed*, each of which reveals a longer-term enmeshment of affects into the appearance of a constitution? The past participle also suggests a passivizing reception of slowness, a force from without. The "intoxicated" of the title is both a process and a state. The title is meant to serve, however, as an indictment of the state told as a feature, retelling it as process—in my version, a process that might involve self-direction.

What does it mean to think about developmental time, global economic time, and delay together, as Down did, commingling racial delay with developmental disability to the point that they cannot be separated? What kinds of temporal politics clashed in the case of Down's patients, and which temporal politics emerged as dominant? And what does it mean to ask questions about legacy effects, to take such thinking as not exceptional in the present but instead as actively structuring that present?

Finally, where does sexuality, in the form of Down's understanding of his patients as all looking so densely similar to one another, like "children of the same parents," inform the understanding of delay, and similarly of race, which is itself constituted on the fundamental basis of an increasingly biologized understanding of heterosexual reproduction—of breeding? In fact, reproductive time was a central aspect for Down for mongoloid idiocy and the lessons that could be drawn from it. I return to Down's phrase that, owing to the resemblances among affected children, "they must be children of the same parents" and the accompanying allegation that that phrase makes of a queer *or* racial density. A queer density compresses the familial unit—to allow other, similarly affected children, perhaps by a shared look, to enter into each other's families, thereby expanding parental identities. Similarly, a racial density allows for race and disability together, as in the "white Mongol" who bears intellectual difference, to assemble more ulterior kin in genealogical place. Thus, we see sexuality communing in a particular way—in a fostering of newfound genealogical densities—with racialized disability.

Intoxication is also a kind of density—a threshold amount, in blood percentages or parts per million of some sampling, upon which one can be said to be intoxicated. Medicinal dosing presupposes the possible range of intoxication. I don't yet know how to reconcile this condensation, this transversal, of kin with the likeness/absence of opium intoxication itself, except to want to meditate on the mirroring they suggest together. To think only in terms of appearance or phenotype might disallow the affective—if you will—vibrations across media. Slowness and density. That latter happens to be another word, in English, for intellectual incapacity. How do these notions carry one another? How do they make things queerer?

For Down, futures did indeed matter for such conditions. He wrote of guileless medical practitioners that they would be lost in inadequate systems of diagnosis and classification:

> Existing systems of classification . . . will entirely fail [the medical adviser] in the matter, and . . . he will have in many cases to make a guarded diagnosis and prognosis, so guarded, in fact, as to be almost valueless, or to venture an authoritative assertion which the future may *perhaps* confirm.[63]

But there was one aspect of reproductive time unimaginable to Down, despite his having had what could be called a creative and open imagination. It was his patients' own reproductive futurities. For Down, his patients were not imaginable as anything other than the subjects of their parents; they were not the future parents of others. That is to say, the classically nonreproductive queer inhered—and was to halt there in multiple dimensions—within the bodies of Down's patients. The struggle today for many people with Down syndrome to parent their own children without undue intervention might bear now, as then, marks of a carceral state as much as it does a colonial paternalism.

One can consider here the relationship between biopolitics, whose definition is so often imagined as involving a closed populace under a system of governance, and the transnational biologization of governance, which might include the different *heres* and *theres* of British opium, to use M. Jacqui Alexander's formulation of imperial geographies and temporalities as a "here" and a "there."[64] "Here" being London and the Earlswood clinic, though Earlswood also exercised a "there within the here" of Mongoloidness working within the bodies of the white children; and "there" being loci like "Asia" in its vulnerable entirety, but perhaps also London's Chinatown.

Opium, racial specificity, and intellectual delay formed a kind of interiority-exteriority, a (slow) constitution, in the bodies of Down's patients. Opium, racial specificity, and intellectual delay formed an *analogous* (slow) constitution in Chinese bodies entwined with opium through addiction and in pleasure. A transnational imaginary made vivid by Blumenbach, even if he did not innovate it, allowed for the sleight of hand that played matchy-matchy with enormous consequence.

Coming back to the slow time that sits at the heart of the biopolitical traversals of this chapter, for a last time I invoke the conundrum shared by George Estreich's well-meaning acquaintances: Is his child Japanese, or does she have Down syndrome? The "or" here poses an impossible or irresponsible conundrum, whereas an answer of "both" only helps somewhat. And the question of constitution lurks, even as genetics do not rise here to provide answers to uncertain racial or syndromic identity. Yet in formal terms, Estreich's narrative poses a resolution of sorts. The memoir temporally jumps from his mother's wartime experiences, to the time of his daughter's birth and her ensuing medicalization, to moments in his own upbringing, and to his crafting of his memoir. That is, it violates continuous, controlled time, perhaps beyond narrative convention (as in flashbacks). The effect is one of mixing, temporal *and* otherwise, and an overall effect of sharedness that nevertheless registers difference. By book's end, we have not arrived, either at the most developed, refined perspectives on disability, or at the moment of now. Nor has a new typological ordering of disability knowledge been instantiated.

Importantly, we do not ultimately know where the science is supposed to fit (trisomy 21 is not the winner), and it does not arbitrate. In some ways, the circumspection of medical authority is not unusual for a disability memoir. But viewed on the whole, this memoir is doing some other work that makes it both sensitive and unresolvable. The resolution-of-sorts, perhaps, is just right; the jumping may be a method—in this case, one perhaps not designed, and nearly indiscernible, wearing an identity of disorganization and apparent randomness, and yet one that most effectively works to sift nonidentical kin into a tensile yet fragile settling place.

It's an unsettled settling Estreich leaves us with. We might seem to disobey time's determinative logics, rejecting, say, the image of the chronic "developing country" for the synchronic "Global South," and rejecting the progressive narratives of neoliberalism that produce such attributes as backwardness, retrogradeness, and chronicity. But any experiment with "faux temporal latitudes" perforce yields surprising harmonies among different developmental stages that are born from development's logic. This is in part because of the substantiation, the mattering, that timing provides. There is something compelling and satisfying about its explanatory capacities, and it is not surprising that something similarly compelling like race might find good company in time. We might also keep close watch on development's own clock, attending to what it reveals about its multiple fabrications, about the interweavings of the ways that race, geography, sexuality, and disability are the very things that give form and texture to that thing we call ordinary time: that "mundane" face, that "regular" tick, tick, tick. Simultaneously, the notions that time informs flex and bend, revealing their investments, their protean natures, their attachments, their fictions. Whatever is called slowness fills these things. Simultaneously, they come together inside slowness.

Seated in (slow) time's nonidentity, I end this chapter with a gesture. I wish, ultimately, to reject the accounts that posit the continued racialized, disabled Mongol figure—a hybrid of the Asian racial position and the white intellectually disabled position—as a figure of vehement rejection, premised on the alienation of the two, the two that do not live as two (but also do). I would rather hold that we already live together. This is my invitation, then, to dwell where we are, in slow time, understanding nevertheless that even as we are kin, we are never always one and the same.

2

AGITATION AS A CHEMICAL WAY OF BEING

Chapter 1 concluded with questions of slow temporalities: temporalized human beings living at distances yet made kin from without, in such a way that the logics of constitution infused bodies, leaving behind the simplified externality of phenotype to form a curious combination of racial stereotype and bodily knowledge. Also apparent was an implicit structuring logic in reproductive, or sexualizing, time, which Down, based on racial misapprehensions, actually took as a sign of hope about the falsity of some forms of hereditary racial limit. In Down's case, slowness functioned affectively in the sense that it was more than simply a cast of representation, but, as I began to lay out in chapter 1, was driven *into* and *through* bodyminds in ways that patently refuse interior/exterior structuration, crossing temporality and medicine, behavior and phenotype.

Lost from that account, however, are the scenes of discontent, distress, alacrity, and freedom—both within Down's clinic and for any of those so reputed (such as "Mongols"), so constituted. That is—slow bodies surely don't stay steady in sincere languor; they are bodies that live in and by multiple temporalities, and as such constantly pose challenges to the temporal image given them. As those familiar with state archives might estimate, and as these archives seem to confirm, many of Down's residents in the clinics were awash in modes of nonconsent. What counts, to a resident patient likely there against their will, as the best response to a nurse making the rounds of intellectual assessment? Sometimes, in the archives, it seems to have been a refusal to honor the assessment. This is not simply resistance *within* modes of representation. The ways in which forms of governance, such as environmentalization, themselves *impute* constitutionality, have effects, mean that "compassion" in its reductive terms will also predictably be met with tumult. Drawing on my previous book, *Animacies*, this becomes a question extending beyond coveted or ordinary humanness, which is itself something of a circular question without absolute reference. As a consequence, the discussions of this chapter, particularly as it closes, extend beyond the transhumanization of people.

When I began to share the Down work with audiences, I was repeatedly asked temporality-based questions that were—perhaps obligingly, since I had talked about slowness and opium intoxication—aligned with the ramifications of speed in a context of chemical alteration. I often received, to my intrigue, questions to the effect of "What about fastness—for instance, the drug called speed?" Above and beyond the seemingly natural oppositional pairing between speed (fast) and opium (slow), it is actually quite indicative of its longstanding patterns of deployment that the primary (most frequently evidenced) senses of "slowness" in English use (OED) are in contexts indicating *intellectual lack*, rather than as strictly speed itself—if there even exists a bare "itself" of speed. (Interestingly, "quickness" does not follow the same use preference for intellectual acuity.) Such usage information casts in doubt a fantasy that speed alone informs something like "slowness." The harder question remains: Why, for the descriptive state or quality of being slow, has English-language semantics of "slowness" turned so determinedly to ideas of intellectual disability?

Note that this is an inversion of a perhaps more expected account adherent to hierarchies of notional scope: that this delimited space of exception of disability (say) would have had to borrow from the overweening structures of already-extant slowness, unchangeable in its pervasive reach in the basal logics of time. So, a provocation: I could do several things here. I might be able to make a plausible explanatory argument to answer this question. It is possible to claim, following others, that capitalism is an intensifying web of speed, read perhaps through ever-increasing demands for productivity and profit.[1] It is not at all unusual to understand disability as having been pitched, within capitalism, as *the* indicator of the nonproductive, so as capitalism goes, disability slows. That *could* be made to answer the question. While such arguments might attain, my position is otherwise: to plead a certain suspension of convictions (or of argument toward such convictions). The reason I turn in this direction is to respect how knowledge works for many of us, and thus to forward, and make transparent, what I could call a crip/intoxicated method.

I am a writer of a book, and yet, to recall my statement in the Introduction, I don't want to convince you of any *thing* even as I write with immense investment about the relations among race, intoxication, disability, and time. For academic book writers, or at least book writers who are also in the academy, to say this is a red flag, and I don't think I am alone. I do very much, however, want to steward you through a series of visits to junctures that in the ensemble may engage you in a different way. Indeed, circulation (not linearity) and indeterminacy have their own means of conveyance, and they have been necessarily usable strategies for anyone who has been straining to pay attention, to sustain and grow short-term memory traces, to force segregations in order somehow to learn about togetherness. There are also critiques about the relations between white supremacy and the force of rhetoric, argument, and linear order. I think back to high school. I regularly got Cs in history. Many of the problems I had were about reading, which had once been the joy of my life but became immensely difficult, almost nonexistent, by the age of twelve or thirteen (I now very rarely read fluently; undone reading populates my ongoing professional regret). For hours I would restart reading the first paragraph of a textbook chapter, then realize that nothing had entered and that I had to start again. It was impossible to keep track.

In a grab for dignity, perhaps, I initially tried disclaimers: that I was less interested in European history than in physics, or that high school US history had an imperial lens in the 1980s. While both may be true, they don't explain enough; I was trying hard to do well and I was tormented beyond proportion in the effort. My teacher had won a prize for his technique for teaching history via the flowchart: a straight line representing the inevitable flow of time. Arrows upon arrows upon arrows between nameable events demonstrating historical inevitability (or something? I still don't understand), from left to right. There was some interaction between events and the gestalt of stories that I (would have) read about them, and simultaneously temporal *and* causal relations that

I could not apprehend, premised on an inconceivable narrowing. Speech did not help to disambiguate, and audible speech, too, has been tricky to process.

To survive, to get the C and not the F, I scraped together a means of looking-without-looking, reading-without-reading. Plucking out words without their woven relation, and inviting them to join my thought, but without the clear guidance (owing to relations between cognition and grammar) of what would have accompanied them. It felt like mimicry, even though it was probably more like interpolation. This feels embarrassing, and for a proper academic troubling to admit, but it feels real and common enough to register here nevertheless. As to thresholds and delimitations: I don't know if this *medically* qualifies, because I have not submitted to testing, as dyslexic encounter; or if any other of my atypical experiences of sensation, perception, and sociality then and now count as neurodivergence, since diagnosis of my capacities with regard to education took a secondary role vis-à-vis my more obviously "medical issues"—my asthma, my bleeding, my sickness. As with intoxication, thresholds do and don't mean that much beyond legal schemes.

To respect neurodivergence as a mode of production as well as a mode of reception,[2] as something that could live between you and me, the moments that can be visited in this chapter do not proceed by a single principle, or a natural ordering as far as standard chronology, judgments of size, or other categorizations that might support a normatively cognitive encounter (the determinant of much publishing convention). They don't ask you to hold something for too long. They can be visited out of order. The point is that they sit together. But should one wish to read sequentially or at least know where things appear, here is an order of events, a random-access guide, for the chapter.

I begin with scenes of resistance for Down's patients, whose constitutions were not only his scientific diagnostic concern, but also his professional charge, to feed and medicate—to calibrate—them. One can say that, when confronted with a cognitive test, some of the patients both answered "correctly" and also answered "incorrectly," with room for "crip" somewhere within. The gap between correct and incorrect can be found in slowness, and also captures an inchoate politic. From there I move to discuss a moment that is signal for what Henri Bergson, a theorist of affect, called the comic, a moment premised on the look of a disability, to think affectively about the focus of this chapter, *agitation*.[3] In fact, agitation not only is familiar but is today pervasive within contemporary biopolitical discussions of embodiment, and I tour the vast domains that it currently serves: Western biomedicine, education, political expression. Within affective thought, Bergson built the comic upon notions of the machinic; aligned with an approach based on reaction, the look of inhumanity might have been particularly tempting as example.

A different way to think about Bergson's turn to the comic, however, is that laughter is also a response to a devastating tension around sacred (white) bodily ideality, erectness, and integrity, within which visible disability (what might be called "disfigurement," which I oppose in its referentiality) becomes intolerable. The question of an acceptable movement is imbued with its racial valence, and I let Bergson's signal figure fade into the shadows as I examine the presences of agitated disability in scenes of racialized intoxication. On the other hand, the intolerability of a "break" of white bodily ideality explains the immensely (for some) "watchable unwatchability" of white working-class, masculine flirtations with disability and death, in "What Could Go Wrong" videos, explored later in this chapter.

Bergson was thinking in a parahuman way about affect. It is why environmentalization bypasses the ideal of human agency, which has long been a certain idealist fantasy.[4] Furthermore, perhaps less so than for slowness, agitation has its own intimacies with chemicality. I consider the gestural lives of disabled, including environmentally harmed, people, in the realm of political expression. Agitated expression's chemicality ranges through the political, whether in "What Could Go Wrong" videos or the occupation of the US Capitol. I conclude with a turn to ambivalently "nonhuman" agitation, in an installation by artist Fiona Foley at the Brisbane Magistrates Court in Queensland, Australia, that ultimately puts the lie to human-nonhuman distinctions.

The Comic

Is it not, then, the case that the hunchback suggests the appearance of a person who holds himself badly? His back seems to have contracted an ugly stoop.

By a kind of physical obstinacy, by rigidity, in a word, it persists in the habit it has contracted. Try to see with your eyes alone. Avoid reflection, and above all, do not reason. Abandon all your prepossessions; seek to recapture a fresh, direct and primate impression. The vision you will reacquire will be one of this kind.

You will have before you a man bent on cultivating a certain rigid attitude whose body, if one may use the expression, is one vast grin.—**Henri Bergson,** *Laughter*[5]

If agitation is gesture, what makes its chemicality political? What acts, movements, gestures does an embodied archive of political agitation comprise? What are the forms and modes of embodiment that can be counted? What might it mean to focus on the embodiment of agitation as a form of living presence (and without prioritizing moral judgment as to its provenance or intention), rather than on the strategies used to kill it? These are admittedly abstract and enormous questions, but I wish to sketch out a broad range of imaginative possibility. Henri Bergson's musings about the disabled embodiment of a "hunchback," in his book *Laughter*, at first seem to have little in common with these questions, and yet they propose an intriguing, and demanding, theatrical set of conditions about durability, disabled appearance, and response—in particular, habitual or sedimented "contraction," "rigid attitude," "physical obstinacy," and, in this case, the primally, unreflectedly, comic.

Wildness—the motivating thematic for my engaging in this chapter on agitation, with thanks to Jack Halberstam and Tavia Nyong'o—and agitation are something like kissing cousins.[6] Wildness, for instance, can be associated with an excess of emotion ("an agitation of the soul"), which can itself be counterposed to notions of cultivation (Bergson's gesturally controlled comic). At the same time, some versions of agitation have the appearance of gestural repetition, suggesting to some observers the machinic over the natural. The term *agitation* has broad use and a broad range of value, crossing domains such as medical pharmacology, securitized educational and child developmental spheres, and political movements, where it is seen as a fundament of revolution. Agitation appears regularly in dramatic, individualized stories of contemporary drug scourges in the United States and elsewhere, which might not be unrelated to the fervor for cultures of resistive contamination seen in contemporary zombie shows. Most importantly, however, by its simplest movement definition, it is a part of everyday movement for a diverse number of people.

Does the term's nonmetaphorical reach across pharmacology and political movements signal a relation other than homonymy? I believe there are connections, in practice. My focus moves from a brief assessment of the nominative and conceptual hold that agitation has in contemporary American/US life to an etymology, followed by reflections on agitation's role in contemporary security discourses broadly construed (and they are indeed broadly implemented). Throughout my argument runs a justified abandonment of body-mind divisions such that it is, of course, legitimate to discuss both interior and exterior, incidental and historical, neurochemical incitements within and across bodies. The disciplinary encounter staged here could be described as ranging between gesture studies, critical race theory, medical humanities, and disability studies.

I stage this modestly, however, as I come at gesture studies from a combination of linguistics and animacy scholarship. This is necessarily a glancing and stubbornly (despite my efforts) ambiguous piece that cannot do full justice—bibliographic, critical, or even textual—to the many sites it visits. This glancing could be identified as a feature of my failure to maximally synthesize as a scholar, or of my attempt to carve a path across a number of traceable critical domains. And, I suspect, it bears the marks of my own intellectual agitations.

The Racial-Disabled Theater of Security

In medical sciences, the term *agitation* is broadly operative in manuals of toxicology, psychiatry, and pharmaceutical reference. In such contexts, the term commonly refers to psychomotor or neuromuscular movement ("excessive motor activity associated with a feeling of inner tension," whether or not "influenced by external stimuli") or conditions or states; one form of agitation, muscular spasms, can result from either "mental disturbance" or nerve stimulation.[7] The term also arises in the discussion of various stimulatory substances, and in pharmaceutical reference it can be a sign that a drug is not well tolerated. Its mention is opposed to the calmer patterns resulting from another set of drugs, such as sedatives. In the most general sense, agitation has been something to treat or suppress from the point of view of a system of control—with the exception of those transitional exacerbations that may be anticipated in medical treatment.

This can be problematic or nonproblematic, depending on the form of assessment. The medical industry creatively generates its own continuation, in terms of defining pathology and treatment, a constitutive problem, and yet it can sometimes offer genuine relief: in some therapeutic use, for instance, muscle relaxants may be prescribed to alleviate the constant muscle tension characteristic of many forms of cerebral palsy. In other medical foci, the gendered pathology of hysteria was defined symptomatically in terms of agitation of mind and body, and both condition and symptom were subject to correction. And indeed corrective medical suppression could be found both within and outside of corrective institutions. Anthony Ryan Hatch's *Silent Cells* examines the use of psychotropic drugs in carceral systems to silence prisoners, part of what he identifies as "technocorrections, the strategic application of new technologies in the effort to reduce the costs of mass incarceration and minimize the risks that prisoners pose to society."[8] Psychiatric survivor and scholar Erick Fabris has written of a form of mandated chemical restraint, or chemical incarceration (using largely sedating and constraining substances like haloperidol, used to treat diverse conditions such as psychosis and Tourette's syndrome) of psychiatric outpatients in an era of post-1950s deinstitutionalization in neoliberalizing North America.[9] Chemical restraint is intended to suppress agitation, which Fabris reads as a pointer to the stereotype of the "aggressive" patient—yet, within this privatized, distributed institution, there is no more than a "hazy line that separates agitation from illness and drugging from treatment." (In terms of animacy, the "aggressive patient," as opposed to the docile patient, violates an expected asymmetry of actancy whereby the agent acts upon the patient.)

While the widespread medicalization of cultural fields extends the meaning of patient, the discourses of security also expand the potential gestural field for what is called aggression. Indeed, apparently aggressive actions are those most obviously tied to the case for violent suppression, to the point of intentional killing, by state or security agents. Most palpable today is the continuing sequence of viewable Black deaths at the hands of police and repetitive police defenses narrating their perceptions of dangerous Black movement, in an era in which social media and readily available cameras have yielded a novel sense of immediacy, even if the deaths have been ongoing. We can note a fluid and overlapping, sometimes interdependent, interplay between "chemical incarceration" and state murder of people of color and those with mental illness.

While a range of human life is increasingly submitted to medicalization, childhood bears a particular sheen of surveillance and management, in mind of its futurity. Here, the term *agitation* is used to describe the states of young people who evince disciplinary disturbance in schools—or who are disruptive at home. Its school-bound imprint is baldly racialized, and is reflected minimally in the set of dynamics and institutions understood as the school-to-prison pipeline. Within the racial orders of education, inchoate criminality takes shape within behavioral circumstance. Where Black children, who have less likely been diagnosed with disability, show agitation, responses all too often align with the punishment of an intending perpetrator; and where white children evince agitation, responses can open more generously toward the diagnostic: the assignation of a state of being "moved by" a pathological agent called autism. Neither funneling is "safe," even as criminality is particularly forbidding in life chances and other schemes of livability. The general schema by which autism is taken to displace an authorial human agent is a pattern generally characteristic of many disabilities, as well as debilities. Pipelining, however, seizes upon the image of agency, or the idealized (white) subject of education, and perverts its means and ends along racial lines. Philosopher Alisa Bierria describes the context in which the actions of Black people are judged:

> This persistent yoking of "blackness" to "criminality" does not merely reflect unjust, uncharitable, or untrue characterizations of Black people, but is a matter of the structure of concepts themselves, deepening the problem for social dialectics of action from shallow to *foundational*. That

is, the persistent and embedded relationship between "blackness" and "criminality" has come to structure meaning that is authorized as "true" via multiple forms of structural and social epistemic power. As part of the structure of the concepts themselves, the relationship primes others before the fact—and before the act—in how to understand intention, curb potential for doubt, "logically" draw conclusions, and accept those conclusions as a noncontroversial reality.[10]

One might extend Bierria's thinking beyond criminality to consider kin that also work within the scope of agency. Here we can consider the conceptual raciality of agitation itself, in the transnational US context and elsewhere, in the same way that slowness cannot seem to help but carry a (racially) disabled load. The racialized, already-agitative may carry with them much more than disposability; carceral and deathly logics also lay in wait.

Agitation has a history as a political term, referring to activity opposing dominant forces and supporting change or to the collective shaping of dissent; for instance, Russian revolutionaries led by Vladimir Lenin considered agitation a key focal and inciting revolutionary tactic, to operate in partnership with propaganda. In communication theory, agitation has been opposed to control, such that one can analyze a rhetoric of the ongoing dance between politically resistive, system-changing agitation and repressive acts by those holding political power. However, agitation has not always been used according to surface expectation; one can observe fascist and antidemocratic strategies used by the US Republican Party, such as the use of mass movements and paramilitary groups against racial minorities, trans and queer people, and leftists.

While "excessive motor activity associated with inner tension" does not immediately correlate to the incitement to revolutionary action, there is nevertheless within both an important relationship between action and actional potential. What links these approaches and subsumes potential, and which I explore below, is a question of gesture: gesture defined as movement that doubles as articulatory animation, though without necessary attachments to clear evidence of (for instance, nondisabled) human intention or agency—indeed, articulation itself includes all of the senses of expression, growth, and arrangement. This definition may seem to oppose the expressive exercise of political agency that is understood as characteristic of some forms of conscious agitation. But the diversity of many gestural ways of embodied living makes such an opening necessary. What strikes me as a critical mechanism for security's theater is the line between intention and nonintention, responsibility and nonresponsibility. In the theater of security, the uncertain expectation that a gesture be expressive (do security agents look for expression or for behavior?) is what stages this uncertainty, sometimes dramatically. Furthermore, as Bierria shows, the intentionality of action itself may be compromised "before the fact—and before the act."

Though etymological compendiums don't have all the explanatory powers that they have occasionally been accorded in humanities scholarship, the historical span they record can still be instructive. For instance, in the *Oxford English Dictionary* (2017) the first definition for *gesture* (n.), etymologically derived from Latin nominalized *gerĕre*, "to carry," is "manner of carrying the body; bearing, carriage, deportment," implying an agent with physical control. Agitation, however, has a mixed etymology of activity/passivity that includes both Middle French ("state or condition of being moved to and fro, public disturbance or unrest, action of shaking") and classical Latin ("violent moving, brandishing, shaking, disturbance, movement, practice or exercise, mental activity"). Each etymological contribution alone suggests that agitation is only the latest concretization of an even longer conceptual tangle between now-distant entities such as mental activity and violent moving or shaking and public unrest.

By comparison, consider Adriana Cavarero's tracing of terror to the Latin root *ter-*, "trembling," and to a verb relating to fear as a physical state.[11] In Cavarero's analysis, the trembling movements as well as the flight attributed to fear are both etymologically linked to modern-day *terror*. There is an "instinctual mobility associated with the ambit of terror" that not only replicates the etymological ambiguity of action for agitation but also suggests its own modulating temporal scope.[12] My ongoing interest in animacy requires a careful look at such unsurprisingly blurred agencies to ask about assignations of humanity, agency, that cluster around certain human or inhuman entities such that only some, for instance, seem to be afforded a "theory of mind." Of course, simply by juxtaposing agitation and gesture, I am aware of the possibility for (hopefully productive) confusion. The question of uncertainly sourced agitation interrupts the question of agentive gesture. As Rebecca Schneider describes the broadened "relational" scope of gesture (I quote extensively, with bolded emphasis):

> A moving or articulate body is thus perhaps always relational in that the movement/stasis of the body (both/and) may be said to necessarily engage a broader scene in which the body is given to exist in space and time. That said, even a minor or unconscious gesture may be relational, and we can think here of the large body of work in psychoanalysis

on the depth relationality of **embodied tics, slurs, errors and breaks**. Certainly, it is not a stretch to say that if my posture droops, or my head tilts, or my feet drag I may alter the environment of my social surround. **These may not be conscious gestures, but they are gestic nevertheless,** and contribute quite importantly to what Brecht termed, as I already discussed, the social *gestus*. Even our minor aspects of bodily comportment contribute to the fields of relation that we engage and navigate everyday—and the large body of work on "marked" bodies and epidermal schema (Frantz Fanon) **gives way to the depth of intersectional relations, welcomed or acknowledged or not, by bodies in everyday movement practices.** This is to say that if bodies are caught in webs of relation, the movements made by those bodies will be relational as well. Gesture is relational, and the ethics of relations haunting our bodies in modes of reiteration make gesture a matter for ethical consideration.[13]

According to Schneider, gesture is not constrained to conscious deliberation; drawing on an endlessly relational (and, I think, conditional) terrain, her example of the "drooping posture" anticipates what Bergson would himself take to be the socially humoristic content of the "hunchback" which, unlike for Schneider, becomes vested inside the figure itself ("one vast grin"). Extending the above, and following critiques of humanist modes of inquiry, I thus choose here to consider gesture as both more and less than the simplest ideal of human agency. I do this not because I wish centrally to reassert the presence of humanness or agency in certain scenes but because I wish to be able to point out the complicity of dubious agency in the formulations of racist securitization. The determinacy of life and death in the realm of animacy is conditioned by other factors. Who, in a given instance, is understood as being animated, or deanimated, or animated by disability or disabled intoxication, and how? What will be done with that animation?

The relevance of gesture deepens in relation to what I am reading as a consolidation of security and medicalizing discourses, particularly around the racialization of disability and the disabilization of race that end up staging, animating as it were, something like agitation, in ways that simultaneously deny and sublimate its own history as linked to resistance or chemical exposure (or both), while failing to acknowledge the history of performance and gesture and, indeed, embodiment as one of undeniable and irreducible experiment constantly crossing the shifting lines of ability, debility, and disability.

As mentioned in chapter 1, I have found it useful to think with a relatively capacious idea of racialized tuning—a form of dis/ability or difference-soaked embodiment or a kind of gestural containment to which all are subject and whose entrainments can be biopolitically managed. For such a scenario, biochemistry and its "agencies" can be counted as active on the scene; debilities and their agencies can also be counted as actively on the scene. We might condition resistive agency simply as an immanent feature of Foucauldian power: rather than resistance extant as/within power, where there is power, there is agitation. Regardless of the chosen analytic, there are ways to locate arguably less classically expressive forms of gestural resistance and to revive discourses that allow for the participation of chemical histories of environmental injustice in a scene of an apparently different kind of violence.

Premises of Bergson's Laughter

In the present consideration of the racial-disabled theater of security, I find Bergson's treatment a fitting occasion to ask further questions of agitation. What becomes of the theatrical nonstage or semistage; the failures of legibility of the comic; the persistence of racialized-abled-classed-gendered bodies who are too negligently characterized by a "deep-seated recalcitrance of matter"; or the implicit felicities that make successful Bergson's form of "comic [encountered] readily enough in everyday life"?[14] One immediate consideration is that of the performative objecthood of racialized and securitized beings. Foremost among these is Black engagement against a history of aggressively securitized existence that begins devastatingly in the US context with slavery.[15] In one particularly creative example, Uri McMillan, in using the figure of the "avatar" to read Black women's strategic deployments of self-objecthood, identifies the explicit presence of disability in a number of gestures and "prosthetic" objects such as poultices that indexed the white avatar of a woman named Ellen Craft during her escape from bondage.[16] McMillan's analysis pointedly announces disability and, in so doing, implicitly names the bifurcation in the structural privileging of disability over debility that in its simpler versions mirrors a racial divide, one a flag toward consideration and acknowledgment, much like what Tobin Siebers describes as "disability masquerade," and the other a flag toward the biopolitical zone of vital abandonment.[17] But what McMillan makes additionally clear is the white cast of this symbolic potency, its power to cultivate concerted actions of civil society that enable rather than curtail passing (through, by, or, in addition, as) and perhaps also fugitivity.

In *Laughter*, Bergson identifies the participation of inhuman and human in the sharp affectivity of an apparent lapse of the agentive, yielding to the mechanical, to the rigid, to the matter within (and thus enabling comic reception);

but, to depart from the proper scope of his work and the craft he attributes to the comic performance, we know that that point of affective intensity at the gap of agency does not yield only laughter. As suggested earlier, the scripts for gestural conduct are, and have been, racialized. I am interested in how race, disability, and performance are made to work together in the everyday in a troublingly generative way. This is the unmarked everywhere of disability, disablement, debility, and occasional impairment, in which so many people are, if not categorically disabled, then in intimately tuned relationships with chemicals, exogenous or endogenous ones, whose management in the body can be temporarily altering and temporarily impairing or disabling—but of these people, some number are further exposed to destruction not because of but in conjunction with them. I emphasize "in conjunction with," because this is not a question of causality. The pervasiveness of these chemical encounters presents other gaps to explore that represent something of a departure from the virtuosically agentive performance—if we were to consider the possible legacy of the Middle French etymological contributor to agitation, "being moved."

I return to Bergson's opening quotation to examine the logic of his exemplar more closely. This comic scene, whose baldness depends on a "primate" lack of language or cognition (only the visual register is allowed—"above all, do not reason"), relies on the apprehension of disability—the hunchback. It is a particular form of comedy, since not only does it rely on a relationship of the spectacle, but its reactivity borrows on the structure of othering (one can see traces of Raymond Williams's survey of intentional and extensional meanings of "culture" as drawing on "cultivation" and "civilization").[18]

The function of removing cognition is to de- and re-temporalize the form before the observer. From "His back seems to have contracted an ugly stoop . . . it persists in the habit it has contracted" one moves to "You will have before you a man bent on cultivating a certain rigid attitude." The consolidation of sedimented time, with gradual effects on the body, to a moment where that sedimented attitude is presented as presentist attitude, transfers the articulation as growth to the articulation as expression and, in so doing, remaps (perceived) time. This telling may be too constrained for Bergson's purposes; as Schneider observes of the striking of a pose within the flow of time: "A pose is a posture, a stance, struck in reiterative gesture often signifying precedent. The pose articulates an interval, and so, in Henri Bergson's sense, is given to multiple and simultaneous time(s)."[19] Yet a consideration of the temporalities of disability invoked here, rather than an invocation simply of the machinic, puts an interesting pressure on the labilities of time in the reception of this moment.

Correlatively, the man's body becomes another attitude altogether, the prescriptive attitude of the observer: "one vast grin." And in cognition's absence, the agency of the back and its habitual contraction has become the ugly willfulness of the man. Bergson suggests that the grinning charge of affect, temporalized and perhaps intensified, becomes transferable, sharable, or blurred, between observed and observer: a formal kind of sympathy. Furthermore, the attribution of disability, understood templatically as an accreted condition of nonagency, becomes inchoate: the audience, the judge, may no longer have to be seen as reactively laughing at the disabled man, even if one had to understand the idea of the disabled man in order to laugh. The stooped man alone, the comic, is responsible for making a mockery of the nonagency of the disabled, the fall, and sympathy runs between the comic and the audience, but not the hunchback.

What if the reflexive laughing were instead a reflexive act of condemnation?

Agitations of Racial Intoxication

By way of demonstration of the consolidation or attenuation of what turns out to be racialized difference (not equivalence), consider three different scenes. The first asks of the reader an extended time in which to imagine the "reflex." White male Brock Turner, in Stanford, California, was witnessed raping an unconscious woman in January 2015. He turned out to be drunk. One year later at trial, he was given a light sentence precisely because, to quote Judge Aaron Persky, "it's not an excuse but his intoxication is a factor that, when trying to assess moral culpability in this situation, is mitigating. There is less moral culpability attached to the defendant who is legally intoxicated."[20] The legal definition of intoxication served as exculpatory in Turner's case: He was so moved by intoxication, and the result was a relative evacuation of responsibility. The judge could not condemn, but laughing might have been more possible: Turner and his actions had effectively made a mockery of durative intoxication, perhaps even of cognitive disability, but/and in the theater of security he was not (so) responsible. If the judge were to have scanned the possibilities of disability, he would have found no comparator.

Korryn Gaines, a Maryland resident and a young Black woman, filed a lawsuit in 2012 against two Baltimore landlords, alleging that the apartments they had rented her had "'a sea of lead,' which contributed to 'neurodevelopmental disabilities or injuries'"; unlike in many lead toxicity claims on behalf of vulnerable children, she was an adult justifying a claim to chemical vulnerability; her high level of expertise about lead toxicity informed her assignation of responsibility for environmental harm.[21] Gaines further connected this claim to her diagnosis of neurocognitive impairment and her history of agitation and mood swings. Four years later, on August 1, 2016, in Randallstown, Maryland, she was killed inside her apartment by police after hours of standoff. While the drama of the case focused on her own use of firearms and her status as a mother, the existence of the lawsuit filed four years earlier suggests that she had a much longer history of consciously embodied living as someone who understood herself as having been significantly affected by lead exposure. Unlike some intoxications, this chemical modulation was clearly one she had not elected and, by pursuing it in the juridical domain, had attempted to remedy. Here is a history of durative intoxication that, rather than working as a kind of attenuator of responsibility, functioned as aggressive debility.

Gaines did not kill anyone, but the point in her having been killed by police seems to be that she might well have. LaMarr Jurelle Bruce writes that he locates a murder of a man committed by Gayl Jones's protagonist in the novel *Eva's Man*, Eva Canada, as a "mad crime within a broader web of Reasonable crimes that are perpetrated by antiblack, misogynist, racial capitalist, carceral, and necropolitical regimes. . . . If we are to conduct an ethical forensics, our investigation must center [the person] while also panning outward. . . . There are violent geopolitical and world-historical systems, structures, and other murderers implicated in this horror. There is culpability that seeps in and spreads out . . . to the end of the world."[22]

In counterpoint to these twinned stories of white and Black agitation is what at first appears to be the seeming gestural impossibility of that of a "sleeping race," Asian Americans. Their images benefit both from a presumptive automaticity (thanks to the legacy of early alien laws and Third World orders of labor) that suggests the deprivation of an alert presence and from a superficially expressive "sleepiness," an immigrant stupor, as has been claimed of and by many women of East Asian descent who sought "Asian eye surgery."[23] This constitutional imagining has a kinship with the opiate allegation of slowness, and as such bears a chemicality even as it lacks explicit participation of drugs. Besides subterfuge, this persona does not beget securitized violence in the same ways. I believe such an imagination underlies the reaction of surprise in cases of Asian-engendered gun violence, such as occurred at Virginia Tech (Seung-Hui Cho) and in Isla Vista, near the University of California, Santa Barbara, campus (Elliot Rodger) by men of East Asian descent, and the desire to "automatize" their subjectivity by way of attempting to ascertain a history of autism—a mode of being that has been not only highly medicalized but also long haunted by pathologizations referring to inhumanity, automaticity, and lack. This imagination is not interrupted in any way by the shooting by a white man of Asian diasporic/Asian American women at the spas in Atlanta, Georgia, in 2020; it joins it in sympathetic rendering.

Gestural Wrongs

An era of chemical experimentation, which is the stuff of medicine, consumer culture, built environments, and industrial commodity policy, is equally an era of bodily experimentation. In a gestural world already conditioned by unpredictability, what bodies will be made to pay doubly for that experimentation? And in these contexts, what becomes of "unruly," "unrest-ful" conduct, bodily agitation? I want to take agitation seriously, in other words, not only as an ensemble of gestural cultures of nondisabled expression or choreographed resistance but also as the movement vocabularies of people living with diverse bodily experience, as well as with bodily intolerances—actively collapsing the apparently segregated domains that agitation has come to occupy, though not under the sign of any one of them.

This is a broad sweep, but consider here what might be defined as "bodily intolerance," while suspending valuation or judgment or categorization. The expression "There is only so much you can take" could thus refer equally to the forced tolerance of environmentally inequitable ingestion and to the forced embodiment of docility, noninsurgency. Relevantly, Jonathan Metzl, in *The Protest Psychosis*, describes the mid-twentieth-century emergence of a novel type of schizophrenia attributed to Black patients by white psychiatrists in a clinic in Ionia, Michigan. In this case, the patients' "agitations" need only be understood in the context of an actual struggle, embodied and felt, for civil rights, and their sheer intolerance of gendered-racialized racisms that surely bore vivid inheritances of slavery. Metzl further notes that advertisements for the antipsychotic sedative Thorazine in the 1970s referred to Africanized figurations of the unruly "primitive."[24] Alondra Nelson shows how the Black Panthers actively contested such "biologization of violence," the entrapments of medicalized pathology.[25]

From another angle, Darieck Scott brilliantly explores in Frantz Fanon a metaphor that repeats throughout Fanon's *Wretched of the Earth* ([1961] 2004): that of "muscular tension" felt by Algerian colonial subjects living under conditions of colonial domination, a tension that engenders resistive value. Through the analysis, Scott insists on tension's purely metaphoric value for Fanon as a psychic element, pointing in spite of itself to "powers in the midst of debility."[26] Scott writes, "Muscle tension is the state of flexure that has the appearance of movement but is in substance barely moving and static, in a state of attenuated atrophy."[27] Asking questions of embodiment that Scott precisely does not ask, I do wonder about the link between tension and agitation, one as the condition for the other, or where tension is the condition shared between a sedimented rigidity and the movement that is then dubbed insurgency.

To think further about the kinds of invisibilized and corporeal debility introjected by certain bodies in a time of environmentally disproportionate harm, what might it mean to think about these forms of chemical being together, so that pollution is rendered not simply a pan-species threat but a specific one decried by environmental justice, working in conjunction with existing structures that serve to intensify or double that harm (slow plus structural violence)? Is it to further, or rather acknowledge, the biologization of violence once we consider civil rights or anticolonial agitation, "muscle tension," as itself more than metaphor, as biochemical process?

In the contemporary animation of security, there seem to be two modes of inhumanism. The first works along the lines of ability's consolidation with agency, intoxication, the workings of an inhuman chemical inside of or through you, Bergson's mechanical encrusted upon the living; the second, raciality, runs through the first mode, but also contributes to delineated gestural economies. These work together such that there exists, on the one hand, a category of the gestural "mundanity of whites" (or, to refer to Bergson's comic, a kind of white slapstick broadly construed, without durative effect), which bears a history of the autonomic, the mechanical, the suprasession of human agency, and, on the other hand, the gestural "monstrosity of others," which bears its own history of the autonomic, the mechanical, and the absence of human agency. I contend that these bifurcations of agitative motion feed into contemporary security states in ways that, given their histories, are unsurprising (both to historians of gesture, perhaps, and to communities and individuals forced to engage in lifelong gestural entrainment).

The systemic encoding and legitimation of murder by police is made most stark given the standard police injunction "Don't move" (understood in movies, perhaps no less accurately, as "Freeze"), such that movement itself becomes an act of resistance or aggression. To some observers, the accusations of aggression after the fact only legitimate a preexisting judgment of racial insurgency.[28] Here I meditate on the life before the death—in an attempt to address the conditions that privilege his example—of Keith Lamont Scott, of South Carolina, who lived a full life with family, including a wife of 20 years and several children. A motorcycle accident in 2016 had caused a traumatic brain injury (TBI) which affected his memory and speech, and other major physical injuries led to the use of a cane. Mere months after the accident—meaning, while he was still in recovery—while he waited for his son to return from school inside his car, police noticed the car and chose to investigate. Claiming later that he was armed—his family said that he was reading a book—they drew guns. His wife, Rakeyia Scott, who had been nearby, ran to the scene and started recording, calling out to police that he had a "TBI," "don't shoot him"; she later stated to a reporter that she knew he was "sitting there, looking forward. He is confused. I know he was. He had just taken his medicine."[29] These words did not prevent the shooting. His movement—indeed, his disabled movement—had been not only criminalized, but found to be aggressive.

I think here not just of disabled movement, but of the ways injuries extend time to a prospect of uncertain return, uncertain healing, uncertain transition. In what ways is the question: "How long does healing take?" delimited to certain circles? Who else is left vibrating to old injuries, to transgenerational harms? The economic racism of institutionalized health care preconditions access to care and healing, and amends the fantasy of "cure" differentially, splitting care and guarantee from other forms of institutional correction, and carcerality or elimination. In this context, Scott's "gestural wrong that violated rules of racial attunement" is but a small feature of a scene that foretold the presence of seemingly violent agitation regardless of whether it could take place. Though Scott's death had as much to do with the racialized structuration of (the impossibility of) cure as with security itself, it also underlines the fact that gestural improprieties blanket the terrain of racialized security, and they can occur anywhere and at any time and yet are heightened where security is territorialized. Think national security, security of property, the designation of violence in criminal justice and not in capital, and you are everywhere in the here's of coloniality: Khairuldeen Makhzoomi, an Iranian student who had attended a United Nations meeting, was removed from a Southwest Airlines flight for speaking to his uncle in Arabic on a cell phone call while waiting for the plane to depart. During the conversation, he said that he hoped, "inshallah [God willing]," to be able to return for another meeting. According to a flight staff member of Middle Eastern descent who scolded him for speaking Arabic on a plane, he had essentially committed a gestural wrong. Security discourses run deep and wide, and such is their holistic and previsory threat.

In my last case, Charles Kinsey, a therapist, was treating Arnaldo Rios, an individual diagnosed with autism. In Miami, on July 18, 2016, Rios had attracted the attention of someone who then alerted the police, and when they arrived, Rios kept rocking and moved "agitatedly," while Kinsey attempted to calm the situation, explaining that he was a therapist. It was Kinsey who was shot in the leg by police and survived. The police had been notified of a dangerous person carrying a gun; Rios had been carrying a toy car. Kinsey held his hands up over his head and lay down on the ground. The police officer shot him anyway and later claimed that it was an accident, saying that he actually intended to shoot Rios.

If this was a gestural wrong that violated rules of racial attunement, whose was it? Should we be asking questions about racial scripts here as well, and how to define that raciality? At what point does physical agitation, racially improper gestural conduct, suggest a call to the authorities, and when might it so easily change hands in a police officer's own gestural imagination, as it perhaps magically did in the case involving Kinsey and Rios? When does time consolidate and agitation transmute from observed to observer in an encounter? For which bodies does the demand "Don't move" most directly lay out the terms of living and dying, rather than the beginning of a negotiation?

I have already mentioned the tracks of state guidance, abandonment, entitlement, and criminalization that have been described as "pipelines." They are certainly a useful metaphor for describing a structural channeling of bodies and forces along an overwhelmingly singular path, and even as metaphors they are not without power. However, following environmental activists, I'm even more interested in the friable or corrosible constitution of pipes, and the work that it does in relation to what I call "environmentalization," which collapses people and environments such that health, on the one hand, or malignancy (and toxicity), on the other, becomes a fixed feature of a neighborhood and the people who populate it. As events in Flint, Michigan, showed most egregiously, pipes can play a role in the environmentalization that partly constitutes the mindbody. I cannot fail to be struck by the importance to activists of the chemical materiality of the partially constructed Dakota Access Pipeline in Standing Rock, whose oil, upon the next leak, would threaten the Missouri River, the Standing Rock Sioux tribe's primary source of water, and the health of the surrounding sacred land. Both the metaphor and the constitutional work merit consideration, together.

Like many other forms of management, securitization is linked to a field of chemicality. Slowness and agitated being are not mere metaphors; they do not exist without material surrounds. The forms of harm and consequence that attend toxic exposure cannot be disassociated from the imposition or allegations of compromised capacity in ideational spheres.

Given the above, how to pitch the need for toxic remediation without notionally attaching that lead templatically to certain bodies on the basis of a partial, environmentalizing, truth?

A Direct and Primate Impression

What is virtuosity? Improvisation? What of gesture, agitated gesture, that lies between these two things? How to locate and value disruption, especially when that disruption is a violation of a racial-gendered script of embodiment and movement? Where does mildness go? How to replenish the rich sphere of gestures of life, of thriving, amid the violences that contain it? To want it, however, is to take full consideration of the full range of lives that must bear these gestures in an economy of movement and stillness, an economy whose different actors wield disproportionate powers of life and death, and within which the crip and the queer and the raced lose diagnostic clarity.

Perhaps it is useful here to adopt a notion of "bodily insurgency" after Daphne Brooks's *Bodies in Dissent*.[30] Brooks refers to the use of "opaque" performance in order to "defamiliarize" the narrow binds of racial expectation, in this case by Black and racially ambiguous performers in the late nineteenth- to early twentieth-century United States, demonstrating the "insurgent power of imaging cultural identity."[31] Critically, Brooks records a proto-afterlife of Black minstrelsy and its later whitened, deracinated invocation within Jekyll and Hyde productions as horrific, no longer comic, performative cultures. Again, the line between comedy and horror, as well as the absenting of a historical figure, surfaces. Could the mobility of harm and harmlessness in the endless translation of gesture enact something against the seeming recalcitrance of skin?

As for agitation, I argue that the contemporaneity and pervasiveness of rampant biochemical modulation (for some, but not all, biochemical unwellness), the ongoing experiment of the industrial age, combined with the ongoing complicity of state and cultural imagination alike in the obscuring of perceptible and imperceptible forms of debility and disability integral to lived lives, does strange things to the reflexes proffered by the state in relation to its internally or externally acting bodies and minds, leading to clashes of systems—states as "immunitary" bodies, individuals and collectivities as neural actors subject to agitation. These clashes of systems, however, do not exacerbate willy-nilly, but all too often accord to certain coherences of racial segregation and racialized bodily order that themselves have fed extensive histories of chemical and environmental injustice that have ultimately kept no one from being affected. Some analysts may claim that the clashes are proper ruptures, proper violences, that precisely exemplify the ongoing subjection of a population or subpopulation to the state.

In this new midst, what to do, again, with Bergson's urging for the reactive spectacle for an enhanced strength of example: "Try to see with your eyes alone. Avoid reflection, and above all, do not reason. Abandon all your prepossessions; seek to recapture a fresh, direct and primate impression"? "Primate" here might serve as a categorization at the level of a taxonomic order of species, at least for perceptual phenomena. Perhaps Bergson is seeking a reversion to some idea of basal sensation that abandons some, but not all, degrees of critical intelligence. It may be however that this aesthetically pure, fresh, freedom of impression is a style of primitivism that only furnishes freedom of perception for a few, liberating the laughing instinct with only a slight mental trick.

A Fanonian resistive muscular tension, agitation as its release or its intensification, the muscle tensions of disabled movement, the trembling of intoxication. The geneses and timings are unambiguously different, yet their role in the theater of security is inchoate and somehow distantly kin.

White Agitation: Two Tables and a Ladder

Above I wrote about agitation as a feature of the entanglements of race and disability, a response to racialized oppressions and environmental inequities and ordinary disabilities in a proto-gestural world. It is in part an argument for the allowance within the scope of the political for a mindbody literally poisoned by the ills of colonialism and capitalism, rather than barred from legitimacy. And for the allowance for those remade by it, constitutionally. It is just one emblem of the intoxication of the blood and of the body. In addition to intoxication medically defined as physiological damage by way of a chemical substance or impairment by ingestion of substances, I am also thinking about the mimicry of intoxication by endogenous bodily substances such as the endorphins, said to behave like opiates, and epinephrine/adrenaline, which are integral to an affective being: that is, agitation works affectively, disregarding the boundaried interior, working across and not only within or without bodies.

While previously I have focused on recognizing justified agitations from within queer, crip, and nonwhite, particularly Black and brown racialized being, I turn here to revisit the comic side of Bergson, exploring the potential field of its own suppositions. By examining a region of the white ludicrous, I want ultimately to find ways to think more substantially about white supremacist agitation.

Comic physicality—and more generally, the most profound capacity of the physical to be *moving*—has always enraptured me. Over time, I've become an avid student of the motional incitement to laugh—whether the classic flat-on-face fall (also known as a pratfall, with a historical trace in burlesque and vaudeville) or the gestural microcosm of a lip pucker registering a sense of dawning failure. More generally, watching stunts or tumbles is for me a guilt-free pleasure accompanied by vivid mental self-animations and sweaty hands. I also identify as a physical comic and as a stunt-double hopeful. In my adolescence, forms of physical abandon, defiance, and surprise were a way for me to throw off—in a way that felt literal—a constantly imposed submissive, gentle, Asian female embodied stereotype. Yet I know that stunt-like movements can incur injury, too. (The OED rejects etymological contributions from "stump" to "stunt" yet credits the United States with this prevalent belief in this relationship.)[32] I have asked myself, why aren't these harder to watch?

In fact, the dual valence of so much popular contemporary media seems to be that of simultaneous unwatchability-watchability, even as each of these qualities has been the nonobjective result of cultivation, market, and taste.[33] Much discussed is the watchability of the ongoing spectacle of racial, gendered, sexual killing in news and serial entertainment; they disproportionately and perhaps pedagogically rehearse certain deaths, staging relative vulnerabilities, grievabilities, and murderous intents. In *watchability*, *-ability* makes of the word a nominalized adjective, meaning the quality of being watchable and perhaps grammatically sidelining the question of the witness. Another reading, which would key in on nonsuffixed *ability*, refers to capacities and incapacities, as well as the dynamic line between disability and ability: watch this ability, watch this disability. Both of these senses are relevant for WCGW (What Could Go Wrong?) videos,[34] which are largely in the form of purely visual looping GIFs. There are a limited number of videos that have the fuller sensory element of audio, for example the hoots or sympathetic moans of onlookers, who may also be filming, and evoking silent film aesthetics.[35]

WCGW videos exist in a subreddit on the social media platform Reddit, reddit.com/r/whatcouldgowrong. The pleasure some ascribe to these videos is akin to the schadenfreude of writings about Darwin Awards "winners"—that is, egregiously self-canceling acts. Attributed here is a form of mental failure, or constitutional incapacity, in the sense of a lapse of judgment, foresight, or awareness of risk. In WCGW, there seem to be combinations of mental and physical problematics, even if mental allegations appear mostly in the form of textual comments. In both cases, the distinction between the lack of "situational awareness" attributed to certain lifestyles of privilege or modernity and the possibility of an immanent difference becomes quite complex. How much does disability do hidden work? And to what extent is it racialized? The resemblance of some tumbles in /whatcouldgowrong to the pratfalls represented in comics suggests an obscured contribution of minstrelsy.[36]

In the WCGW video "Two Tables and a Ladder: What Could Go Wrong?," a white man in a T-shirt and long checkered shorts partially appears in a fixed-view shot of a large grass backyard scattered with patio tables and chairs, a ball, a yellow slide, and a lawnmower.[37] A superimposed late-afternoon date-time of 28/9/2016 in the upper left, and "Camera1" on the lower right, suggest the unmotivated recording of a security camera. To the lower right, closest to the camera, are positioned a wood picnic table on the ground, atop which rests a long folding table, above which is perched a ladder at about a 30-degree angle from the vertical. An orange extension cord dangles to the ground where a thick coil awaits, then trails off to the distant right. As the man begins to climb the ladder, cord agitating, a blond child, perhaps a son, walks out from under the ladder around the table, looking up, and then moving out of sight to the left. The man has now climbed the ladder high enough to be out of view. After a pause, the ladder gives way, following gesturally the agitating cord and tiddlywinking the white table on its sidelong end, and the man plunges down into the mess, leg caught in the ladder, which is for a moment horizontal, then bouncing off it toward the earth, arms out stiffly. The ladder extension skews off kilter, tracing a possibly parallel injury experienced by the man. The GIF ends abruptly—and begins again—just as the man nearly reaches the ground.[38]

Are there pleasures in this? What could they be, dare I ask? He'll be all right, won't he, after a period of accessible care and rehab? I think about what "all right" can mean; it's never so simple. While I find police murders or violence against feminine people unwatchable in the sense that they are too painful to watch, other sequences can be surprisingly fair game. It's partly because, with repeated viewings, there is a pedagogy of physics, a way to learn what not to do—look at the placement of the objects, look at the genesis of the fail, learn about friction, learn about momentum, learn about rotation, learn about the placement of limbs, look at the ways that sequences spiral into the zone of hurt and damage. It is this pedagogy of physics that holds my fascination; here I avidly learn, with specific attentions to movement, perception, and balance, how I will try to survive a like "accident" when the time comes. Despite a vivid imagination, I was not able to activate the script quickly enough to jump, spin, and roll out of the way of an oncoming car in 1999, and my knee and hip remain quirky (I broke the front of the car, which shared our damage). However, I *know* that when sliding off a metal pitched roof, I'll maximize friction and anticipate, grip, and steadily increase my distributed force on the flimsy raised lower edge.

Scrolling through the WCGW archive, one is treated to a tour of ostensibly nondisabled (at least at the outset) white masculinities, with some nondisabled white women and nonwhite people here and there. While five years ago the all-time top posts in this archive were almost entirely populated by white people as their subjects, more recent polls record increasingly global engagement in

Reddit, as well as increased participation by people of color in this subreddit in particular, overcoming insistent racist gatekeeping in some quarters of Reddit. Yet one continues to see the flagship variety of beer chuggers, golfers, skateboarders, BMX bikes, agricultural machinery, casual stunts involving rotation, and so many white men on ladders. Viewing these in rapid succession, the effect is not unlike, I imagine, what happens in *Jackass* (2000–2002). Except that I never saw what Jack Halberstam would call the "witless white males" of that show.[39] Nor have I ever had the taste for the nominally representative, also white male, slapstick comedians The Three Stooges, Buster Keaton, Laurel and Hardy, Charlie Chaplin, or their contemporary comparator, Jim Carrey. I didn't know that slapstick comediennes of color such as Bertha Regustus, or white comediennes such as Marie Dressler and Sarah Duhamel, existed (I turn later to Regustus).

WCGW videos, unlike elaborate filmic productions, occupy an entirely different space (even if the choppy frame rate could be seen to approximate that of silent film): both the "performer" and the documentation share an identity of the aleatory, the DIY, what Scott Herring in referring to queer life might call the "rustic"—spaces outside of metronormative, chic sexualities.[40] Sometimes the amateur-framed view wanders away from the accident in progress and returns just in time. The GIFs often end before we know what has happened to the fallen, so that in comments, the question is often, "Did he die?" More infrequent are musings about permanent disability. (The coarseness and injury of white pratfalls, and the lack of sympathy in viewer comments, suggest there is not a lot of compassion here, either.) Commenters ask what happened, but rarely does an original poster have inside information, since all they did was produce a GIF of someone else's video for fast consumption. By the sheer continuous animation of WCGW GIFs, "Did he die?" is countered with the certainty of renewal, a lifely repetition also found in greater variation in video game cultures since the time of Atari.[41]

Perhaps this is where the whiteness that is all over these videos comes in: Regardless of a viewer's politics, one is invited to entertain the question: Can and do white people, even poor white people, bounce and get back up as if nothing happened? I suspect they generally do not, but the question falls on the representational value they have to others as well as to themselves. The political distinctions in how this is answered may lie in how vulnerability and optimism are understood, but from the pandemic time I am writing, I feel resonances between the WCGW videos and the white appeals to "natural" means of acquiring immunity from infection with COVID, preserving strength as the reigning affect (this even as deaths accumulate, and are to some degree acknowledged as the price of freedom). One can level the broader sense of socially produced neoliberal capacity against disability, such that the first could make less consequential the second.[42] The optimism of unperturbable (masculine) being fantasizes whiteness beyond its classed idealization and attempts to belie the realities of white disabled poverties and other depleted capacities. And the story of the day seems to be that limited capacity for empathy, for long sentences, for honest exchange, for multiple pieces of information works just fine for some white folk, especially if the illusion of power or freedom is there to provide endless renewal. The WCGW archive suggests, finally, that vitality was never the point.

I return to the early archive of slapstick to meditate on an earlier instance of racial meaning. The comedienne Bertha Regustus's archive might well be taken to have a different tack on these questions, even if it might not hinder racial closure. In the silent 1907 film *Laughing Gas*, at a pivotal time for film in the shift from a focus on sensation to longer narrative formats, Mandy, a Black woman played by Regustus, is the central, solitary persona binding several scenes together.[43] Initially she comes to a dentist's office for help with a painful mouth. In a room-scale view, we see the setup of the procedure, during which Mandy, to combat her fear, requests and is administered laughing gas, which puts her to sleep. While she dozes, the dentist and his assistant perform acrobatics to remove the recalcitrant tooth, which, when it emerges, is enormous. When she wakes, Mandy tumbles off the chair and to the ground, shaking with laughter; the two men begin laughing, too, but it's not clear whether because of the sight of the tooth, or the leaking of laughing gas. What one surmises to be in the air at this stage, and the ambiguity therein, are both telling.

The dentist eventually struggles to place Mandy's hat back on her head and amicably sees her to the door. As she stitches through town and encounters other groups of people, they start to shake and laugh as she does, suggesting that the opening scene in the dental office was one of a similar contagion. The initial chemicality of the gas, a kind of interior affectivity, has transitioned with Mandy's travels into interhuman or collective gestural contagion—or perhaps joyful agitation. Maggie Hennefeld credits the super-sized inciting tooth with the same combination of comedy and horror theorized by Brooks: "The image of the tooth as the locus of this racialized difference, an internal object to be extracted and expelled, further intermingles the comedy of minstrelsy with the terror endemic to dentistry and the fear of losing one's teeth (which Freud associates with castration)."[44] Mandy's gas-induced apoplexies, on some level, seem to rehearse Black agitation as a regular feature of Black embodiment; as Jacqueline Stewart argues, the closure of the film in a Black church resolves Mandy's gestural infectivity as just one of many problematic naturalizations of Black hysterics, "virtually indistinguishable from the gesticulations of Black religious ecstasy."[45]

At the present moment, the image of sharable joviality emanating from the body of a Black person can echo a minstrel politic in a US national culture that denies its history of slavery while continuing to take an extractive attitude toward Black movement, especially in furtherances of disposable labor and cultural production. But Regustus's *Laughing Gas* also hints at the inextricable, and fundamental, role of Black creativity in US cultural life, and is an argument for the potency of Black joy that is both hard-won and ever present. I further find myself reflecting on the role of the nitrous oxide in inducing the very agitations that become naturalized. Is there a proposition here, too, about the agitative *chemicality* of Blackness; and if there is, is it at all reconcilable with environmental injustice and the question of environmentalization? Is it of a piece with, or does it live within a cacophonous family alongside, the substance life of Asian contagion? In the case of *Laughing Gas*, the allegation of chemicality, whether or not it behaves in or across bodies as gases are known to do, does not go without narrative consequence.

Occupations of Space and the US Capitol

If Regustus, as Mandy, was roaming throughout civic spaces, presenting to viewers a quandary for the regulation of Black women's movement, and enacting contagious hysterics, I am brought to reconsider the spatiality of the WCGW videos. Their physicality depends, it seems, on soaring or tumbling through space or in a rogue fashion across land. I would less call this athleticism, especially given its message of failure, and maybe even less thrusting masculinity, than consider it flamboyant, carefree occupation, even awkward occupation. There is little virtuosity here, if we define virtuosity as an intimate, learned relation to space and how one lives in it, which has nothing to do with what kind of body and how nondisabled it is, and could even tip toward the side of those forced to find means of being in spaces that were not industrially designed for them.[46] In WCGW videos, one senses even the underside of the weekend warrior. It is not unrelated, then, that white supremacist agitation can be even more dramatically entangled with the (settler right to) occupation of space, of publics. Landscapes become racialized spaces of nature, rather than perceived as occupied ground.

There seems no stronger recent example than the occupation of the Capitol Building in Washington, DC, on January 6, 2021. I remember this well, because I was working on this book manuscript while playing the news as background;

the background became foreground, and I had to step away from the writing for what eventually became months. In the scene of the occupation, and in snippets shared since, there was so much piling on, so much climbing, so much tumbling, so much hitting, amid articulations that this was "our house." Without needing the singularly contagious politics of Regustus's *Laughing Gas*, we also know it was determinedly *also* an intoxication, a shared one, an adrenalized constitution in the frenzied occupation of the spaces of government that looked ridiculous and frightening and comical on video, but one perhaps experienced as a soothing fire for those heading into the maw of it. The frenzy of the crowd as a shared intoxication.[47]

There have been other occupations/intoxications, of course. On March 22, 2017, a group of ADAPT (American Disabled for Attendant Programs) protesters occupied the Capitol Building's rotunda. This was one of a series of disability protests around and inside the building over the years. In this case, they were protesting the Republican health care proposal that, among other things, would make cuts to Medicaid, dump preexisting conditions, and more. Unlike the January 6 protesters, as the ADAPT protesters were occupying the rotunda area and chanting, they were engaging in rules of peaceful protest, lying down as a die-in: a kind of slow agitation for care and state support for disabled people. Promptly, forty-three arrests were made; many protesters were simply wheeled out or dragged out by Capitol police, which one commenter described as "condescending."

Nonhuman Agitation: Fire and Ash (and Meat)

Speaking of maw, a point of revisitation: "Edibility" is a register not only of the substance eaten, but of the credibility of the eater (for instance, in chapter 1 the zombies shouldn't eat at any cost, unless it's to save their own life), and the promise of transformation by the act (the eaten, in the case of zombies, may also become the infected eaters).[48] Eating is a registration of matter, what it is as it enters, what it then becomes. Eating is itself tested by a kin process, breathing, in their dual status as forms of material or chemical internalization. It is no wonder that chemicality often uses eating, or breathing, as its dramatic (human) stage. In this section I set to abrading the edges of human/animal, meat/air, substance/flight, allowing them to pass over the uncertainty of ash. Ultimately, in the work of the artist Fiona Foley, ash engages a form of agitation that pulls all these dimensions in, and spits them back out in the form of indictment and challenge.

Recently I served as a visiting professor at a small liberal arts school, teaching a seminar in critical animal studies. This was a time when racially gendered injury and the perpetuation of ignorance in the school's administration were creating pain and distrust and inspiring remarkable Black and antiracist activism, while the national and global tightening of oppression continued apace. To talk about animality at this time—to think about creatures, human and nonhuman, to think about histories of oppressive dehumanization, to meditate on lines of difference and union that are not species lines, to ask why rats are used to spatialize homelessness, why a people's worth in colonial calculus banishes them to animality or humanity, to think too about the strength, vulnerability, and resistance that might be felt to reside in animality—each of these moments had tendril ties to things we felt happening around us.

In all the turns, one of us noted, we kept coming spontaneously to the as yet unthematized word *interconnectedness*—as a means to wrest animal valences past a sealed species divide, to allege undeniability, an indication of complicit ties within a broad system of seemingly disparate elements. Interconnected was also, I suspect, a gesture of hope and affirmation, and inevitability in forms of shareable harm. In my observation, "interconnectedness" most represented a kind of secular tracking of capitalism and its structural coconspirators. This is something the students were very good at. We discussed race, disability, industrial agriculture, capitalism, class, and how they mapped to one another—all the while being quite certain of the elements we discussed, what they were and were not, convinced of their integrity as things or structures.

Then one student said, with hesitation because of her perception of the ill fit of her comment: "I'd just like to know what you all . . . believe. Because for me interconnectedness came first out of my belief—which is Buddhism. It's that interconnectedness—you know, the grain of rice . . . ," and her voice trailed off. Then she commented as if in apology, "Look, I've taken up so much space to just talk about that." But another student picked up where she had left off—and, in a kind of rhyme, told a similar story that had no end, rather an ellipsis. Just an experience, one laterally, associatively, metonymically linked, but linked nevertheless. In this doing, we started to realize a different form of interconnectedness, one lurking beneath. It wasn't all what might have been called Buddhist, it wasn't all anticolonial, and it certainly was not moving along a single axis of critique. What it was—perhaps unnameable even in retrospect—transformed. The room shifted. Other emotions: laughter, surprise. Words faded, silence came in.

She/we had not only reimagined but reenacted, somehow, what interconnectedness could mean. Along the way, we could lose some of the resolute edges: of species, of programmed and overdetermined relations, of value—that substantive web of determination. We could, among other things, begin to shed the blanket of capitalism's and colonialism's animal meaning. There are notable aspects of this story. One is that, in the middle of a liberal arts school committed (and structurally restricted, to the point of bodily conduct, civility, proper to education and made into habitus) to secular theorizing, something that could be called "spirit" broke through, and despite professional suspicions (particularly of religion), I am not quick to dismiss it. Two, we didn't end up anywhere. We didn't know quite what we were saying. Maybe that's another drag on my quick dismissal; I liked it. Our takeaway point was to note the nature of the shift, to know that it constituted a reach for a different kind of interconnectedness—even while not knowing what it was.[49] This is what I would call a moment of unlearning, anticipating the concerns of chapter 3.

Are We in a Time of Unique Urgency?

My colleague and friend Abigail De Kosnik, a media theorist, revises James Dator and Michael Ruppert's assessments that collapse may well be underway by specifying that the current uniqueness of this collapse is that it is occurring at the global level. She notes that collapse is something that colonized people, people subject to genocide, and enslaved people know well in their histories and presents. "Another way to understand Collapse theory is as the term for designating the Global North's moment of having to confront the same degree of destabilization and uncertainty that it has long compelled other peoples to experience."[50]

The common—genuinely global in the sense De Kosnik raises above—sense of overwhelm at such a political moment as this suggests there is a need for many things, all seemingly at the same time. There is a need for clear, nameable perception of what is happening and what has happened, and meaningful and direct means of remedy. There is equally a need to recognize what has begun to break or dissolve, what no longer works as diagnostic as we strain after conviction. But that recognition might withdraw from ambitions for clarity, for fear of fixity or misapprehension; it might rather show traces of the collapse it observes. That is, method might come into sensory, analytic, or affective alignment with its subjects. Systemic knowledge, habitus, infrastructural expectation, or any relationship between these may not necessarily operate so well when their subjects shift in novel ways, pitching remainders of structuralism into knots. In an essay thinking with infrastructure, Lauren Berlant described this sensation as a "glitch," a troubled transmission in the reproduction of life.[51] Even within familiar frames, we face a shifting coagulation, perhaps even in metaphysical order. Sometimes such shifts beckon the affects and orientations of what are felt as the spiritual.

What I wonder that the students were feeling was the presence of relations, relations whose prescriptive ordering and perhaps leading categorizations they nevertheless wanted to refuse. Sitting in the affect of the blurring, the nonidentity, might have been a way to release biopolitical obligation that had already begun to devastate them. Animality, for many, is also a formula for eating, eating that has been comprehensively and unacceptably industrialized. It is not only fleshly, but spiritual consumption; and what *cannot* be eaten is a form of increasingly molecularized expulsion in the management of self. This means that one of the students spoke lovingly of her pet rat, and the rest sat with this recognition, awash in feeling and uncertainty. Buddhist relations to the eating of animals are a thoroughly spiritual matter. The substance or matter of an argument is its necessary grounds for operationality. When there is no substance, there is "nothing." If substance is the grounds for argument, for constitution, then what is its inverse (and hence its quiet co-substantiator)?

Air

Here I am thinking of the brilliant work of Tim Choy, who has written precisely on the quality of air—and the apprehension of that air, the variable "substantiation" of Hong Kong air, as he puts it—by different parties and communities in Hong Kong. Air is not undifferentiated nothingness, but quite lively in its own way, and it contains substances. Choy writes of a journey of epistemological revision following his and his partner Zamira's illnesses by way of the polluted air—he had to reject his "initial attempts to disavow difficulties with the air," because, particularly in social theory, "air is left to drift . . . neither theorized nor examined, taken simply as solidity's lack . . . air can only be insubstantial."[52] Notwithstanding more recent attentions to airborne pollution, I wonder what other effects await for the application of this insight across domains of social theory.

Substance and air meet, not only in, say, the conceptual or ontological traffic of co-substantiation or the place of representative pollution like Hong Kong, but also in the closed spaces of the slaughterhouse. The hacking and grinding of animal killing yields "ground meat" and airborne particulates, a soup that bears the mark of processing consequence, an abstraction that must be assimilated by the worker. And substance and air meet in all the other ways that animal substances travel into the air, or in the ways that air recirculates into settled substance to be absorbed, managed, and sometimes kept by the human and nonhuman animal bodies that breathe or otherwise receive, that are porous to the world around them, which is everyone and everything.

These are not fictions, nor are they limited to either science or religion or practical life, for that matter. In the last few years, California, another nonintegrity, has been burning regularly at the scale of international spectacle. If climate disasters become characteristic of a given place, California's will henceforth be fire and landslides. In the few fall semesters at Berkeley before COVID hit, I would buy bulk masks to distribute, in the midst of thick sunless air, to my nonplussed students who had been told that (1) school will be canceled only according to federal air quality guidelines (thus it used a conservative guideline of reaching an Air Quality Index of 200 before closing, whereas most other area schools more seriously exercising their duty of care, including other UC campuses such as Davis and the University of California, San Francisco, actually closed before Berkeley), and (2) only the "sensitive" should take care when outdoors, because they were the ones who might experience difficulty breathing. Sensitivity has been critiqued before within disability studies, and by feminists too; not only does it presume individualistic, atomistic visions of health, but it requires one to imagine that only some have it.

And what does sensitivity mean if what is burning, what incinerates into the air, is not only some fantasized exterior "nature" of trees, grasses, dirt, and other distant flora and their seemingly mundane chemical contents, but also built "environments," including houses, cars, barns, garages, and their chemical contents, such as paints, fuel, solvents, insecticides, as well as living beings—insects, salamanders, bears, deer, frogs, *and also people*? So that not only are the absorptions particularly frictive (as in asthma, for instance), but chemical (a form of intoxication)? What kind of ruddy, capacious eater is the normative student supposed to be-in-becoming? (Is this the literalization of whiteness's incorporation?) Should only "the sensitive" be kept from eating/becoming differently, even if the advisory might keep them hale for just a little longer? If people are burning and the winds know no bounds, what of the comment that this inhalation of cooked fleshes reaches the level of cannibalism? Yet given that cannibalism has been deployed as an exoticizing, racist popular anthropology, isn't it simply a continuation of how we are—contiguous, intersubstantiating?

Particularly during fire season, but also during the drier otherwise, it feels as if California's air has become closer to something like meat (though I suppose the commonest metaphor has been that of "soup"); if, on a given day, the sky looks clear and the air feels clear, we've had the exceptional luck of a meatless

Monday. Wildfire specialists concur that there will not be a time in California's foreseeable future in which there is no fire happening anywhere in the state. After years of drought, any generous helpings of rain only now seem to feed the tipped balance in which tender new kindling is grown to feed the next fire as it comes. That is on top of the "kindling" making up the housing built into fire zones, pushing back the front of nature in order to be near it. One irony among many is that this meat bears the marks of its own history of asserted erasure. The periodic prescribed burns, called "cultural burning," that were the regular practice of Native Californians made such extravagant meatification so much less likely, before the typically misbegotten system of scientific-ecological absolutist state fire prevention and its conjuncture with the rapidly changing climate. (This is not my time to take on a tentative Anthropocene argument, by which, teleologically, the whole earth has become a slaughterhouse that the geological record will reflect.)

Contiguously, within the final pages of this chapter, "Agitation," and the next chapter, "Unlearning," I will attend to the art of Fiona Foley, an artist whose (Badtjala) people are the traditional owners of K'gari,[53] near Brisbane, Australia. Her diverse work encapsulates, demonstrates, and teaches across these two; it has also taught me some profound lessons precisely about the politics of unlearning. The first work I refer to is a permanent installation by Foley at Brisbane's Magistrates Court.[54] Called *Witnessing to Silence*, it is the story of a victorious misdirection. The call for art projects for the new Court building called for the inclusion of at least three elements: (1) environmentally sustainable design, (2) the integration of art, and (3) support for victims of crimes. In the competition for the commission, Foley had initially responded to the call by way of proposing inclusion of a natural disaster, the Australian bush fires, represented by a display of ashes in suspension. In figure 2.1, one can see shards of gray-black-brown inside five vertical glass cabinets mounted into the ground, with further closeup of varieties of ash in figure 2.2, and an even further closeup on one section containing black shards of ash in figure 2.3.

What didn't become apparent, what Foley didn't reveal until later in the construction phase—when it would have been much more difficult for the Court to cancel the commission, for instance—was that the "bush fires" marked genocidal acts. The suspended ashes in fact represented the ash, not of, say, the ecological management's canonical objects of trees and scrub, but of Aboriginal bodies that had been "removed," to use the euphemistic scientific language of colonial operations, by way of government-instigated massacres all around Queensland, after which the bodies were burned. In the ambiguity of "bush" might be a wry comment on the colonial conflation of Indigenous people with

FIGURE 2.1 Fiona Foley, *Witnessing to Silence*, 2004. Partial view on columns of ash. Photo: Mel Y. Chen.

"nature," as if to capitalize on Indigenous relations to land. Arrayed on the ground, partially visible in figure 2.4, are ninety-four stone panels, each bearing the name of one site of Aboriginal massacre. One is thus positioned to meditate anew on the varieties of ash distinct in form and also presented in distinction as seen in the three-sectioned column in figure 2.2: What beings have perished, and by what fires? Nearby the towers of ash are groups of cast bronze standing lilies.

Foley has written, "Any analysis of Queensland's laws is repetitive with injustice and continued hypocrisy. The state played a dubious role in both its denial and evasion of the truth."[55] Further reflection on Foley's use of "hypocrisy" reminds me of the risk of considering Foley's application in terms of "subterfuge," as I originally did, and the history and present of criminalizing colonized subjects as constitutionally deceptive. Instead, I now perceive an in-

FIGURE 2.2 Fiona Foley, *Witnessing to Silence*, 2004. Partial view on a single column. Photo: Mel Y. Chen.

sistence on highlighting the conflations made by a hypocritical state, its mode of forgetting, particularly in the law.

One can detect, in Foley's deployment of an asserted truth-after-all, an insistence on the traffic between human and nonhuman ash, their nonidenticality, but also humans' and trees' enduring copresence in country. In her recent book, Foley writes of the once-resplendent bunya tree, on Bunya land, which was a place for food, gathering, and alliance among nations before the arrival of the colonists and a center point for the exchange of social, ritual, and cultural life; the decimation of country included systematic human murder by colonists and the destruction of the ecology together. This included the loss of the bunya tree and its food source of nuts when the settlers took over its use for building.[56]

Jack Halberstam writes of the use of "bewilderment" as an aesthetic strategy, enabling a quality that suffocates colonial modes of knowing. It emerges

AGITATION AS A CHEMICAL WAY OF BEING 95

FIGURE 2.3 Fiona Foley, *Witnessing to Silence*, 2004. Partial view on a single panel. Photo: Mel Y. Chen.

"out of precolonial notions of space, orientation, and navigation; and refers to an immersive sense of being lost or of standing outside of a system of knowing or of merging with other systems of space and time that linger in the background to those we have selected as meaningful in the contemporary world . . . a becoming that moves in an opposite direction to colonial knowing."[57] The taxonomic and relational disorientation of tree, body, and the land itself as a place out of which Indigenous law arises before State law, appears to promote and entice such bewilderment well outside of the modes of Indigenous incorporation typically deployed by Australian State entities.

I might also suggest, however, that Foley's dual presentation of "natural ash" is not just structural ambivalence, but a before-and-after pedagogy by which the relative (but only relative—what are the preferential hierarchies of urgency?) mundanity of and sympathy for burnt trees gives way, necessarily

FIGURE 2.4 Fiona Foley, *Witnessing to Silence*, 2004. Partial view on distal view of cast lilies and floor plates. Photo: Mel Y. Chen.

and pointedly, to charred bodies of genocide (including trees). There is also a pedagogical collapse of time, a reminder that (legal) history is being made with certain occlusions that must not be allowed, if the senses are to leave an impression, perhaps even a thrusting forward of country and its denied world of intimacies and relations. Foley's "meat," then, once bitten, forces digesting, in spite or because of the contents, for the lifetime of the Magistrates Court. The ash: reanimated, submitted to eternal labor, and suspended again, wrapping time tightly within its frozen agitations. There are folded and layered lessons then of the inseparability of settler colonialism and ecological management, a non-neutral mutual enfolding of peoples and things of the environment around them, and the segregated fiction that the lay definition of *environment* (as nonhuman) has come to inhabit.

Ash, suspended in air. To substantiate air in ways like this is not to ignore the predictive density of certain relations—of the way blood travels, of the selective porosities of human skin, of the differential scales by which rock becomes air. But if we remember, say at bottom rather than exceptionally or provisionally, the nonintegrity of things, the work we do changes quite dramatically. There are exclusively scientific ways to describe this—porosities, particulates, dust, smoke, wind. But then we are still stuck in the conceptual words of scientific-ecological management, using them for perhaps compromised ends and ever again ignoring the consistent call to Indigenous sovereignty and decolonial possibility in a world whose apparent dissolutions too often seem only to serve the urgent rebuildings premised on broken universals (informed by already-default ableisms, settler ideologies, capitalist formations, and white supremacist patriarchies).

In the context of a discussion on presentist, contemporary genomic models of Indigenous identity, Kim TallBear writes of Indigenous notions of peoplehood "as emerging in relation with particular lands and waters and their nonhuman actors differ from the concept of a genetic population, defined as moving upon or through landscapes."[58] In the light of such ecological devastation, the meatiness of air, however perverse in this present circumstance, requires so much rethinking, and I feel suspicious of the urgencies that may predominate. If the adoption of Indigenous land management techniques, particularly in terms of cultural burning, has already begun in Australia and California, it seems only the beginning of a deeply needed epistemological shift and recognition of the multiple layers of violence, settlement, and resubstantiation beyond present-day capitalist mappings—the simplest forms of complex "interconnectedness"—that need first to be accounted for and addressed, even mourned, especially mourned, differentially mourned, with all the emotions and ellipses that obtain. On this, as I am among those of us in the San Francisco Bay Area who have settled on Ohlone land and who participate in academic and institutional epistemologies that require radical undoing and redoing, I have many of my own accountings to address.

This incinerator has many bodies. As they burn, they seem to become one, yet they are not the same ash. What to make of this historicity? How to recognize it, record it, face its differences? How to enflesh this air-meat's nonintegrity, to embrace it viscerally?

Molecular life has in it a kind of ordinary storm. Sometimes things crash and separate; sometimes they crash and gently coagulate; sometimes they generate new collectivities, if but for an instant. I am thinking here of molecules and their physics, and the agitations they undergo in the course of ordinary existence, but also of the behaviors of particulates that play a role in intoxication. In my previous work on animacy, molecularity was linked to sometimes spatially microcosmic and yet massively effective agencies such as toxicities, and represented one of many ironic potencies from the lower end of hierarchical orders of being. It might be useful to contrast this use of molecularity and the kinds of constitutional shifts it allows with the imagination of what Deleuze and Guattari called the *molar*, which would be most aligned with the positive categories and actors of the university, including the unmarked human package itself, who is white, nondisabled, masculine, "functionally" social, and creditable.

If I were to draw on what this offers, I might want to think about the ways in which agitation is not equivalent to the exertion of long life, even if it points to the right to one. Foley's ash agitates suspended, marking and mourning lost lives even as it indicts the operations of municipal law. And in a queer kind of way, agitation may not last. It may be poorly resourced, but it is vigorous in its own way. It may live (as ACT UP protests did) with grief as much as fury, depression, slowness, and even inaction. Agitation as collectivity, no matter the durability of every body within it, manages a form of political expression not dependent on individualistic virtuosity and promise of longevity; here I'm referring to the evanescence of queer liveliness, and the political agility that is neither dependent on permanence nor even, arguably, agility itself. And indeed, that may be its key.

3

UNLEARNING — INTOXICATED METHOD

It takes imagination and courage to picture what would happen to the West (and to anthropology) if its temporal fortress were suddenly invaded by the Time of its Other.—**Johannes Fabian**

Perhaps in another room you may come upon some about whom there can be no doubt—blocks which no educational razor can cut; vacant minds, into which you can infuse nothing; and you pity the poor teacher condemned to spend her time in the middle of such a group, labouring apparently in vain and spending her strength for nought. Many of the pupils are on half-time.
—Christopher Crayon

It is an odd thing to embark on a chapter about unlearning when it feels as if the world as it has been known is coming undone. But if "done" was late capitalism in the Western settled world, if "done" was industrialism gone sour, if "done" represents the exploitation of nature's materials for industrial capitalism (according to Marx), then undone is perhaps a necessary means to something else. Done means made; made means made of. In this chapter I want to think about unlearning specifically in relation to intoxication, race, and disability; like the rest of this book I contend with whatever blurry nexus they occupy.

I hope to find good company in efforts to imagine worthy forms of experiment in the humanities, but this is equally a plea for certain forms of experiment to count, and to already have counted; this is not advocacy for innovation so much as revisiting how and for whom innovative or virtuosic form is marked.

Returning to the art of Fiona Foley and her investigations into histories of black opium, I further think about the materialities that attach to race and disability; in this way, the unlearning that I am interested in is woven in with the material environment, and with nature and its players. Alternative, or decolonial, pedagogies in fact require the rejection of control kinds that force a desire for coherence. Learning well, to me, is the unlearning of those tropes. This chapter is thus in part about exploring the rejection of majoritarian coherence.

Tempted as I am to invoke the present as a kind of ending (a climactic ending, no pun intended), I withhold it here. The rampant deployment of the end times, even if in wry concession, does little, fixed as it is on a scope of loss and tragedy that would seem to suggest nothing but fatalism. It seems to carry on the affect of the Anthropocene, even as we learn how better to critique its ultimately "useless," to redeploy Ahmed, species universality.[1] What becomes of survival in the present? What must be unlearned, and what must be learned, for the revolution, or for the welcome?

Differential Being, Institutions, and Pedagogy

In chapter 2, I explored the nature and productivity of agitation, which lives at the conjunction of being and chemicality, disability and the political. Here, I turn to consider the operationality of what I call "differential being" in a schema of becoming undone, unlearned. How does differential being charge unlearning? How does securitized or subjectivized difference become unmade? In the pages that follow, I examine the relationship between differential being and the environment at large of the contemporary university that must be navigated as a part of the normative educational process. "Differential being" refers to ways of being—in space, time, and sociality—that allow for variabilities that in themselves are not cognizant of social difference, and yet manage to interpellate those differences. Differential being allows for cuts like slowness that, on the one hand, do not attach securely to either race or disability but engage in traffic with both, and, on the other, still expose bodies to the management and discipline of the university.

In asking questions about the collective entity of the university, its institutionality, and the bodies—human, nonhuman, and inhuman—within it, I am concerned with the ways in which fluency or its interruption become marked, as well as ways in which the systemic maintenances of difference are adjudicated.[2] By difference, here, I do not refer to a singular dimension of segmented, segregatable, or even centerable identity. Rather, differential being finds itself arrayed across many dimensions, nameable and unnameable. Chapter 2 laid out radically different scenarios for variously agitating bodies. This chapter broadens the terms by which these bodies are imagined in their variety, beyond intersectional factors almost consolidated in their regularity: race, gender, nation. I am grateful for studies of institutional difference and diversity, resistance, chemicality, illness, and disability that have given this current approach an appreciable orientation.

The agitation of chapter 2, in its diverse forms, did not constitute a collective program or a politic. While I am not convinced that it should bear the responsibility for *fabricating* one, as some kind of processual completion, I am nevertheless interested in ways that agitations might together take flight—or, rather, take to crawling. In their introduction to a recent issue of *Social Text*, co-editors Nathan Snaza and Julietta Singh call for attention to "undergrowth," which they define in relation to "myriad encounters, relations, and affective shuttlings that enable 'education' even if they happen at a scale . . . that is outside of traditional humanist ways of viewing education."[3]

Inspired by considerations of undercommons,[4] as well as meditations on those subdetectible regions below the marking thresholds of being that congeal around identity, I am particularly interested in the forms of undergrowth that, in denying, challenging, or circuiting cogitation, summon the "risk" of disability or incapacity, such as questions of development or more broadly the narrative progression by which a learning body must undergo ordered changes. Underdevelopment (and delay), by strict definitions, marks a failure of the encounter between body and institution, and that failure is too easily cast upon a neoliberally individuated human/inhuman body rather than, say, the neoliberally configured institution itself. More importantly, there are forms of ostensible failure that turn out to be wholly generative if one is open to perceiving them.

I build on the treatment of agitation in chapter 2, which takes account of—to use the superficial categorizations of agitations—self-evidently political as well as physiologically emergent agitations. These include the incitements to movement of mind and body—intolerances—brought about by pharma drugs or insupportable levels of pollutants; ocean water in a strong wind; the unruliness of children already subject to securitizing impulses in early education; and the collectively choreographed gestures of street protest. The attribution of agitation travels through all of these, and keeps intention, and its cousin agency, at bay. Indeed, that is the trick of the use of *agitation* as a label: in helping to allege the machinic, or forms of mental incapacity, it can assist in processes of inhumanization. Instead of accepting the common discursive segregation of these examples, I actively consider inviting their agglutination or at least a remapping at larger scales, as well as consider why etymology might suggest a meaningful way to relate them.

Recall that I am treating disability as a notion. In this light, it feels important both to expand what is meant by disability, precisely beyond the capitalization of medicalized or securitized categories (ones taken up in regimes of security), as well as do the work of translation for various long-standing forms of material oppression and the contemporary novelties of becoming. It is also a moment for caution, at the disingenuous promise that disability advertises—like any domain with legalized right—when it is in practice open only to some, whether culturally or legally. I write at a time when President Joseph Biden can sweepingly say that "long COVID" will be covered by disability law—so far unproven—and the centrist *New York Times* regularly publishes a column on disability.[5]

Disability can confer a selective entitlement, or reveal an interior hierarchalization, because as a social and administrative category it tends toward the recognizable. Iconic disabilities are taken as more legitimate or valid, particularly in a system that attributes properties to recognizable subjects, and counts someone as having one or another disability, as if all forms of bodyminded difference can be encapsulated atomistically. And then, taking seriously the reflexive impulse of disability studies, disability can and should be itself examined, disaggregated, in the interest of understanding its own fluent traffic in relation to the *racialized* workings and accountabilities of institutions. In all of these discussions, considering materiality and affect can make palpable some cherished forms of Snaza and Singh's "undergrowth."

Undergrowth, undercommons. Undergrowth (one take, anyway): the apparent relative slowness of the universe that nevertheless makes good on what it suggests. Undercommons: what can be found in and around the university, in spite of the canceling tendencies of the settler state found within it. That is, by pointing to the universe before the university, I celebrate an undergrowth that defies value judgments or quantitatively shriveled takes on its beneathness and instead owns a promise of subtension, a vastness of potential that remains in spite of everything. As those studying the university's dependency on diversity have pointed out, the tyranny of names includes those of *race* and *disability*, which, along with a few other exclusives, are tethered to the work of co-optational diversification. Undergrowth and undercommons recognize that as much as these tyrannical imaginations may lay claim to something of what's there, there is always a supplement or a fundament that escapes their reach.

I hold on to suspension, dissatisfied by the stubborn exclusivities attributed to human embodied-minded being (such as skin boundaries, the apex of sentience), as well as the easy promulgations of presumed exteriorities (such as air that is not of body) across a swath of educational domains and lay pedagogies. I take suspension to offer, for the purposes of this book, that the very materiality of human being—as well as the presumed externality of the stuff with which it engages—must remain in suspense, casting continued doubt on, for instance, the facial phenotypes of race and the visible prosthetic determinants of disability, as well as the forms of becoming involved in, for instance, *breathing things*.[6] My respect for the ample mysteries of suspension that escape contemporary epistemological closure is tied to in some way to my having been influenced by discussions on the right to opacity and wiliness: the project of exhaustive knowledge for its own sake mimics the rapaciousness of colonial desire, and one response to it is to reject the obligation to be known or knowable.[7] These are anticolonial discussions that wax and wane in the literature, but remain necessary due to the sticky coloniality of what has been established as scholarly.

There is nothing mechanistic about the grace and the magic of this indeterminate (as far as the nominalist is concerned) place of undergrowth, as I see it. But it is certainly a place that has—in addition to structures—mechanics, pathways, emergences. I return here to agitations. As suggested in chapter 2, agitations cross the realms of the human, inhuman, and nonhuman, and capture some form of unrest. That unrest can be naturalized as political activity, but traditionally only in certain predictable senses attuned to favored definition. And when unrest is either indicted or dismissed, accusers can borrow precisely on discourses on materiality or mechanicity to allege mental loss: agitators may be doing, but they can't grasp (I use this word intentionally, to refer to the illusion of the essential character of consciousness) what they are doing.[8]

In the university, agitated gesture—whether in the form of politically legible protest, aggressive physicality, or movement (including stillness or slowness) inopportune to favored class habitus—has no proper home, save perhaps in practice-oriented dance training or intramural sport. And on the choreographically imagined stage of political demonstration, disabled gesture is too often removed from the possibility of the political, except when it is disability protest. With the exception of non-normative movements domesticated for the purpose of representing the value of minoritized disability in the university—for instance, the rolling of a wheelchair—illegitimated expression, as wrong or slow cognition, or as nondeliberative or ill-classed gesture, co-conspires to begin or complete one's removal from the university or to guarantee that joining the community is not possible.

And yet, as I argued in chapter 2, agitations of all kinds deserve the mark of the political insofar as their evacuation from the political has delegitimated them, and insofar as they may exist precisely as a response to the constrained environment of the extended university or to a broader history of institutional violence. What I describe as emergent agitations, then, are those that reside in or emerge from regions of undergrowth. As an occupant of the university with the illusorily central status of a professor, I try in university spaces to invite forms of movement or stillness in any mode but what we have been trained with. When I begin classes or deliver talks, I have developed the practice of opening them with an invitation to be otherwise, while speaking to the disciplining of bodies in a place that would seem to care only for their complement, the mind; the raciality of that disciplining; and the removal of bodies defined as improper or insurgent.

The more outright militarization of the university's spaces and bodies—the panoply of campus police actions—is complemented by a securitization of movement falsely, and dangerously to their targets, sensitized to class, race, and disability, such that measures of identity difference alone could signal a danger to "the community" (which is presumed thus to exclude race-marked, class-marked, gender-marked, and disability-marked people). Within the university it remains all too easy to be a Black student taken to be in the "wrong" place, such as a dorm; a non-national student taking "too long" to answer a question at an exam; a student whose physical twitches and adventurous intellectual jumps, as if they were of a piece, serve together to discredit. If all of these scenarios have happened (they have), the structuring of security suggests that most such incidences go unreported.

While there are so many incidences within the university I have witnessed in my years there, I want to turn to think especially, in this chapter, about the undergrowth that *isn't* considered to be housed inside a neatly boundaried university or active only within its particular, teleogizing terms. I am interested in thinking about spaces perhaps kin to the university and carrying some of its mandates, invested in productions of knowledge, but not believed to operate by its fullest norms. After all, if so many spaces of higher education have shied from the insurgent knowledges that they once threatened, undergrowths and their pedagogies can still—perhaps especially now—be found everywhere.[9] My commitment to the potentials found in even the most thoroughly institutional university must be complemented—first and foremost for myself—by a pedagogy of spaciousness and a memory that most knowledges have *not* come of it; rather, the learning in this place is but one version, full of tools and precise vocabulary, lexical and bodily, that could be repurposed, yet is woven into mandates of capital and hierarchy, and implicated both historically and in the present with unambiguously eugenic and colonial exertions of dominance.

That reflexive pedagogy is there to remind me why there should be no surprise when an Asian nonbinary student performs an absolutely unusual (again, for the university) dance at the conclusion of my "What Is Queer Cultural Production" class and a white cis-female student who has in our classroom rarely ventured beyond convention is the first, not the last, to pronounce it "amazing"; there should be no surprise when one of the first two nonverbal students at Berkeley is randomly assigned a presentation about Temple Grandin's work scientifically likening the prevalent anxiety characteristics of agricultural animals to the anxieties of autistic people (she problematically adheres to dismissing the potential of "low-functioning" autistic people, a cline linking autism and "function" to which many autistic people object), and pronounces that the only thing that makes him anxious is Temple Grandin. That these things (still) happen in my university is also why I remain, attempting to help cultivate these moments, zones, cultures of possibility. In a space where it takes courage not only to be a racialized isolate, but also to rock, to twitch, to stand when others are not standing or to sit when others are standing, to laugh out of sync, to lie down, to have any kind of a discernible smell other than racialized class-appropriate scents, to make intellectual connections between circumscribed domains and across accepted genres that "sound mad," undergrowth must remind that it is not only there, it constitutes a ground by which the "there" of the university may be defined.

Fiona Foley's *Black Opium*

So here I deliberately turn, not to a canonical scene within the nominal space of the university, but instead to a place closely associated with its elements of legitimated knowledge, inheritance, enlightenment, and archive—the State Library (within the English Commonwealth)—a kind of institutional and knowledge-legitimating proxy. Though in some instances libraries adhere even more to the radical commons of "public" in ways that many public research universities have recently seen fit to abandon, the State Libraries of white supremacist, settler nation-states such as Australia have a messy history with these dynamics. I will wonder about intoxications working within the State Library, for reasons that I hope will become clear.

The Queensland State Library sits in the heart of downtown Brisbane, Australia, and is located near several universities, among them the University of Queensland (UQ) and Griffith University. Some elite universities in Australia are dubbed the "sandstone universities," a reference to the local stone found in prominent display in buildings in campuses such as UQ and the University of Sydney—an architecture conferring ostensible dignity, solidity, permanence (through settlement!), and the tying of land's resources to the nature-transforming trick of masterful "human" knowledge. The history of education for Aboriginal and Torres Strait Island people is one of many stories of exclusion from the sandstone universities, stories of the combination of occupation of land and denial of entry, and is far from being remedied.[10]

In this context, the Queensland State Library appears as a stage for commissioned art in the permanent installation *Black Opium* by artist Fiona Foley.[11] I believe that I first became aware of Foley's work from casual conversation in the Queensland State Archives in Runcorn, which had been my research destination from the United States and occasioned my stay in nearby Brisbane. Viewing *Black Opium* in Brisbane not only shook me profoundly, it began a process of inversion in my relation to the research archive, as well as a repositioning of archival knowing—both in how I thought about it, and in what Foley did with it in her artworks.

As shared in chapter 2, Foley is a multidisciplinary artist and scholar; she is Badtjala on her mother's side and of Irish heritage on her father's. *Black Opium*'s central historical material, leveraged for the present, comes from more than a century ago: Queensland's 1897 Aboriginals Protection and Restrictions of the Sale of Opium Act, which was the original subject of my archival visit. This Act ostensibly addressed a perceived shift in economic and racial being, casting as a scene of danger the trafficking of a harsh form of opium called black opium from Chinese to Aboriginal and Torres Strait Islander bodies, many of whom became addicted. However, Foley notes the paternalism of protectionist attitudes: "To treat Aboriginal adults addicted to opium as incapable of making decisions for themselves is another layer of white virtue."[12] Black opium was the name for a post-use product, the actual ash of smoked opium, that was exported from China to Australia by a web of traders. There are multiple chemical intimacies in this scenario, from Indian growers, to Chinese users in China, to the ash in the cargo of traders headed for Australia, to Chinese shopkeepers, to Aboriginal buyers in Queensland.

Foley's attention to the legacies of this 1897 Act, which includes many independent works, has an insistently pedagogical thrust in the sense that she is, across the diversity of forms and implications of her artwork, also invested in getting Queenslanders—especially white Queenslanders—to understand the impact of this law on the history *and* present of the state. Its administration profoundly impacted Aboriginal and Torres Strait Island life in Australia; it rewrote not only the uses of drugs, but the very terms of governance, the handling of Aboriginal and Torres Strait Islander, as well as Chinese, capital; the management of space, and interracial sex and kinship. Reserves were formed, children extracted from their families, and training programs established for the girls to later become domestic servants to white families. Stricter, and extractive, licensure systems made it nearly impossible for Chinese to sell opium to Aboriginal people, leaving whites free to engage in the trade. Rules on the living arrangements of "half caste" girls were racially coded so that they would be seen as being "harbored" illegally. Police protectors took money from their Aboriginal charges, presumably for purposes of supervising the funds responsibly—and never returned it. The scope of the Act was devastating.

Previously, white Queensland employers would pay Aboriginal and Torres Strait Island workers in the form of opium ash that they consumed by drinking in suspension,[13] in ways that were tied to the keeping of a chemically *docile*—noninsurgent and indeed nonagitating—labor force.[14] They became aware, however, that the workers were turning to Chinese sellers of opium ash, insisting on, as I saw in the state archives, dealing only with Chinese sellers, not white suppliers. It's unclear whether this shift coincided with the explicit danger of death faced by some Aboriginal and Torres Strait Island people who became addicted to this poor and harsher form of ash, but the government determined that the Chinese were part of the intensification. The criminalization of Chinese commerce and sold goods followed on existing racist ideas of Chinese moral pollution.[15]

While this circumstance yielded vastly different economic lives and freedoms for the Chinese and the Aboriginal communities,[16] an undergrowth-based account requires that one simultaneously note that Chinese communities and individuals were managing to form independent relationships—of trade, collaborative work, and intimate lives—with Aboriginal and Torres Strait Island people and also, in so doing, threatening a form of commercial exchange that deprived white traders of their stronghold on opium. But the protection law, already suspicious in its paternalism, turned into a radical form of abuse that was copied across Australia: the establishment of Aboriginal reservations, the breaking up of families and communities, the control of sexual activity and movement particularly of Aboriginal and Torres Strait Islander young women, the expropriation of Aboriginal wealth by so-called police protectors, and the forbidding of interracial union between Chinese and Aboriginal and Torres Strait Islander people, notably in the form of control of the residence of Aboriginal and Torres Strait Islander girls.

Foley's work has a diversity of forms, including sculpture, video, textiles, and architecture. Much of it recently has focused on the form of the poppy (some appeared in the Magistrates Court commission in Brisbane, described in chapter 2). Both the poppy and the Act feature prominently in her Queensland State Library installation. The installation, entitled *Black Opium*, begun in 2006 and completed in 2009, deploys large-scale dimensions in works below, across, and overhead, and much of it is thus visually accessible from a fairly large part of the library—particularly an infinity symbol of aluminum poppy buds cast from molds and hung directly over the courtyard that unites all four floors; there is almost no way to avoid seeing it if you visit any part of the library (figure 3.1). Because this installation is located in the library, in some fairly obvious way it stages the politics of knowledge or knowledge production. But there is something pointedly embodied, too, about this knowledge.

Down a third-floor hallway skirting the courtyard (figure 3.2), small trapezoids of different heights the size of a doorway open to shallow individual cubbies, most of which have some kind of seating inside. Each cubby names a material player in the entanglements of the law: "Mangrove, String, Silver, Shrine, Gold, Slow Burn, Bliss." When I went to photograph those rooms, there were students busy at work in almost all of those cubbies. There are two rooms that segregate Aboriginal and Chinese people, one with documentary and ethnographic photographs of Aboriginal people around that time, and the other with documentary and ethnographic photographs of Chinese people around that time (figures 3.3 and 3.4).

On the back wall above the work table in the cubby depicting Chinese people is, hauntingly, an enlarged letter to B. D. Morehead, a legislator, condensing the logic of the Act (figure 3.4). Not only does it condense the paranoid and "compassionate" logic of the Act by pointing out that the Aboriginal people were sympathetic but free of moderation, and that the impudent Chinese sellers made a great profit, it describes the Indigenous people with what is today described as the "n-word." The proximity of Chinese documentary photographs, of which the central image is of a Chinese opium smoker, is in tension with the narrative presented by the letter writer. Finally, obscured to the right, the date 1848, not visible in the figure, looms large. This was date of the arrival of the first ship containing free (not convict) English settlers to the land of the Yuggera people at Moreton Bay.

Each student or pair of students seemed to be enjoying the privacy and perhaps, just perhaps, maybe unwittingly too, a certain sensorium, an aura of environment. There seems an explicit invitation to embrace a change in institutional space.

FIGURE 3.1 Fiona Foley, *Black Opium*, 2006, interior courtyard. Photo: Mel Y. Chen.

The most vivid and obvious example of a sensorium is the room spatially set off at the end entitled "Bliss" (figure 3.5), a markedly darkened space in which one seat faces a video screen playing a loop that shows short, phrasal excerpts of the 1897 Act as well as other commentary, including an explicit nod to modes of sexuality and contagion, the "red plague" as a white venereal disease. The video loop has continuous shots of swaying poppies (filmed by Foley on GlaxoSmithKline fields in Tasmania), mostly from a low angle, sometimes with a focus on one or a few poppies in a shallow depth of field or wide aperture (figure 3.6). This is a sensoriality: The long focal length or wide aperture—suggesting the subjectivity of an intoxicated, dilated pupil. And there is a kind of blurred intimacy and locality rather than mastery of the entirety of the visual space as one would see in a god's-eye view ("god's-eye" because the mapping projects of colonial imaginaries that had to do with religion, resources,

FIGURE 3.2 Fiona Foley, *Black Opium*, 2006, hallway view. Photo: Mel Y. Chen.

conquest). Instead, there is a relationship to the ground, and perhaps to land and landedness.

Foley also invites the enormous question of what a drug *does* for life, experience, and resistance. Was the red plague a disease in the way opium addiction was a disease? Or was the dis-ease of opium also a disassembling, or dissembling ease? Some accounts point to opium's resemblance to a plant used by Aboriginal people as a medicine.[17] While I feel in no position to morally define opium's rightness for any particular people, particularly in a historical context of such difficulty, it does feel my responsibility to affirm the potential of sovereign acts. It should not be unthinkable that plant use can have profound, and sovereign, purpose, whether or not medicinal. It was unthinkability in part that facilitated the confidence of the 1897 Act.

In that way that visits are never strictly archival, but lively, during my personal visit with Foley, the artist mentioned that her mother, who was a Badtjala activist engaged in multiple projects of land care and who also wrote a Badtjala–English dictionary, was engaged for decades in a struggle to establish environmental stewardship classes on K'gari, a determined struggle for sovereignty and a pedagogy of Aboriginal caretaking.[18] I have begun to feel the ways Foley's attention to the 1897 law and its effects on the present day involve a kind of transtemporal reminding that feels more complex than the unidirectional form of Western historical agency of a legacy event: that thing happened, and it happens again, in a different form. Perhaps this has to do

FIGURE 3.3 Fiona Foley, *Black Opium*, 2006, interior view of a room with framed photographs. Photo: Mel Y. Chen.

with the pedagogy of Aboriginal time, connected to place, that may inhere in Foley's work, which has managed to penetrate my own dissolving sense of masterly Western time in the shifting pandemic.[19] And in deploying intoxicated temporalities in Bliss, Foley directly engages the experience and politics of memory as well as event.

In June 2019, K'gari came into the news: A father had wrestled his child back from the jaws of a dingo. Their family had been participating in the tourism on the island, which is today billed as an ecotourism destination and a UNESCO World Heritage Site. Its management follows the common pattern: ritual ownership is held by Badtjala people, but management remains in the authority of the Queensland Park Service. In the wake of the dingo incident, the authorities consulted were the Queensland Park Service, not the Badtjala people. An online parks page on dingoes refers to three conservation management factors of *education*, *engineering*, and *enforcement*,[20] which dictates the killing of offending dingoes in such cases of conflict. The Badtjala Traditional Owners stated that in their efforts to communicate about the dingoes, they

FIGURE 3.4 Fiona Foley, *Black Opium*, 2006, interior view of a room with the elements of the study space. Photo: Mel Y. Chen.

had been kept at "arm's length" from the management of dingo species on the island. They insisted that the sacrifice of dingoes for this encounter had not been necessary.[21]

In this instance as in so many others, settler colonialism has been materialized through durative policies of what Jonathan Goldberg-Hiller and Noenoe Silva call "scientific-ecological management," a relationship first identified in the wildfire policies of California described in chapter 2. Working with philosopher Giorgio Agamben's notion of the "anthropological machine," a species apparatus which relentlessly produces the recognizability of the human being as against the animal, Goldberg-Hiller and Silva analyzed a case of a shark attack on a boy, the sequelae of which unleashed scientific-ecological state law over Indigenous law of the Kanaka Maoli. As a response, they advocate the potential held by the Kanaka ontological concept of "kino lau," defined loosely as "having many bodies, human and nonhuman."[22] Goldberg-Hiller and Silva's "kino lau," at least in the Hawaiian context, also hints at a potential for Agamben's approach to unlearning—namely, "destituent" power, which has as its end the devolution, or dissolution, of a dialectic between constituent and constituted.[23]

FIGURE 3.5 Fiona Foley, *Black Opium*, 2006, exterior view of "Bliss" room. Photo: Mel Y. Chen.

As the above suggests, the worldmaking of settlement tied knots between questions of race (including the designation of racial groupings, such as whites, and the racialization of Indigenous people), species (how species mattered and exclusions of species from personhood), ecology (knowledges about taxonomy and relation, and what was alienable), capacity, and kinship (ancestral genealogies and their governance in different forms of state and Indigenous law) in ways that bring together animal studies, critical race, and Indigenous, disability, and sexuality analytics and accountings in complicated ways. That omnipresent sense of legacy not only has come to preoccupy my own work, but also haunts organizations such as Link-Up that point to this Act's scale in Queensland and its role in expanding the breaking up of Aboriginal and Torres Strait Islander families in numbers that are purportedly outdone today by modern child welfare and child removal laws. That is a pedagogy whose form may have an impact on how that knowledge carries forward.

Returning to Bliss, then: Ultimately Foley has crafted an *intoxicatory* sensorium in "Bliss," an agitation that works "underfoot," that in that dim room pointedly refuses any kind of programmatic textual study that students might want to do on their own books. Keeping in mind Foley's nod to pedagogy, this

FIGURE 3.6 Fiona Foley, *Black Opium*, 2006, photo of video in "Bliss" room. Photo: Mel Y. Chen.

is a form of different "study" that allows only the apprehension—in terms of text—primarily of the law and its paraphrasing that flashes over the screen, but always in combination with the swaying intoxication of the poppy buds from below at the level of the ground.

Notably, that explicit text inevitably *fades* as the poppies come into focus, suggesting a giving-way of law and of anointed forms of knowledge, and a giving-back to opacity. It is a "study" that is also a way of breathing the black opium, alchemizing the ash, ash that has been breathed in and out by Chinese bodyminds before its journey to Queensland. Foley is known for her particular combination of beautiful aesthetics and challenging provocation. If Bliss works as the final, rather than first, room in the sequence along the hall, a set-off place where a "blotting or indeed blacking out" of the norms of "literary, visual, or rationalized enlightenment" might be imagined to take place, the materialities, visualities, and sheer arrangements of the other, previous rooms come in to sit with you: a kind of agitative unlearning.[24]

I turn here to augment this account by thinking through the frame of transmedia storytelling. What happens if we look at this work in this way? As the experiencer of the installation, as you move through the rooms, the artist offers a first-level mediation of the opium history—which includes the land—in the tools, trees, photographs, legal texts. You take them in, one by one; perhaps you are given a task of documentary duty and commitment to memory as you traverse aspects of the ecology of the land, more direct factors that participated in the opium trade and use, the images of people living within this drama and nightmare, a reproduction of the text of the law that so impacted them. And then at the end—arguably in "Bliss"—there is something of a transmedia synthesis of the individual mediations.[25]

What is compelling about this moment of arrival, Bliss, is that it is not full of information in the way of documentary conclusion. If there are occasionally words, they are eventually outdone by poppies swaying and blurring in the breeze, almost a rejoinder to the informational or representative approach that one might have made up to this point. This final synthesis, if we call it that, is a very underspecified thing, not so faithful to the information, but more faithful to the disabled event of intoxication. I gather that much of transmedia's attributed richness is assumed to be in its multivariateness, its voluminous interfacing, its rich multiplicity. Instead, here, the documentation stops, the informational noise quiets; "Bliss" might additionally signify here Buddhist nirvana.[26] Disability, along with its spiritual register, leads a way out of the able-bodied maximization of labor. Or as a way through labor. And perhaps as a way not to work. You're in a space, a dark one, one of the few dark spaces in this enlightened place of the library. But/and maybe, just maybe, you have come to know better.

Unlearning and Racialized Intimacies

Black is a moniker for Aboriginal and Torres Strait Island peoples in Australia. In that context, "Bliss" possibly animates the form of *contrary relief* that black opium offered to Aboriginal people, many of whom were laboring in gendered and sexualized terms under unsustainable conditions. On top of suggesting, for me, questions of disability in the encounter with debility, "Bliss" presents an indictment of the knowledge base (and basis for knowledge) of the State Library, taken as a place of conventional study. Instead, the room inverts enlightenment with darkness, a fading of words into blur. It is a kind of unlearning.

This is not to suggest in any way that Foley is in any way against education tout court; she is fully identified as a Badtjala, Indigenous researcher whose doctoral dissertation at the Queensland College of Art led to the published book *Biting the Clouds*.[27] This is research compared to which my own pales, not only for its comprehensive attention to the non-Indigenous literature on Aboriginal and Queensland history and the Aboriginals Protection and Restriction of the Sale of Opium Act, but also for her deep integration of Indigenist

Research Theory and her unpacking previous erroneous accounts by non-Indigenous researchers. Foley's curatorial activism has pointed to the complex responsibilities of the sandstone universities, which generally continue to function as places of exclusion for Aboriginal people despite having been literally built on and with Indigenous land (including the sandstone that features in the highest universities' campus buildings).[28] Unlearning happens in the heart of the educational space, as well as beyond it. Unlearning can thrive in a dark cubby in the maw of the State Library.

I continue to sense relations between "Bliss" and Black study, for the ideas each presents in relation to the educational scenario and the broader one of learning. There is a vibration perhaps between this juncture and the turns within global Blackness. There is a history of Black (or the more differentiated spelling, "Blak"), as in Aboriginal, affinity to Black, as in US/African Black diaspora or Black Atlantic, political life, that does a kind of uniquely positioned transnational work vis-à-vis recent ventures with respect to the ways that Black and Indigenous theories and movements might engage one other. Aboriginal Blackness and the Black Atlantic diaspora come together in one capacious figuration of the "shoal," in Tiffany Lethabo King's assiduous and reparative crafting. With attention particularly to the Black Atlantic, the shoal is an ecological juncture bearing weight in histories of slavery and also known to Indigenous peoples, and is a theoretical and methodological intervention: "a disruptive mechanism that interrupts and slows normative thought and violent knowledge production" that has been premised in part on binaries between land and sea, "aesthetics and theory."[29]

In a comment on the racialization of Aboriginal people in Australia, Patrick Wolfe notes that "the specificity of the Aboriginal category cannot be reduced to colour, any more than Aborigines' historical maltreatment can be trivialised as 'colour prejudice.' Beneath the indeterminate signifier of colour lies the historical continuity of dispossession, an irregularity that the inclusive regime of race has sought to neutralize."[30] While Fred Moten notes that the Atlantic slave trade drew on an Indigenous African population, the enslavement of Aboriginal people—deeply linked to the Stolen Wages cause—had a different temporality and valence from US forms of slavery. Yet movements such as Black Power cultivated transnational recognition of and openness to connected/shared causes, such as that of Palestine and its struggle against colonialism. Aboriginal activism had its own resonant (not derivative) Australian Black Power movement for self-determination in Redfern in 1968, as described by Aboriginal scholar and Black Power member Gary Foley.[31] Considering "Bliss," and more generally *Black Opium*, together with Black study is to suture Australian Aboriginal forms of revisory and anticipatory unlearning to the webs and histories of knowledge intervention in the Black diaspora.

Crucially, Foley's video's effects blur the strict edges of what one has seen before. Mangrove, String, Silver, Shrine, Gold, Slow Burn; Bliss. There is an argument there about, for instance, whether the idea that the segregation between the Chinese and the Aboriginal-Torres Strait Islander rooms, or Chinese being and Aboriginal being (note I do not refer to a denotative "identity" whether or not the documentary segregations of photos could be collated among themselves to suggest that), could ever actually be as perfect or permanent as the installation rooms seem to set up, and the "queered" families that resulted from their nonsegregation—their mixing not only socially but constitutionally—bear such witness. Such a questioning of constitutional segregation, and the histories of racialization, shows up in her other work, particularly in a photographic series called *Nulla 4 Eva* (figure 3.7), which Fiona Nicoll has analyzed in terms of sexuality.[32]

More broadly, the communities joined together commercially, carnally, in friendship, and otherwise. There were many moments in the archives that bore this out, and in a powerful way, even if inextricable and painful ambiguities live on in the state archive. One petition to the colonial treasurer by Chinese shopkeepers, filed in the archives and dated June 26, 1903, was a plea to reinstitute their capacity to sell opium under the existing (pre-Act) restrictions, such as caps on opium stocks and licensing, which should have been adequate. "We are thus placed in such a dilemma as to practically preclude our dealing in Opium, much to the prejudice of a very large section of the Chinese community." It was hand-signed by eleven petitioners.

As mentioned above, I saw repeated mentions that Aboriginal people insisted on buying opium only from Chinese shopkeepers. Sometimes the justification was that Chinese shops were open "at all hours," but in most cases this insistence went unexplained, perhaps because no answer would have been reasonable to the court system. I do wonder about the emergent and then lived temporalities that took hold among Aboriginal, black opium-opiate, and Chinese bodies; in such an examination it becomes clearer that slowness as a reference to life affected by opiates is but a general (and, again, indicting) cast over a complex and contradictory tangle of modes involving the variable timing of life. While the concept has been used more capaciously in terms of multispecies ethnography, I think here of Eben Kirksey's broadly applicable notion of "chemosociality," which he defines as "the altered, attenuated, or

FIGURE 3.7 Fiona Foley, *Nulla 4 Eva I*, 120 × 80 cm, 2009.

augmented relationships that emerge with chemical exposures."[33] Bracketing the suspended (legal) application of human concepts to any of the grouped beings taking place in this extended scene is both a refusal of settler modes of articulation as well as an opportunity to explore the ways in which relational lives might have taken shape in the context of an exposure that only under certain conditions strikes me as capturing a form of agentive voluntariness that is both favored in law's criminal treatments as well as utterly denied to Aboriginal and Torres Strait Island peoples subject to legal "protective" measures.

Another legal case involved an Aboriginal and a Chinese man, on March 18, 1902, as a case against "Ah Chie" in a breach of the Pacific Island Labor Act. The two men, Ah Chie and Narveah, had been accused of being proximate in a way that had been deemed illegal, in this case the allegation that a Chinese man was employing an Aboriginal man. Remember that the 1897 law was significantly about reasserting white control over labor, as well as radically expropriating it. In the case are records of the Aboriginal and Chinese men's protests that, in fact, they were equal owners of a garden which they had decided to keep together, for their sustenance. Figure 3.8 shows part of Narveah's testimony, I quote here:

> I have been in Mr Hobler's Office this morning. I have been working in Defendant's garden, I told Mr Hobler I had a paper which may come alonga Court. Mr Hobler ask me what I was going to say. I worked alonga Ah Chie last Christmas. He was fined for employing me. I saw Mr Bryan out there the other day. I was working there that day cleaning a boiler. I stopped in your Office this morning about a minute. I just came in and go out. I wanted to see the Agreement. I can't read I put my mark on that put a cross. You were in the Office when I made the mark. Ah Chie was there too and some other boy four fellow Joe, Charlie Sang.... I lease boiler, plough and everything there. Ah Chie is not my boss. We work like Company in partnership. Ah Chie sells the vegetables and gets the money. We get half and half the money. I no sell nothing yet, too dry, haven't sold anything since Christmas. Mr Hobler was not there when I made a mark on the Agreement.

Eventually Ah Chie and Narveah won the case, a rare victory. This case, one of friendship, perhaps love, and collaboration, moved me nearly to tears in its forthright defense of care and communing. Yet it coexisted with another clause from the Chinese shopkeepers' petition to the Colonial Treasurer mentioned above. It is a clause, shown in figure 3.9, that speaks directly, and hauntingly, to the relationship that some Chinese drew between their constitutional capacities and what the medicine enabled: after a list of conditions they used opium for, including malaria, colds, chills, and rheumatism, they "find it so efficacious that they cannot do without it [opium]." A further line of writing has been added in later, with a different pen and in a more cramped fashion, sitting upon the red line that had previously been used to mark the end of the numbered entry which gives it the status of accentuated afterthought or a phrase once missed then unwittingly emphasized: "especially whilst opening up new scrub land."

Though much in the archives refers to Chinese shopkeepers positioned as possible sellers of opium, this addendum accentuates their work on the land. There is a chilling resonance here between the question of Chinese farmers "opening up" (whose?) land as phases in agricultural "development" or urbanization—a known participation in settlement—and the question of the settler's (whether as laborer or owner) modulated suitability for it. I think here about Chinese expertise in monocropping as a fundament of early Chinese ecological practices, and what trails of history may be traced between Chinese immi-

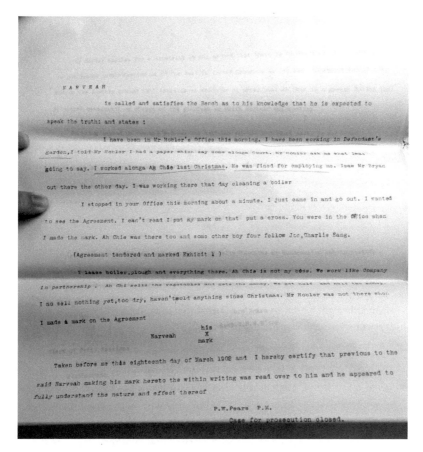

FIGURE 3.8 Narveah's testimony for the court. Photo: Mel Y. Chen.

grants to Australia and what they did with the land. Furthermore, the idea of collective tending to gardens productively haunts the settler colonial project in Australia. The Torres Strait Islander (Meriam) Eddie Koiki Mabo's lawsuit for genealogical Meriam land sovereignty and the rights of Indigenous law, won after his death, was grounded in a deep knowledge of land care that included gardening; it resulted in an overturning of the terra nullius principle in the favoring of Native land claims.[34]

The slowness of the opium here has a trace in both race and disability. I mentioned above that the opium was used in part to ensure a "docile" working population, one crucially not subject to (recognizable) political agitation.[35] But there were other slownesses that came to bear the legislative heft of the state. In the gradual inclusion of Aboriginal workers into the managed legalized labor

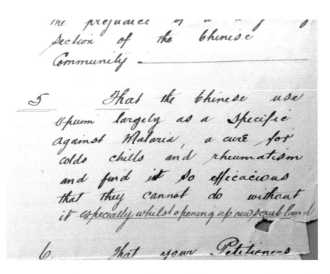

FIGURE 3.9 A portion of a petition in defense of Chinese usage of opium. "5. That the Chinese use opium largely as a specific against Malaria, a cure for colds chills and rheumatism and find it so efficacious that they cannot do without it especially whilst opening up new scrub land." Photo: Mel Y. Chen.

system, the Slow Worker Clause from 1972 was essentially a negotiation or conspiracy of cattle ranch owners and labor law to allow them to continue depressing Aboriginal payment for work: an "Aborigine who is an aged infirm or slow worker" could *still* work for lower than "minimum" wages, provided they successfully became permitted.[36] To think of the Slow Worker Clause as strictly "disability" law is to ignore the inseparability of disability and race in its very conception. Thornton and Luker note that in a 1965 case whose existence was owed to major strike and union actions by Australian Aboriginal cattle workers, Aboriginal workers could thenceforth be included in Cattle Station Industry awards, and yet were still—continuing the effective exclusions of 1951 it was meant to undo—considered as a racial class to be slow, and by the following quote, slow in two senses: in work itself, and further ("retarded") in the *understanding* of work: "at least a significant proportion of the aborigines employed on cattle stations in the Northern Territory is retarded by tribal and cultural reasons from appreciating the full concept of work."[37] Considering "appreciation" as a form of knowledge simply underlines the depth of insinuated (and legislated) attributions of lesser knowledge capacity on the part of Aboriginal peoples.

The Slow Worker Clause instituted disability pay on the backs of Aboriginal workers by a circular trick of definition: Aboriginal workers were slowed *as workers*, and even if they weren't, they were collectible with the aged and infirm. On the one hand, employability under the new system might be protective against off-track forms of enslavement or indenture. On the other hand, what wages existed were now legally systematically depressed below minimum wage levels, and furthermore, any winnings were captured and held by the supervisory and "protective" state, with steep requirements for their retrieval, resulting in an ongoing struggle to regain "stolen wages."

At the strictest level, it could be argued, in a narrowed and universalizing formulation of disability, that legal instruments like inclusions of "slow work" in schemes of remuneration allowed for "disabled" people to be newly employed, albeit at wages lower than those for nondisabled people. In order to hire a disabled worker, an employer might have to mark, for instance, how many fingers were missing compared to the norm; this calculation thereby determined the reduced wage rate, since the assumption was that productivity would be reduced in comparison to nondisabled laborers. Disabled workers' labor was thus worth less, even if recompensable. However, just as in the case of the Slow Worker Clause and its use to suppress Aboriginal people's payments, "other"—and the language of segregation fails here—legal inclusions of disabled workers within Australia were similarly keyed to the success of the economy rather than exclusively on individual or group rights per se. Several Australian legal devices related to disabled work were a response to the establishment of a minimum wage law which was understood to create new forms of competition that would result in unemployment for less competitive workers: "every less competent and aged and slow worker is thrown out of employment as a result."[38] But note the muddiness of the meaning of "slow," which could be informed by its association typically with agedness, incompetency, inexperience, raciality, and more, through their grammatical conjunction; or by its mutual exclusion from those categories.

The same author, a US government scholar of Australian labor history, notes that in regard to the furniture trade in Victoria, it was reported by the New South Wales Royal Commission that "[t]he consequence of the Chinese and other (slow worker) competition is that factories where the cheaper kind of furniture is made are in a bad way."[39] Who *could* be, or *would* be, a slow worker? Though a close study is beyond the scope of this book, in my brief survey of twentieth-century laws and discussions of slow workers, this kind of muddying ambivalence seems to be the norm. The use of slow worker categorization of Aboriginal workers as a means to evade even antiracist legislation such as the Racial Discrimination Act has continued until the 1980s, if not the present day.[40]

The defense of the interest of disabled workers in the wake of minimum wage laws was regarded as a growing problem around the turn of the twentieth century, right around the passage of the Aboriginals Protection and Restriction of the Sale of Opium Act in Queensland. In this simultaneity, note that I am not here alleging causality between, say, sedentary opium ash use and later Aboriginal categorization as slow workers. Instead I point to a kind of conceptual and affective soup of policy marking racial and disability status, mediating between rights, perceived competitive populations of workers, codes of labor value, and materialities of time, and generating pre-legal potentials. The imaginary flexibility of slowness and its mobility of referents have served the interests of racial capitalism so thoroughly and insidiously that I am motivated to bring a critical curiosity to every "innocent" characterization of slowness today, particularly to ask about its involution of muddier historical meaning.

It is appropriate here to reflect back on the valuation of slowness in the university. Certainly, being marked as slow renders some mindbodies unsuitable for the university—this seems increasingly true for humans and inhumans with any form of disability, whether marked or unmarked, visible or invisible—since the university's rushed temporalities create ever larger zones of exclusion marked as incapacity. Beyond any intelligible interpretation of disability, slowness is an experience of some kinds of thinkers who might be invested in the meditative, or require time to live within modalities of undergrowth.

Partial Cognition, Cripistemology

Using slow thought or slow being in the university as a fulcrum, I turn here to inquire to what degree that which is dismissively or apologetically called "brain fog," or other cognitive states of difference, must be excluded from method, and the presumed activity of epistemology, given its active suppression particularly within academic spaces, including disability studies. Brain fog has re-entered the national consciousness in the United States as a feature of long COVID. In turning to cripping partiality, I attend to the concomitant importance of addressing questions of racialization and decolonization.

Years ago, I had a work obligation that included a degree of public performance. I was grateful to be able to attend, as for some time I had doubted that I could. What I first thought to describe as "extenuating circumstances" in a prefatory disclaimer, I realized would have to be treated quite differently. Just two days earlier, I had gotten stoned—for the first time in more than ten years. I think the word is "toke." I took a toke, or I toked. Dictionary.com says I could say, "I toked some grass." So it is.

It was a great pleasure. My toke did not choke, as they sometimes do, by inducing fear and paranoia; instead, I had a lovely giggle about nothing at all, or at least nothing that I can remember, and eased my way into and then out of sleep with nary a worry about how I was going to do a good job that coming Friday. That was radically unlike the daily dance I lived then, even more now, between anticipation, apprehension, disarrangement, and fog that together constituted the brinksmanship of my existence as a working academic on a very packed schedule of (then five, now twenty?) interwoven ongoing administrative, social, pedagogical, and intellectual activities. Instead, I had no care that way. I just kept repeating the phrase my friends and I had come up with the first time I, at age twenty-three, ever got high, the mysteries of which I am still trying to unpack twenty years later. The phrase: "More ice cream than you can remember."

I live in California where flora—including grass—are various and plentiful and are so wonderfully weird that they challenge fauna/flora divides. And yes, the West Coast of the United States has a long tradition of experimentation, of knowing how to "go cosmic," with not a small dose of orientalism. That is all true; I am a product of my environment. But the most remarkable thing about getting high was the next day, Monday. After a miserable six weeks of ongoing migraines and nausea, accompanied by wiggy visual and auditory distortions, I suddenly felt better, suggesting that getting stoned had been exactly the right treatment. For the respite, I thank a friend who spirited me a joint left over from a prescription she used to complement her chemotherapy the previous year.

The migraines announced themselves with a visual signature: if I looked just to the left of someone, I could make that person simply disappear, amid shifting zipper lines within my field of vision. Soon after this aura came the extraordinary pain, and then came the sequence of rolling migraines. My visits to doctors and acupuncturists, my ingestion of meds, and my otherwise widespread attempts did little to stem the tide of migraines. In that six-week period there was exactly one two-day stretch in which I was free of major head pain. I had to email excuses in advance, when I was able to read a screen and not throw up at the same time, or retrospectively apologize if I had not been able. Even harder was that it seemed extremely difficult to think, both before and after the migraine itself. "Feeling stupid" is a phrase I do not use, for its palpable antidisability sentiment, its violent rejection of a particular cognitive range of being. Yet what better phrase is there, sometimes, for my force of disappointment and self-repudiation in comparison to what I expected of myself—particularly in this type of academic employ?

Feeling and reporting that "I can't think," in fact, is something I have undergone since I was young. By now I've learned to just stop working when I have an illness event, because it is too hard to keep track. Whatever the specifics, many call such a cognitive state—or style—"brain fog." Whereas I once led a class in which I hid an occasional inability to process what my students were saying, today, having summoned pragmatism and courage in part derived from immersion in a range of locations, including the collective work of disability studies and disability community, I am open with my students on days I feel far from intellectually optimal, heightening our awareness of the shared project of pedagogy. It is then that my wish for shared epistemologies that can be developed together among differently cognating beings becomes most acute—even, or especially, in the university.

The kind of intellectual work we are asked to trade in, I venture, requires a comprehension—a word that suggests both finality but also wholeness of grasp—something that feels impossible when brains are foggy. As an example, university exams vary greatly. Some depend on recall of comprehensive knowledge of an entire domain, while others ask for methodological performance. I mention this comprehension again because I want to ultimately ask after the methodology: the operands and instruments of theorizing. To what degree are brain fog and other cognitive states of difference excluded from the activity of epistemology, given their pervasiveness? And how integral a role does cognition's racialization play in such inquiries?

Like others, I had trouble reading in school when something shifted in my mind and body around the age of ten. But I can only suppose that because of my middle-class mien and a certain racialized model-minority position, I, unlike many others, was forgivingly credited with having come up with smart, if eclectic, alternatives when in fact I was having so much trouble with the information, was full of not-knowing, and had to find a way to learn differently, which was associatively, because the direct path felt blocked. While I am cautious about telling this as a "disability history," I have started to tell it as a history that has surprising connections to disability and that is one of the things that push me to think about disability as a thing that has more than four square edges. Disability is morphologically contingent—in its very constitution, its narration, its historicization. Mushing and pulling at disability and disability theory's own complicit norms seems to answer particularly well the call to craft *cripistemology*, a term introduced by Merri Lisa Johnson and further considered by Robert McRuer.[41]

You might guess at this point that I am less interested in moving directly, as an identity gesture perhaps, to sheerly revalue this experienced cognitive "partiality," experienced as a "less" of rationality. Rather, I wish to consider this partiality in relation to an ideal and also to a demand of a particular kind of cognition called comprehension, which academic thinkers are supposed to foster even as we pursue "a single line of thought." Donna Haraway's language of "partial perspective" in her article "Situated Knowledges" is useful to think with here.[42] I do not know if Haraway's work from three decades ago is a cripistemology, but it might be one provided its use of sight be bracketed as a structuring metaphor for knowledge probes and nothing more. When I teach this text, I draw on the humility made necessary by partial perspectives, as well as on the necessity of working together among diverse embodiments and cognitions on shared projects—projects themselves that, I genuinely hope, will not be comprehensive.

Back to the migraines. This migraine series produced for me a new, extended illness profile. In fact, all that seems regular in this "chronicity" is its phasal nature, marked by an occasional shift into a new unfamiliar terrain of symptomatology, at least for a while, of what is understood as chronic illness. Each phase of chronicity—with its characteristics, its temporalities, its surprises and nonsurprises, and its socialities—needs learning anew. Those of us who work for wages and who have lived or even thrived within such crip departures from normative time can then be stunned by the revenge of the clock: we are, upon "improving" beyond that mediated threshold of capacity that says "work/don't work," tasked with finding ways to renavigate standard timeliness, as well as prompted to analytically help others work with our changing versions. And we catch up on what is owed other decent folk who have every reason to expect something from us because we have promised to do it. Rosalind Gill and others have traced the injuries of neoliberal academia; this is, of course, the common experience of what perceivedlessness—described by some as disability, by others as illness, by others as pain, by others as gender departicularization, or gender deterritorialization—obligates in a labor or social profile.[43]

How, then, does cognition's racialization more explicitly complicate the picture I have already sketched? The (racialized) nationalisms related to some conditions proximate to disability, like the toxicity that threatens disability, are such that toxins, and thus the toxicities that may accompany them, are exported to other places, as in the logic demonstrated within the notorious 1991 memo signed, if not authored, by Lawrence Summers, then of the World Bank. Quoting it partially: "Shouldn't the World Bank be encouraging MORE migration of the dirty industries to the lesser developed countries? I can think of three reasons . . . 1) a given amount of health impairing pollution should be done in the country with the lowest cost, which will be the country with the lowest wages. I think the economic logic behind dumping a load of toxic waste in the lowest wage country is impeccable and we should face up to that."[44]

That Summers, when challenged, quipped that this memo was "ironic" does not affect in any way the underlying logic of chronic indebtedness, coded as "low wage countries" and "high mortality countries," as if these conditions emerged without the help and insistence of the World Bank and the World Trade Center.

There are at least two reasons why identifying nationalism within disability cultures is critical to a transnational analysis of disability's complexity: one, the ongoing fact of war and impoverishment and the varieties of impairment they deliver (on top of sheer death), such that disability pride can seem to ignore the ties between Western rights-based identity formations and the United States' role in constructing international dependencies to furnish its constructed dominance under the guise of democracy; and two, industrialization, mass-commodified agriculture, and the injuries they deliver to their generally socially or globally peripheralized and disempowered, racially gendered laborers. Toxicities are integral to both. And both of these—particularly the former—have been part of the kind of objects called forth to witness against a disability nationalism. Damage to life and limb—that is the phrase that comes up in war talk—amputations by munitions, permanent scarring from roadside bombs. These are the wounds of war. The "flying limbs" dramatized in the bombing at the 2013 Boston Marathon, the stark reversal of super-ability to the loss of the very limb that made you super—these are the players in the transnational drama of war's production of disability.

I bring up these examples because cognition is so very often part of what happens, what changes within them. I do want, in a disability-studies inheritance context, to insist on the words *damage* or *harm* while registering the ways cognition changes, while suspending judgment on those changes. That is, I want to insist on the harmful and indeed transformative function of the act, however complex the agencies and histories behind that act, even if the result may not be experienced as harm. A cripistemology needs to weigh questions of value carefully, well beyond a sheer reversal of negativity that can accompany some neoliberalized but otherwise highly capacitated identities of disability.

Disability rights often takes place, today, at a distance away from certain sites of damage/change, such as the harsh, disabling and unprotected conditions of commodity manufacture, or the cancers and other chronic conditions that impact laborers who deal in pesticide intensities and combinations (toxic combinations) that are virtually unstudied except by those who must cope and strategize under these particular working or living conditions, for instance through intuitive survival practices, or in community-based research and other community advocacy projects. These multiple conditions come with a deeply hybrid transitional profile in which the mind and body undergo their own effects. The head injuries of war, likewise, which Jennifer Terry has described as occurring in ever-changing ways due to the development of new kinds of munitions, have their own neural and cognitive effects.[45]

Let us think not only about chronicities, toxicities, and effects, but also about points of bodily departure, particularly what integrities are proposed by what haunted presumptions of essence. Who gets to begin, in the regard of others, with a body? And who gets to begin, in the regard of others, with a mind? I refer here to profiles of race, gender, and labor that produce variable "body-mind" distributions that are keyed to their proper place in a hierarchy.

The kinds of transnational felt resonances that might cripistemologically inform one's approach to people positioned as conventional "others" (through racism, coloniality, class, political geography, or, indeed, disability) become less palpable precisely because of the differential corporealization of "good"-minded selves and "other" possible embodied subjects—other possible experiencers, other possible bodily situations, other possible cognators. I imagine this differential becoming as complementing Margaret Price's work, for instance, in delineating the hidden but pervasive figure of the "able mind" that prevails in the academy within a context of production, collegial sociality, and more.[46] Price's delineation of the privileging of rationality would apply well here, though her focus is primarily on mental disability as a diversion from that academic rationality, rather than intellectual ability/disability and its racialization. I also consider Nirmala Erevelles's work on the stickiness of the racialized school-to-prison pipeline and its relevance for various considerations of disability—both the impossible registration of disability and the impossibility of services for select racialized intersections.[47]

To be clear, cognitive or intellectual disability—and its broader matrix of cognitive variation—is the near unthinkable for academia. What are we to do with the brain fog that has become our troublemaking partner in this context, more prevalent than we were told to believe? What if we cannot cancel it, for those of us who arrive here on more secure cognitive ground? Or those of us who have experienced cognitive change with various shifts due to age, illness, injury, or other bodily transition? What about the cognitive imposters who have always thought "I don't think" while somehow getting through? And there could also be the fact that cognitive imposters are us, in that we have all trained in an unfamiliar specialty of cognitive style for which we have paid, not necessarily life and limb, but certainly money, passion, and labor. Finally, what about those deemed cognitively deficient their entire lives, about whom definitions, sometimes insidiously, vary; and what about those trapped by the strange trades between cognitive disability and race? Where and how do all these differences fit into this picture of cripistemology?

I began studying cognitive science from the perspective of linguistics in graduate school, just before neuroscience began to predominate the field. Today the commonsense acceptance of a biologized and hence neural basis of mind is in part why I think the terms *neurodiversity* and *neuroatypicality* are used with such pervasive commitment by community members, activists, and disability studies scholars, and in part why experts appeal to neuroscience for insights on autism. And yet some characterizations of neuroatypicality seem only tendentiously neural in character and seem to have more to do with old-school cognitive elements such as information retrieval, calculation, and the like. Thus, even in neural approaches to cognition today, there remains a notion of information being acquired, held, sequestered, and corralled. I know that calling it all "information" is a rude reduction of what was going on in cognitive science then and now—or, rather, it bears mentioning that the "information" matter of cognitive science itself is continually protean and under revision. And yet, information has prevailed, I think, by and large.

An information-handling reading of cognition, rather than being a remote disciplinary feature proper only to cognitive science, is integral to the prevailing mechanisms for the contemporary production of knowledge. As humanities and social science scholars we are tasked to work with a fluid cognitive tool set: taxonomies, namings, retrievals. Ultimately the academic institutions we inhabit are at this moment adept at producing what I would call disciplined cognators. What happens to us in that process? I do not mean that some people simply become canonical or affixed to disciplinary frameworks. I mean that our disciplining goes much further than disciplinarity. We know this, but to what degree have we explored its consequences for our production of epistemologies? What kind—perhaps even, what cognitive kind—of epistemologies do we wish to produce? Must we consider brain fog—or other kinds of cognitive states deemed improper—necessarily punishable in an epistemological, or even cripistemological, context of collective devising?

The concept of cis-ness might help us move toward tentative answers to some of these questions because of the ways in which it opens up questions of time, change, and transition. *Cis* is a term that within popular gender-forward practices indicates not only "same" but a singular originary-to-present "homeness" in a given gender position as assigned at birth, as in "cisgender man." But monolithic cisness is in large part disingenuous; we are all too complex for such linear transhistorical sameness. Then what could a venturesome term like *ciscognators* mean? Someone who has the same style of cognition as assigned (such as "normal" or "not delayed") when they were born? Maybe not with full sincerity; but maybe we can use it as a conceit to talk about an expected temporal trajectory, not consistent throughout but—like sexual development narratives—having its own proper spurts and ebbs, a mapped journey of cognitive elaboration (known to cognitive scientists and pediatricians as development), such that a cognitive identity can be felt and affirmed in a way that produces the effect of a "cis." But the becoming that neurotoxicities, for instance, invite, is something else. Yet Marquis Bey extends the critique of cis to point to its ineffable racialization; or, rather, that both trans and Blackness—along with cis itself—refuse cis's simplicity.[48]

We are all becoming, and I credit trans studies for helping me think through body- and self-becoming's rich complexities. Trans studies helps to open and critique beginnings, middles, and ends—such as in "cis"—to meaningful inquiry. It asks fundamental questions of temporal projection, certainty, and closure, precisely for epistemology. It helps to frame ways in which we are becoming environmentally, too, and in a way that transitions seem harder to sort into good or bad if we were to rely on characterizing the materials that move them along as toxic or not, endogenous or exogenous. Already in 2011, Eva Hayward suggested that transing frogs—frogs whose sexing appears to be correlated with densities of environmental toxins—might represent an opportunity to see who and what we become together, as opposed to simply an indicator species for what might become of us. She wrote:

> I don't believe that a single environmental factor could explain transsexuality; the assertion is ridiculous. But it does open the realization that bodies are lively and practical responses to environments and changing ecosystems. Instead of toxic sex change as a sinister force that threatens all life, it might be about reinvention, as well as about political and economic systems that affect everyone, including animals.[49]

That process of "becoming together" is particularly relevant for disability and its edges, especially if we can bracket the properly human.

To extend the inhuman, I want to conclude my reflections on cognition by turning to a text that had a major impact on me as a graduate student: *Cognition in the Wild* by Ed Hutchins, a cognitive scientist at UC San Diego who had spent a number of years serving in the military.[50] He was particularly interested in navigation, and the more he looked at it, the more he realized that cognitive scientists were not telling the right stories. They were still imagining cognators as solitary humans, with interior thoughts, in that classic figuring. But the successful navigation of the ship involved many directional shifts among equipment, men, and material culture, such that "cognition" started to look very different. The men were starting to think "like" the machines; they were "becoming machines." They were not only or ever controlling agents, and no single individual could possibly have mastered the entire schema of operations. What stories are disability studies scholars telling?

Partial knowledge emerges, again, as an alternative, post-human form of cognition. Ultimately Hutchins describes what he calls "distributed cognition," such that cognition is distributed throughout the culture of the ship, and humans are one important part, but still just one part of it. This view of cognition suggests the usefulness of shifting away from the perfect fantasy of repetitious and continuous comprehension; it gives up on this fantasy, reminds us of our shared thinking, and ensures that no "thinker" is actually a thinker as they are imagined. This has implications for the shared cognitive labor we do, and it also could have unexpected and generative implications for the single-author system, the unmarkedness of collaboration, and ultimately what cognitive disability could or should mean. Dystopian machinic visions of manual and nonmanual work notwithstanding, my hope is that it could somehow mean very little someday.

Intoxicated Method

Throughout this book, I have made repeated gestures to the questions regarding intoxication, wondering what is lost when it is treated as a zone of exception or exclusion. I have constantly asked myself what it means to be or become, say, "intoxicated" by a substance like opium—temporally ingesting and thinking with its inter-human temporalities, its urgent demands, its soothings, its very pace, and its extensive consequences—and what it means to treat it as method.

These are not straightforward questions, however. In practice, asking about intoxication's effects in knowledge also requires not only approaching the critical boundaries of the toxic versus the nontoxic, but also exploring the affects and other categorial blurrings in that *production* of the toxic. For entities defined as toxic, this attention to its conditions means to examine not only the toxic–nontoxic axis, but other axes of equal importance, such as disability–debility, incident–chronicity, human–inhuman, constitution–interconstitution, quickening–slowing. In every move from a first to a second term, a sharply defined exceptional state shifts toward something much more complex, inviting estrangement from privileged values. If my goal is more toward intoxicated presentism than a kind of drug voluntarism, I am not sure I can fully leave aside the question of prescriptive intoxication for the benefit of learning or unlearning. I am thinking here of the ordinary, socially legitimate uses of attention drugs, speed, antidepressants, anti-anxiety medications, and wine after a talk, to liberate other knowledges and knowledge performances.

What above seems potentially an indulgence becomes more justified in the context of a critically disabled provocation to ask about the workings of our own memory and, more generally, apparatuses of what we consider as knowledge. For instance, if critical medical humanities calls for examining the knowledge forms of notions of health, illness, and disability, one might be led to reflect on the methods of medical humanities research, particularly given the early ethical motivation of the medical humanities to humanize the scene of treatment in the clinic. In the case of toxicity, what might it mean to take seriously an embodied approach, whether we call it witnessing, approximation, occupation, to the living or dead subjects of our study? What if we were to consider, for instance, the iterative quality of cognitive and perceptual effort that accompanies some forms of intoxication?

This is not an attempt to advocate for a kind of sensory cosmopolitanism or a singular, self-departing dalliance as a way of understanding the lives of interest, but instead an effort to approximate a method that may converse with other people's methods of survival and/or thriving—to recognize, for instance, the trade in alternative temporalities and perceptions that may already be present. This provocation is, of course, tentative, but it is inflected by a deeper reflection fostered by disability studies: that even though it is absolutely problematic to attribute a priori intellectual "deficiency," it is equally problematic to assume that none involved have been thinking in difference; both are the products of the radical segregation of the observer.

And further: What does it mean to elect or enact a kind of cognitive idealism in the work we do, if or when we know that this is not always our thinking home, not always a reliable capacity? And is this kind of struggle to perform cognitive idealism different from the "hard work" required of any specialty? I would wager that it is. As a scholar with illness that reflects intoxications of some forms, and variable cognitive difference, whose occupation is temporally stringent enough to require my working *during* these variances of capacity, I have been led by necessity to meditate on reigning presumptions of research method, in particular on the ways in which idealities of scholarship value cognitive elaboration, purity, and clear thought over blurring capacity/incapacity and associative thinking. Disability theory urges the unraveling of ableist methodologies; and besides the corporeal experimentation that we could describe as the practice of allopathic medicine, a decolonial approach avoids the positing of hierarchies of medicating systems (for instance, the prioritizing of allopathy over other entrenched systems). This rejection of colonial hierarchalization itself brings merit to the valuation and aesthetics of anticolonial ambiguity. A decolonial disability theory may ultimately avoid the positing of a particular, idealized, uniquely temporalized cognition as one of its methodological givens, and relax into the dual modes of intoxication and intellectual difference.

Back to Grass; or, Decolonizing Cripistemology

What cognitive kind of epistemologies is wanted? Ever since interdisciplinarity, as a kind of characterization of an intellectual space such as a university or a realm of fields, or a trope for scholarly transformation, as well as a refuge for odd ones out, has come into itself, and those interpellated by it have gotten into the swing of it, a trajectory of epistemological culmination has been taking place—one in which, for instance, critiques of intersectionality, which articulates almost orthogonally to disciplinarity, have entered. Intersectionality and interdisciplinarity could be said to coexist today within a common era in which favored typologies have become solidified and stopped being animated so that race, class, sex, sexuality, and nation could be felt as comprehensive and could thereby become didactic. Yet critiques of intersectionality, timely as they may be, should not undercut the fact that the term or concept remains a useful heuristic that can at times caution against unconsidered rehearsals of privilege, or forms of ontological packing. There is a sense in which intersectionality might find itself at the heart of cripistemology, animating some of its core questions.

The next logical step, another phasal experience of the agnostic chronicity of academic production, might be something that looks and feels roughly like transdisciplinarity. I have elsewhere described transdisciplinarity as "broadband epistemologies."[51] What role should or might transdisciplinarity play in a shared cripistemology? One of the promises of transdisciplinarity is that canonical vocabularies become gently imperiled within such imagined spaces, potentially to a much greater degree than within spaces of interdisciplinarity.

Such a vocabulary-mushing project, with its suggestions of slippery ground and the impossibility of a standpoint, may sound risky in the sense that multiple embedded projects of dissembling do not by themselves magically unmask insidious projects of coloniality, and I think it is certainly true that they do not automatically do so (this was the nature of the rejoinder to deconstruction, for example, by women of color feminists and queer of color theorizing). We might even tell a story about interdisciplinarity as a style arriving precisely in time to defang the efforts of specifically feminist and critical race interventions, in that way that certain developments appear convenient or easeful to certain people in ways that turn out later to look like the reproduction of patriarchal whiteness; this echoes Barbara Christian's skepticism toward "The Race for Theory."[52]

Christian's dry critique of the strained advancements of Western literary theory-making, so often complicit with leaving race (and its own racialization) behind as if it were literally a drag, remains a striking account of the commodified movements of many strands of theory at the cost of race analysis, including their own practical racisms. Even though today one might identify a growing consensus among many fields that decolonization, for instance, and its racialized ramifications are in fact ever-more critical pursuits, it is also possible to identify other crests of scholarship for which a descent into race is intolerable, or reeks of bad taste or excessive particularity. Cripistemology must also ask: what practical colonialities may quietly sustain within it, even as it turns headlong toward the promising partiality of transdisciplinary communing?

Cripping the acknowledged partiality that Haraway theorized has the effect of blurring dearly held vocabularies, whatever they are. That recognized and shared partiality feels cognitive. There is, therefore, a cognitive blurring relative to our former seat of comfort for those of us who have at some point resided more or less disciplinarily and in disciplined vocabularies, a blurring that certainly reads as "I can't think" or "I don't think," that comes part and parcel with this kind of coming together.

But in light of a shared project of cripistemological making, I do want to ask what kind of cognitions, what kind of information management, what kind of memory retrieval will we require to do the theorizing that will be important to move forward? I think this has something to do with what Jasbir Puar asks of the new cripistemologies, that they will have to define "the "crip in cripistemology as a critique of the notion of epistemology itself, a displacement not only of conventional ways of knowing and organizing knowledge, but also of the mandate of knowing itself, of the consolidation of knowledge."[53] What knowing is desired? What would a decolonized or decolonizing cripistemology—one that took that decolonization seriously by recognizing coloniality's serious attachment to typology, identification, and orders of knowledge—look, smell, and feel like?

Is it possible that we could talk about partial knowing working agonistically against, and thus also with, comprehension, almost as the queer works in odd partnership with the straight and narrow? And then recruit from these forms of knowing to devise a cripistemology that takes seriously its own cripped reach, or rather, crips its reach while still feeling the stars? And make even a further turn to identify a different arrogance of partial knowing dissembling as whole, as the surely revealing condition of majoritarian knowledge, about which our frictive cripistemological partial knowing offers a devastating, holistic if not quite comprehensive, rejoinder?

Redacting Empire, Giving Way to the World

Having established key questions about epistemology, I return now to Fiona Foley's art installation *Black Opium*. Fittingly for this third chapter, I find that it captures a precise mode of slow agitation, slowness and agitation together, a provocation that insists one understand the *present* moment in altered temporal terms that go all the way back to 1897, and beyond to its own shaping. There is an argument about what it means to be both grounded and engaged in an avowedly political intoxicatory witnessing—that is, neither canceled as a form of disablement, nor frivolously entertained as a form of luxurious voluntarism or consumption. Opium is one of those drugs that, under certain conditions, had as much to do with creative European cultures of nineteenth-century self-induced literary making as with racialized debility, survival, self-care, and chemical incarceration.

If redaction (again, blotting or blacking out) is the removal of information for official purposes of confidentiality, I think of *Black Opium* as enacting an epistemology that in my view "redacts" secular or paranoid facticity, as well as perhaps even precision, in favor of a novel account of the scene, allowing the queer sexualities of Chinese-Aboriginal-Torres Strait Islander opium trading and bodily transgression to soothe, retort, and shine. Against the languor of the poppies in the wind, the words of the Act, pushed into silence, would seem to have had no chance.

We can consider here the battleground between distinction and indistinction, or perhaps blurring; blurring and indistinction entertained as visual disability incited by intoxication, but also by so much else; distinction as the exertional result of histories of property relations, trainings toward absolute segregation and perhaps also repeatability of scientific experiment that Vine Deloria made so clear; that terrible divide between ability and disability that is maintained within the academy as a first point of division. That may be the battleground, but what Foley offers is something else—the conjoinment of zones of disability and liberatory modes of knowing; the merit of not willing to know exactly precisely before other conditions of knowing are in place, a desired state that for many never arrives; the power of knowing not through the lexical, taxonomic, informationally accretive, or experientially documentary, but through a transmedia arrival of blurry force and feeling that is summary without being precise at all. Indistinction.

Yet "traditional," "normative" forms of knowledge making are themselves frequently members of complex exchange. Rosalind Kidd, who wrote a history of opium legislation for Aboriginal and Torres Strait Island people that was ultimately drawn upon by artists like Foley, leveraged in her own attempt to remedy continued failure to return moneys taken by police protectors through the institution of the Act.[54] The fabled divide between scholarly apolitical work and nonscholarly resistance that haunts so many graduate students *and* activists has in so many ways been a false one, even if there remains controversy on what counts as legitimated knowledge. Foley's project demonstrates the fertility of exchange of forms of knowing, and indeed of scholarship, across ostensible divides of institution, pointing directly to the potency of undergrowth.

Foley's poetic work might even be seen as suggesting a complex Indigenous-Asian epistemology, not necessarily based on a shared objective analysis so much as a kind of being together out of nonintegrity or paraintegrity: as Foley writes, "Forgotten was the cohabitation and mingling of Chinese and Aboriginal populations."[55] A being together rather than identitarian collapse; undergrowth does not claim nondifference. I say this in a non-utopian way, since in the context of this research I am also thinking about accountability. And this brings me back to meditate on the underside of the blurring intoxications of Bliss and the interest in an undergrowth free of obligation to collapse even as it enriches less regulated knowledges of differences. The Australian scholarship on this period does not seem to deal directly with the kinds of questions I have about forms of Asian settler colonialism. A parallel discussion about mutually impacting capitalizations of "racial" difference in the university is due, particularly in light of the racialized groups at hand in Foley's work.

I have been studying this Act and its ramifications since approximately 2014, with visits to the Queensland State Archives in Runcorn outside of Brisbane and the Queensland State Library. This book is my first substantial publication on this Act. Though I had many opportunities, I committed to not publishing anything on this work until it was far more than an object of scholarship, or an "archive," but something living today that deserves consideration under a commitment to Aboriginal sovereignty, not least by me. The legacy of the Act is found in the articulations of race and indigeneity in Queensland and Australia, the profound alteration of Aboriginal life in Australia, Chinese economic and racial being in Australia (as well as forms of diasporic accountability), and the transhistorical urgencies of Link-Up, an organization that reunites Aboriginal and Torres Strait Island people with their families, from whom they may have been separated eight or nine decades ago through the Act's enactment. Most importantly, I wish to credit Foley with bringing so many of these elements home for me—for literally allowing me into her home and engaging with me in significant conversation about her work, which was very meaningful to me as well as deeply informative. In the midst of my research, seeing the *Black Opium* installation, as I told her, "changed everything." The opportunity has been for me to rethink study, art, archive, and knowledge.

Aware of my possible biographical alignment with diasporic and settler Chinese people in Queensland, and their participation in the black opium trade and to Aboriginal addiction, I asked Foley her thoughts on Chinese accountability. I said this even while feeling surprise at the degree of rise in my body propelling this question, for I hadn't known it would be so significant. I still don't know how the agitation that rose at that moment might map itself: How was I, a child of mid-twentieth-century Chinese immigrants to the United States, binding myself to nineteenth-century Chinese migrants to Australia? And was that enough? Enough for what, exactly? Foley, perhaps wisely, gently put aside my question, insisting that both Chinese and Aboriginal people lived under the oppressive structures of white governance. This may have been a way for her to say, "not my work, go on and do that." And in part by re-envisioning race and constitution, by thinking of shared epistemology, I do consign to continuing to think both about alliances, and about accountabilities—such as of Asian settler colonialism both in the place I live and work and abroad, in Australia, where surely some distant relatives live, where surely my ancestor Lin Tse-Hsu's incitement of the Opium Wars in an effort to remove British-Indian opium from the shores of China set off a peculiar chain of events, including the trade in opium ash. And I commit to not just unraveling or analyzing, but also sitting with, the scenario by which my intoxicated present witnesses Foley's blurred transhistorical appeals.

"Intoxicated method" is at once an acknowledgment of the chemical present of intellectual engagement, and a set of questions about chosen ways of doing research and coming to knowledge. Ways that could involve something like the academic unthinkable of "categorial blurring," which is normally marked as incapacity or intellectual slowness—or a sincere attempt to embrace sensorium, embrace one's intoxication in such a way that it is not a form of temporary, voluntaristic pleasure—a blurring that in the usual sense would only be a point of arrival, a precise achievement for the creator, rather than perhaps a retreat from incessant taxonomy in one's own ways of reading and naming, a disabled loss. It is a giving way to the world, a resignation of educationally cultivated agencies. Indeed, it is automatically ironic to raise this question of blurring in research venues (such as elite universities or ranked peer-reviewed journals), where the business of precision and analysis tends not to be questioned, and where moves away from them are read as anticognitive and thus somehow failing. I understand this as distinct from, but fully sympathetic with, Kandice Chuh's deeply consequential articulation of illiberal humanism, which comes to the fore through relational logics: "the common experience of disidentification rather than solidarity through identity.... It is the relationality of the felt, often wordless connectivity that occurs among minoritarian subjects because of misrecognition, and precipitates the sociality of being with, of entanglement; it is that commonality necessary to persist, to thrive."[56] While it seems to me that Chuh's account is hesitant before what might be called the nonce blurring of disabled being, I want to affirm a path exists that does not collapse blur or indistinction with false equivalence. Blurring, and intoxicated method, are experiences and praxes that can certainly live in radically different ethics. They should not be seen as fundamentally equivocating, but forms of opening: they are modes of being with, of concatenation and assembly, and sometimes collectivity.

Witnessing Foley's installation *Black Opium*—in a welcome and rare sense—puts me in a kind of suspension, as well as inside a rendering of materialities whose relations are unclear, blurred, but also contingent—in the sense not of causality, but of touch. Intoxication's plant-human-aerial-bloodborne materialities inhabit suspension. Whether or not such materialities align with "human" should also be relegated to suspension, insofar as their analysis in human terms (much less Sylvia Wynter's "Man") constitutes a loss of sensitivity to undergrowth, including the slanting potencies, both resistive and oppressive, of intoxication.[57] The undergrowth of education can be felt, immersively, in the stage of the Queensland State Library, and is made both real and inescapably contingent at the hands of the students who populate *Black Opium*'s rooms.

Reflecting on the uses of difference, it is also worth asking whose agitations then "become" whose, in the perceptive/immersive encounter. These are agitations—whether or not by the visual or by poetry or the sensory and experiential timespaces of ingested substance—that may never be cognized as such, and yet remind a bodymind of its fundaments of being, ones that may have their own history of environmental injustice as the implantation of substance-borne rhythms, impingements of attention and thought, ulterior (as versus majoritarian calculation) cognitions, forgettings, rememberings. Taking agitations in their informative breadth and their urgency—while bracketing exclusory accounts of the human, of agency, or of politics—allows transversal forms of differential being to "breathe" in an analysis, or in the stories we tell. And accounting for differential being allows attunement to emergent agitations that bear the marks of, and seek to act against, the exhaustive projections of colonial histories and presents.

Returning to Snaza and Singh's phrasing of undergrowth: "myriad encounters, relations, and affective shuttlings that enable 'education' even if they happen at a scale ... that is outside of traditional humanist ways of viewing education," and "fugitive ungovernability," we have seen a canonical site of knowledge production that was not *the* university but bore its students; that engaged in essentially ungovernable affective shuttlings in direct (if complex) relationship to the university's knowledge mandates; that served up an intoxicated archive. There is no reason not to think of these as gifts, or in fact the ordinary unmarked turns of *education* at large, that perhaps includes unlearning, even as one agitates against the violence of the doubling of indictment, criminality, and medicalization of multiplied difference. If this is true, however, then new questions enter the fold of deliberation regarding what constitutes desirable education, the relation of difference to its multiplication *and* narrowing in the contemporary university, and even what constitutes the favored developmental narrative for a student's individual progress, whatever the political program. No less, the stapling of securitization and medicalization to the ostensibly core runnings of the university's educational processes requires that those of us who live with it must also find how to be with agitative being.

Considering how such agitations are staged in the university raises questions about accumulation (and its partner, extraction), permanence, progressive development, and the durability requirements of difference (race and disability being either permanent, as a favored appearance of the university's self-image, or short-term at the limits of its tolerability, administered as opportunities for nonpermanent labor or as a requirement that disability cannot last beyond a semester else it renders the person permanently inefficient and the university permanently and thus intolerably generous). Agitation is valuable, in some sense, precisely because it refuses identity, exists more comfortably as its undergrowth.

AFTERWARDS   TELLING THE END NOT TO WAIT

We are near the end. Where have we been? Where did we go? How did, and didn't, things take shape? I feel compelled, after all this, to retrace a journey that did not exist. Up to now, I've only mentioned the very rough contemporaneity of Down's diagnostic innovations in England and Queensland's institutionalizations of chemical governance. So let's tell a story, presumably about the past, and for conceit's sake deploy some simultaneities at least as far as colonized time would have it. This story is populated by incidental players who haven't yet appeared in the book. The story/fantasy ends, and then begins again, at the site of the pandemic, a place where time got lost. I know that you will tell your own stories.

In this story, there is a child. In England and Wales, the Lunacy Acts of 1845, made out of welfare interest in "care" for the intellectually disabled, has led to an investment in county institutions with a specific mandate to care for the poor when they had no funds. In pamphlets requesting donations from the wealthy, this is advertised as benevolence for the constitutionally pitiable, and yet it is societal poverty that has created the conditions for many people's more durable categorization as "idiot" or "imbecile." For example, some people living in the areal domains of asylums found employment in matchstick factories, inside which the exposure to white phosphorus damaged the brain and other organs (most of which went without mention), and to the asylum they were sent. The rest were, we could say, environmentalized. Much like the contradictory pressures of contemporary incarceration, many of the former "inmates" (the language used for the mental asylums) would eventually, upon release, return to polluted environments, irregular food provisions, and insecure housing (note that this sentence presumes an equivalence between "pollution," "food," and "shelter" internal and external to the institution). Queen Victoria herself has supported the foundation of the Earlswood Asylum for the Feeble Minded, in 1855, and subscribed to the asylum in the name of her son Edward Prince of Wales for the right of presentation of one bed. It is the first institution of its kind. The child arrives in 1856, placed in Earlswood by poor parents who learned that the institution, rather than their home, might be the appropriate place for her. Care thus displaced. Superintendent Langdon Down and the nurses give her drug cocktails designed to ameliorate her condition, but their insistence makes her suspect that their regularity is meant to make the institution run smoothly. Soon it will be known that she is an Asian child of sorts, she is a white Mongol, though it will not be clear that she herself is told this.

The child has been registered at the asylum amid a flurry of international activity. Building upon the riches of colonial plunder, plunder seemingly without end, Queen Victoria has certainly not stayed local. She has been busy. She has been overseeing a flourishing opium trade for two decades already, as Britain seized control of cultivated crops in Bengal in 1750 and restricted Indian sales exclusively to the British by 1793. In 1837, just as she settled onto her throne, the new queen received a letter of protest from Imperial Commissioner Lin Tse-Hsu, complaining of the British-borne infusion of opium into China (where opium use was banned as early as 1729), a poison that Lin claimed the queen hesitated to welcome in her own country. It's not known whether she actually read the letter, which was written in traditional Chinese characters, vertically on the page. Two years later, presumably without meaningful response from the queen, Lin moves to expunge the opium, confiscating and burning all the stashes he could find in and around the ports of Canton, leaving ash in their wake; this act is considered the start of the Opium Wars. The first Opium War,

1839–42, is won by the English, and the Second Opium War, 1856–60, is won by England and France. The opium trade continues in China, where political and commercial opportunities are rife. Within China, cultures of political resistance to the long-lasting Qing dynasty develop that are centered on the cultivation and use of opium. Many users save the opium ash after smoking. That ash becomes a commodity. Beyond China, traders begin to export this post-use opium ash, including to Australia, where it is called black opium. Once it reaches Australia, it becomes an item to be traded, by anyone who can. Among these are white settlers and Chinese settlers, some of whom work as shopkeepers.

Queen Victoria has remained Very Busy. She is also continuing the unimaginable project of the Australian colony, England having seeded it in 1788 with shiploads of convicts to Bunnabee/Bunnabri/Gwea,[1] alternately seizing, murdering, alienating, and displacing Aboriginal traditional owners of the land and founding Sydney town. In 1898 the concerned legislature of Queensland, still a commonwealth under Victoria, institutes into law the Aboriginals Protection and Restrictions of the Sale of Opium Act. From this devastating law, with its presumptions of concern about Aboriginal people's addiction to black opium and the role of Chinese people in selling it to them, the idea that new controls with the interest of "protection" and supervision of those affected by the opium are necessary. Combined with the reserves systems of other states, this Act accelerates the radical and vast expropriation to white people from Aboriginal and Torres Strait Island peoples as well as Chinese populations, including the establishment of reservations, the institution of a sexual racial order with particular surveillance of young Aboriginal women, and the control of sales traffic among racialized populations other than white.

Aboriginal addiction was quite clearly seen as a disability, functionally discrediting the right of Aboriginal people and Torres Strait Islanders to their exercise of sovereignty. In some basic sense, the reservations were not so very different in rationale from the asylums of England and Wales. Both systems participated in reeducation, as well as forms of substance delivery and control, and had very little to do with self-determination. Here is another girl, in 1910; she has been taken from her family, one of the early members of the Stolen Generations. She has been moved to a reservation and is being trained for servitude. Her sister now lives in Cranbrook House, in Brisbane's West End, and is a domestic servant to white families. Her mind full of thoughts, dreams, and losses, she walks by a part of the reservation called "Chinatown" every day and wonders what happened to Uncle Chin, the Chinese man her mother's sister loved. Two years later the Qing Dynasty is dissolved, and a puff of dust rises from Chinatown.

These queens, they last and last, fed indirectly but very well by poppies and poppies' many intimate kin, and the descendants of those kin. It's always been about money.[2]

One century later, Queen Elizabeth's two nieces, Katherine and Nerissa Bowes-Lyon, are formally registered as deceased, but are in fact living, having been deposited at Earlswood in 1941. Two years later, Mao Tse-tung would take office as chairman of the Communist Party in China. The presence of American GIs in Canton during World War II meant my mother was among a gaggle of children to be given chocolate bars and snacks, and that she got to dance with other children in a cloud of DDT that was there to protect the American troops in Asia from typhus: they fell within the (affectionate, protective) circle of chemical management wherein American soldiers' temporary robustness was prioritized to serve the war effort. Separated by race and nation, this relatively brief occasion means that they will forever be bound by chemical intimacies that consigned them to different, if bodily overlapping, futures.[3] Katherine and Nerissa lived most of their lives in the same institution. Katherine likely was moved to a care home in 1997 when deinstitutionalization led to Earlswood's closure; she died in the care home in 2014.

Nearly two centuries later, at the time I write, Royal Earlswood Park is the new name of the place, having been converted into a luxury complex of residences. My sister Brigitte, my parents' first child, has been dead of childhood leukemia for fifty years. The rest of us, including my brother, have been constituted in part by her absence, tender toward the space she left even as we attend to the world. The world's biggest poppy plantations are now found in Australia (Tasmania) and Afghanistan; the claim to which is "bigger" has everything to do with the claim to legality in the opiates trade ("they" do heroin, "we" do pharma, says Australia). But maybe 1898 should tell us everything we need to know about that. And it's claimed that in fact the Stolen Generations have in fact never been so great in number as today, under rapacious welfare policies that just as readily separate families. The 2017 poster for a Stolen Generations event at Cranbrook Place in Orleigh Park in Brisbane (figure A.1), produced by Link-Up, an organization that works to reunite Aboriginal and Torres Strait Islander families, on Sorry Day in Australia (a special day in the year when settlers sign books to say they're sorry),[4] used as its graphic background/underlay an excerpt of the text of the 1897 law, which established Cranbrook House as the site of a housing unit for Aboriginal girls and women domestic workers—and sex slaves—from 1899 to 1906. The sister kept there will become one of the escapees and they will never find her. At another stop in Brisbane, the

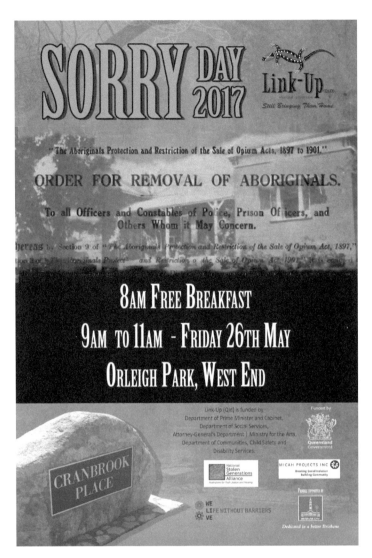

FIGURE A.1 Graphic for Sorry Day 2017 for Link-Up. A black bar across the image reads, "8 A.M. Free Breakfast / 9 A.M. to 11 A.M.—Friday 26th May / Orleigh Park, West End." Link-Up Queensland Facebook page, https://www.facebook.com/linkupqueensland/.

Queensland State Library, the same words overlay an image of blurred poppy plants, dancing in the breeze. Students, some of them Chinese
　(The story ends abruptly.)
　Was that what you call contemporaneity? What does it mean that we often say an "honestly," or "frankly," transnational story feels dizzying? What kind

of knowledge makes it less, or more, responsible? What if it feels like, and also is, one of the kinds of dizziness that make my life, and my accountability, possible? Then again, the dizzy feeling is two temporal sensibilities joined: simultaneities of colonized time, and Bliss. I finished—or at least I drew a close to finishing—this book, which was a long time coming, during the COVID-19 pandemic. Finishing it came in fits and starts, or one fluid run, depending on how you choose to represent time. Like so many others, I "fell apart," mental health mirroring the dissolution of fabrics of partially concealed interdependency under public health mandates wending through the neoliberal fabrics that despite their toxicity I still relied upon. Just as many beings fall apart with the dissolution of natural choreographies—climates—that are increasingly pressed to wrench awry, collecting and dissipating nontrivial forces.

Tim Choy and I, in a fit of temporal confoundedness, co-wrote a piece "about" the pandemic we were living with, the sense of needed pause amid the accelerations of some parts of "essential" capitalism, the ironic mode of "catching up" that fails to recognize crip, and the frictions we felt in the ways in which the modes of productivity our professions were somehow *more* insistent, *more* resurgent.[5] From within blurred time we tried to make sense of it in three temporalities: Quick and Dirty, Not Yet, and Never, as a kind of response to the question: Will you produce this scholarship now? And this confounding no less captures the irony I experienced of making a unitary book, perhaps *the* classic university commodity, during the pandemic, but also a thing that was an urgent act of reaching out. In the following section, I explore the modulations of public knowledge, particularly feminism, in the no-time of COVID, and the chemical intimacies that COVID and its companion wildfires impute today.

In These End Times

"In these times / in these end times,"[6] I was heartened to witness complexity, along with hesitancy, in much of the initial popular response to COVID-19, or the novel coronavirus, which has achieved significance in relation to its global scale and ready participation in existing international coordinations, and its reception as a general "threat to life." Its arrival, however, did not occur in a vacuum of attention to the politics of life. Rather remarkably, increasing parts of the mainstream have been learning how to think intersectionally, not only taking in the regularity of police brutality against Black people in the United States, but also considering the ways in which hierarchies of class and race functioned as drags on George Floyd's life well before he was murdered;

the divergent life chances of Black transgender women and other women of color; and the particular challenges faced and creative challenges posed by Black women. The inclusion of Asian women in mass murders put into relief the hazards of continued allegations of foreignness. During COVID-19, Standing Rock Sioux leaders and other Indigenous allies have successfully applied Native land care practices to resisting the poisoning of the land and waters around the Dakota Access Pipeline. Tied to polluting industrial projects such as these is intimate knowledge about unjust burdens and chronicities that appear to compound the virus's effects.

The very question that was being asked in 2020—Who will get the vaccine first?—acknowledges the capitalist power of biotech and the privatization of the vaccine effort, and profiles the divide between the access of the moneyed and the neglected class of essential workers who are overrepresented in terms of racial and gendered minorities. The bulk of effective pedagogy has been due to the sustained work of so many activists making palpable this formulation.

But one can remain wary of the idea that progress has been confirmed or that justice is within reach. Recall Capcom's skillful use/mimicry of disability-compassionate language in its marketing for zombie shooting games. And while a feminist response of any kind should be a minimum, it's also true that some feminisms head further into territories of domination and capture. It should be clear that registering women's participation does nothing to remedy the drag of whiteness or imperialism on an antiracist or just future—or to, for instance, counteract a property-invested liberal settler mindset. I prefer a feminist account that readily indicts the gender-reveal's explosive binarism and its ritualistic invocation of an entire community of witnesses to determine the spatial, material, economic, racial, and social details of a future gendered life on the basis of one or maybe two medical determinants of sex. And I prefer a feminism that connects this to entire swaths of land-air and their living residents disproportionately going up in flames, and the associated accelerated death, over an account that connects Jacinda Ardern's identity as a woman (one apparently of a global community of women on some vague shared basis) to her success at managing the pandemic in New Zealand; the Navajo Nation, Rwanda, and other sub-Saharan African governments also did remarkably well. Out of the desperation and melancholic pragmatism of the COVID moment,[7] at stake is a series of questions about the "about" of feminisms whose imaginations promise something in the end.

All of these concerns have been present in recent memory, so that, one could argue, COVID-19 both is and isn't the name of a virus. It is many, many things—many histories, many bodies, many politics. It is also the name of differential bodily burdens, differential state resourcing, and differential state securitizations under terms that create bifurcations between care and murder. Above I used the descriptive *is*, as if COVID-19 were explainable in a knowledge domain, even as I gesture to the richness of referents it contains. These viral particles have a physical and interactive character segregatable enough to be called "novel," and yet so much of what is being witnessed feels old and familiar.

Unlike the declarative *is*, a more familiar feeling for so many is incomprehension. "I just can't wrap my head around it." "It's impossible to understand." I have said those words, and I have said them mostly as a comment on my inability to form a singular, consistent shape out of the tumult of accumulated and novel violences that accrete to something like the phenomenon of COVID-19. Even while equipped with critical race theory, cultural studies, feminist science studies, Asian American studies, queer studies, animal studies, and disability studies perspectives that together might allow me to make a certain quick sense of this fast-developing catastrophe, I am simultaneously compelled to register exhausted grief and a newfound hesitancy about analysis itself, or its regathering into synthesis. Against the iterative beat of horrific circumstance, any scholarly gratification from newfound comprehension simply escapes me these days. Here again is the blurring, the confusion. I feel somehow duty-bound to resist resolution, "figuring it out," and to instead sit in the "nothing,"[8] for as long as it takes.

On top of analytical traffic jams there is material tumult, too, including a mixture of actual *things*. COVID-19, in my localized experience, has joined in a duo with another happening of equally spectacular, and perhaps confounding, scale: the seasonal fires of the US West, which I mentioned in chapter 2. COVID-19, because it has managed to thrive in the US human and nonhuman population, and the California seasonal fires, which intensified due to human-induced climate change as well as poor fire policy, are two airy phenomena that dance together, aloft, touching. And they make contact in actuality, sometimes crossing around and in the bodies of human beings and other "breathers."[9] In one conjuncture, smoky air intermingles with the exhalations of an infected, unmasked pedestrian, creating a doubly potent inhalant for someone else; in the next beat, wildfire smoke is also inhaled into that infected pedestrian's body. The smoke and virus intermingle such that a body, and its differentially responsive organs, represent several (chemically) modifying nodes—not a single barrier—in a continuous traffic. Epidemiologists are already concluding, tentatively, that the presence of California wildfire smoke has been linked to greater local COVID infection and death.[10] More broadly, the two phenomena touch at dense epistemological crossroads or matrices.

These matrices include environmental burdens and their relation to chronic illnesses (beyond COVID) that confound mainstream allopathic medicine; medical racism and colonialism; policy-borne failures to provide egalitarian forms of care; modulations of bodily constituents and their biochemical interaction with inhalants entering the lungs and bloodstream; the ability to account for exceptional zoonotic (nonhuman animal to human) transmissions, such as those species and scenes ("wet markets") in China made again globally spectacular, while slow to properly conceive means of *intra*-species (intrahuman) viral transmission, or of the relation between "spillback" (when a virus moves across a biological species boundary from a human host to a nonhuman one) and "spillover" (the best known zoonotic form). We find two cultural images of sexualities, a queered "wet" interspecies commingling in China and a straightened image of neoliberal and asymmetric "dry" monospecies independence that makes impossible forms of white transmissibility while racially othered people continue to be marked as eager or careless vectors.

That is, colonially informed segregations of "nature" from "culture" remain generative, such that live animal markets (including pangolins, believed by some to be a source of COVID-19) become seen sites of perverse and primitive sexualities while gender-reveal pyrotechnics that incite "wild" fires and indoor hetero wedding celebrations do not; and so on. This second form of touch (of analytical matrices) is represented, for example, by the emergent social justice knowledge that COVID-19 has affected Brown and Black people (and, sometimes when registered, Asian and Indigenous people) disproportionately in severity and death, such that Black Lives Matter protests can be affirmed as benefiting, rather than threatening, public health (which pertains to the first form of touch, actual intermingling).

What is more, at the level of policy, much of the incomprehensibility of the early months of national experience with COVID-19 seems due to a fatal confluence between an (especially former) administration embracing white supremacist nationalist exceptionalisms and a public health infrastructure that had long been inadequately provisioned and tied to only certain forms of "public." Simultaneously, the history of privatization of government agencies and the deferral of health care to self-care sit comfortably beside the framed exceptionality of the pandemic and an admittedly remarkable swath of disease effects that corporeally ground and haunt the unknown. Here, various observers, from newspaper essayists to TikTok creators, have been illustrating the painful impossibility—again, that word—of following public health advice:

To protect yourself from COVID-19, "stay outdoors," but to protect yourself from wildfire smoke, "stay indoors," not to mention the type of mask an individual might seek out for proper protection from either ill (another clash, given available supplies), whose recommended management appears only in isolated modes of control.

The COVID-19 guidance, especially that from the World Health Organization, only slowly inched toward acknowledging the primacy of air as the means of COVID-19 infection. As if surprising, we learn the "disgusting" fact that blowing on birthday candles will drench the cake's surface with droplets of your breath; speaking to one another, much less shouting in a room, unleashes both droplets and aerosols whose range can extend meters, enveloping an interlocutor. Here, even public health for the masses can yield no certain calculation for safety. This public confusion is not an indication of the rarity of having to handle two forms of risky chemical intimacy; it is a snapshot of knowledge in the making in a community that isn't accustomed to its novel conjunctures. It should also be a reminder that many who face environmental exposures rarely face just one, and must find ways to manage, if not thrive, under multiple burdens.

Incomprehensible: from the Latin *comprehens*, "seized, comprised"; perhaps air itself is flagged an unimaginable assembly. Air, in this circumstance, comprises both aerosols and particles; gases, ash, airborne virus. So why does airy thinking feel impossible here, in the East Bay of the San Francisco Bay Area, in this current moment? Has air itself been seized? If land were opposed to air (which it is not), we might say that in the Bay Area, among social justice circles, there has been an increased opening to a recognition of Indigenous (Huichin Ohlone) presence and unceded territory that aligns with and augments, rather than fricates against, the common learning about Black disenfranchisement as collated forms of white supremacy. In such terms, the real estate value of this Bay Area land depicts it as that which can be property; the financial losses of COVID-19 lockdowns are attributed to the shutting down of storefront retail and the foreclosing of homes. This is an indirect logic by which land becomes meaningful to majoritarian narratives of COVID-19.

But rather than be a distraction from airborne justice, attention to a reimagining of land must be *augmented* in order for those who live in this place to be fully resident in the traffics, solaces, and violences of the air, or between both. After all, fire's rapid transformation of living beings such as trees into forms of ash and gas is a kind of transformation between "land" and "air" that, despite my allusions in chapter 2, is not categorically unwanted. The perverse binarisms that inform what land means also yield continued perverse constructions of "wildlife," that fantastic realm that supplies a pangolin at one end of this moment and, at the other end, vulnerable forest fauna such as orphaned baby black bears that are unable to outpace a fire. Why is it a hard stretch to embrace the otherwise of human primacy, particularly if we take seriously Sylvia Wynter's consequential challenges to the sharply interested figurations that have formed what is thought of as this human species?[11] To honestly appraise the interdependencies that make the fabric of the natureculture "here" that is not geopolitically opposed to a "there," a remote region such as China?

In my 2012 book, *Animacies*, I alluded to being hyperattentive to passageways of air because I need to anticipate chemical incursions in space that would exacerbate my chemical sensitivity, and thus I have a need to move "queerly."[12] Those with certain forms of chronic illness have, of course, long been necessarily attentive to the air and what it brings. But for the rest, it seems, like COVID-19, this is a novel way to think. And we see how slowly a habitus can be learned; many of my excellently trained colleagues who wield magnificently expansive frameworks for thinking about matter seem remarkably unprepared for and reactive to managing their air differently under these conditions.[13] Disabled people already living in what they describe as necessary and largely self-funded "quarantine" have commented on whatever masking and ventilation policies have managed to be implemented despite resistance from "free air" ideologies. They have asked, Is this what it took for you to make the conditions we need universally available, enforceable, "public"?

In early US-based feminist critique, much of which is now seen as liberal white feminism, private spaces were those assigned to implicitly white domesticity and gendered as the devalued feminine, whereas the public was assigned to the masculine member of a couple, understood to be the one working. One feminist gesture was to assert that labor within the region of the feminized private must be credited as well as remunerated. Black feminist theorizing corrected this racialized gender and economically flattening narrative, pointing out the ways that systems of chattel slavery (upon which white private spaces depended, and which they consumed) had a means of organizing slave labor, sexuality, and property such that the realm of the private collapsed racialized labor, including the space of the domestic and enslaved people themselves, into zones of white property. Race, gender, and sexuality all factored in the *Lawrence v. Texas* (2003) case, which moved homosexual activity and other forms of sex into the realm of the protected private domain. Today, the historically high number of precariously housed, chronically ill/disabled queer and trans of color populations here in the Bay Area tells a story of continued challenge but also creative survival in the face of COVID-19 and the California fires.

Finally, the dyad "indoors/outdoors" mentioned earlier that features in contrasting public health recommendations is itself haunted by public/private oppositions. Any juxtaposition of the higher COVID-19 infectiousness of the "indoor" domain against the unbreathable wildfire smoke of "outdoors," both of which are counted as threats to health, falls flat from the perspective of many unhoused people. Organizations such as the queer/trans-led Mask Oakland are notable for prioritizing the delivery of N95 masks to the most vulnerable residents of Oakland: "We come from and strive to be in alignment with many movements, including climate justice, Black Lives Matter, housing justice, environmental justice, disability justice, queer and trans liberation, Indigenous movements, workers' movements and economic justice, and Black and trans-led feminism."[14] While the striving of alignment with these many movements is likely to encounter complex decision points (that are sometimes negatively rendered as undesirable "conflicts"), Mask Oakland insists on the radical need for an approach that in some loose way looks like the intellectual spirit of intersectional feminism—the surely welcome starting point for much progressive political activity today as mentioned above—but goes arguably further epistemologically and ontologically. Nowhere in their statement are the mentioned toxic illusions and structurations of white supremacy or capitalism or property or indoors or outdoors mentioned; this collectivity keeps those in check. As is needed in this time, theirs is a "necessary mess," an everything, of uncomplicated love, hope, and commitment.

In this moment, what might be some new feminist versions of "public" and "private," and their relation, that could help us move beyond the impossibility of survival in a time of COVID-19 and forest fires? Beyond a biopolitics that naturalizes the view of public services and public health advisories as aimed at the individualized protection of one's "own" health? Leaving behind a binary-gendered, hetero-reproductive, neoliberal, "dry" account of survival and futurity that preserves the supremacies we now live with, for an ecofeminist, "wet," crip complexity of interdependent life and death? Beyond a militant medicalism that vows an all-out fight against bodily vulnerability (which often amounts to eliminating vulnerable lives) and disabled difference, and toward forms of care that refuse to be corralled within either the dignified private or the militarized, necropolitical public? Beyond a racial imagination of differentially embodied publics that means that, in this moment, Asian bodies affectively expand from the mundane (if they ever were—and distant) public into a threat of contagion within private spaces, unleashing responsive violence, whereas white bodies simply occupy all publics thoroughly, with no apparent notice of their violent occupations? Nayan Shah's work on the queer contagions of opium pipes, "from lip to lip," in the smoky opium parlors of San Francisco's turn-of-the-century Chinatown, weaves new smoky tendrils into the present day, placing infection in a stage of dense and racially tinged air.[15] Beyond the "public" occupancy of land-grant universities of unceded Indigenous land? Beyond the viral transmission of video clips that register the insistence by police that Black public life must be transformed into death, while the loss of homes and even of unhoused emplacement threatens Black lives more than ever before? Beyond the idea that air can really be ever imagined as either public or private, but only remarkably shared by both?

Going back to an earlier moment in queer theorizing, I'm reminded of Diana Fuss's comments, responding to the already ample concerns about the gay and lesbian construction of "the closet" (which, in its literal form, is another doubly private feature of the private indoors). Fuss wrote: "The philosophical opposition between 'heterosexual' and 'homosexual,' like so many other conventional binaries, has always been constructed on the foundations of another related opposition: the couple 'inside' and 'outside.' The metaphysics of identity... has, until now, depended on the structural symmetry of these seemingly fundamental distinctions and the inevitability of a symbolic order based on a logic of limits, margins, borders, and boundaries."[16] While Fuss took a psychoanalytic approach to the critique of this implicit opposition, that moment joined sexuality with this spatialized image of interiority and exteriority; thirty years later there is much more critique sitting with us at the conjuncture of sexuality and inside/outside. I also recognize that interior/exterior differences seem fairly fundamental to living in the world's many naturecultures.

But today's easy public health deployments of "inside/outside"—of the two concepts, as well as their binarity—take that for granted and ignore these years of critique, presenting them as perhaps the least complicated givens in a complex decision tree of advisements, naturalizing a propertied approach to land and air that should perhaps be the first to be apprehended (something Indigenous, brown, Black, Pacific Islander, and other Asian people subject to environmental pollution know well). If inside/outside and private/public are so deeply informed by a classing, racing, abling, and sexualizing, not to mention human speciation, of space, how to detach from, release, these substantiating—and pillaging—concepts to allow others to take their place, at a time when our conditions demand it? To pursue the expanded queer ecologies of the present, opening to visions of life and thriving around this earth that have been pressed out by broken imaginaries? To find a way to talk, ultimately, about the *kinning chemical intimacies* of the kinds of multipopulated spaces in which we find ourselves and another, living and dead, without closed attention to species? Here, a reimagining and expansion of the commons must be emphasized.

On the Edge

I am ready to abandon private/public in favor of an imagination less hewing to capitalism's obligations, such as a commons. And while I readily accept that there is something fairly honest about "end times," the likelihood of endings, it is more important to understand this as a predominantly Christian metaphor in the United States coming with its own affective baggage. Awash as I continue to feel with melancholies and farewells, with responsibility for species loss and a global system that puts me near some top, I must also remember that much that is ending may be traditional forms of inequitable and indeed necropolitical governance and relation and that these devastations in no way obliterate energies (agitative and other) that vibrate in spite of those forms.

I turn instead to the potentials of something like "on the edge," to suggest an affect, or a mental apprehension, one that feels also physical, either uncomfortably proximate to falling "off the edge" / "over the edge," or perhaps also exploding, lending to a metaphor of boiling over: "There's only so much you can take." On the edge is also a form or state of brinksmanship. It suggests the "just in time" before the "out of time." And it also encompasses the "edginess," the tension, which I described in chapter 2, that is sometimes a feature of intoxication: being "high," going "cosmic," going over the edge. On the edge could also be the mental health or economic circumstances in which you find yourself, in spite of being able to perform some daily maintenances. The opening invitation to this book, to engage only as you can or wish, has no promise of taking anyone off the edge.

"On the edge" is a fair descriptor for this moment, at least in aligned capital global time, caught on the depleting side of interdependences that blanket life of all kinds and classes (COVID included, but it is far from alone here). Pandemic temporalities in many ways are the pre-pandemic temporalities still present in their ongoing diversity: one waits, one rushes, one hesitates, or, these wait together, those rush together, these hesitate together; but in their assembly they fricate against the choreography of pre-pandemic temporalities.

For those with precarities of various kinds poised to face any direction in the pandemic, there's no telling where and when the next shoe will fall, or what the new form of precarity will be, if one keeps hold of life. There is just a sense of an edge—and being on one, differently or anew. What did I yesterday tell friends who were heading to Iceland? Not "Have a good trip" but "Please, please no crevasses, no novel global warmed crevasses!" I don't want them to fall over an unanticipated edge whose presence I already project and whose fear I experience. Or, there is the edge of a toppling of democracy as democratic capitalism, a system maybe not so sacred to those living under its heel even if voting rights must be fought for.

"On the edge" includes the many who may be experiencing daily time in precarity, the touch and go of the lives of people on ventilators, the hostile and entitled repulsion of migrants at so many borders, white supremacists unwilling to be curtailed in space by identification with a vulnerable community. There is the primed efflorescence of a digital life that we were all realizing was on a steady creep, for better and worse, a steady remapping of time and life and space itself. Amid this remapping we undergo the remapping of physical space in the pandemic, from the convention center or community center where some might have gathered, to the newly frenzied Amazon warehouses, to the domicile and its human and nonhuman inhabitants, to the repeated displacement of the unhoused just as they are forming systems of self-governance under the shelter of cloverleaves and tents carefully and fragilely assembled.

As we know, there's no universal story to tell about the ubiquity of increased social distancing around the world, as if everyone saw fit to follow this recognizable epidemic program. Instead, there are novel intimacies and distances, one which we are inhabiting right now, premised on the reorganization of labor and capital in this provisional pandemic world undergoing active reorganization. The interhuman avoidance of seemingly contagious Asian bodies; the crush of proximities in warehouses on accelerated time and condensed space; more and more and more. The pandemic can't exclude climate refugeeism; indeed, it is arguably responsive to climate change in ways we can and can't determine. These come together, they are co-identified. "On the edge" as an expression also feeds on the experience of actual space, and also projects us to act in actual space in ways that respond to its affects. A kind of spatial imagination, and where it goes and what it does in the pandemic. What becomes of the politics of agitation, the workings of race and disability, when the spatial mappings of both have gone awry?

Underground

What awaits, then? Here, to set a tone about so many edges that may spark recognition from the point of view of this pandemic, I want to turn to a work by the Swiss-Vietnamese artist Mai-Thu Perret from fourteen years ago, a screen print entitled "The Underground" with what looks like a single page of text,

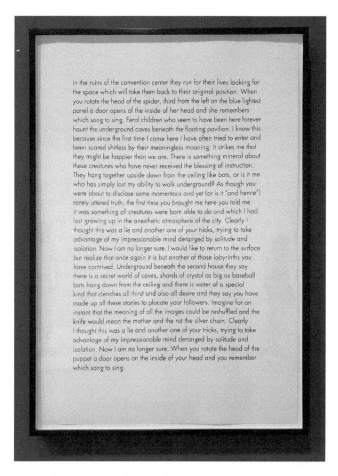

FIGURE A.2 Mai-Thu Perret, *Underground*, 2007, Screen print. 33 × 22½ in. Courtesy of San Francisco Museum of Modern Art. Photo: Mel Y. Chen, 2021.

33 × 22½ inches (figure A.2). This work was the subject of a public conversation with Judith Butler at UC Berkeley on the occasion of a show at the Berkeley Art Museum, and I want to note that in some important way, our authorship is shared around this piece. We chose together to discuss this work because it inspired us both to think especially well about pandemic time. Whatever ideas I share here are inseparable from the preparatory conversations that made them possible. At the same time, I feel responsible for any problematic thinking.[17]

The text reads:

> In the ruins of the convention center they run for their lives looking for the space which will take them back to their original position. When

you rotate the head of the spider, third from the left on the blue lighted panel a door opens of the inside of her head and she remembers which song to sing. Feral children who seem to have been here forever (there are several perversions here) haunt the underground caves beneath the floating pavilion. I know this because since the first time I came here I have often tried to enter and been scared shitless by their meaningless moaning. It strikes me that they might be happier than we are. There is something mineral about these creatures who have never received the blessing of instruction. They hang together upside down from the ceiling like bats, or is it me who has simply lost my ability to walk underground? As though you were about to disclose some momentous and yet (or is it "and hence") rarely uttered truth, the first time you brought me here you told me it was something all creatures were born able to do and which I had lost growing up in the anesthetic atmosphere of the city.

Clearly I thought this was a lie and another one of your tricks, trying to take advantage of my impressionable mind deranged by solitude and isolation. Now I am no longer sure. I would like to return to the surface but realize that once again it is but another of those labyrinths you have contrived. Underground beneath the second house they say there is a secret world of caves, shards of crystals as big as baseball bats hang down from the ceiling and there is water of a special kind that clenches all thirst and also all desire and they say you have made up all these stories to placate your followers. Imagine for an instant that the meaning of all the images could be reshuffled and the knife would mean the mother and the rat the silver chain. Clearly I thought this was a lie and another one of your tricks, trying to take advantage of my impressionable mind deranged by solitude and isolation. Now I am no longer sure. When you rotate the head of the puppet a door opens on the inside of your head and you remember which song to sing.

We can think here, in this perceptive, cognitive, and identificatory blur, this profusion of edges, about the undoing or unlearning of cultivated, infrastructural life in the city. Is it something to mourn, or to fear? Here we have the quick succession and displacement of bats, spiders, feral children, those who walk underground, the effort to be relieved of the anesthetic atmosphere of the city in favor of some forgotten song (Butler reads the sought song as the original song, which Rousseau claimed was language's musical beginning). The disordering of a human monospecies regime that conceals its rapacious dependence on the animal and mineral world. These changes of address and reference, particularly the shifting "you," are not simply confusing; they release us from the labyrinthine fabrications and offer different kinds, moments, of blurring, or of collectivity. The "ruins of the convention center" is but one feature of the radical reorganization of public space/publics in the pandemic, as well as of institution, and sociality.

This underground feels distinctively queer, multispecies or transspecies, in a humming and living or para-living darkness. It's neutral on the question of reproductivity or development, since the feral children have always been here. It is of questionable gravity: How to find a metaphor for bent space? And, of those children, "there is something mineral about these creatures who have never received the blessing of instruction," which suggests a reference to schooling as a disciplining operation that delivers the benefit of citizenship; and that minerality suggests something elemental, or otherwise, lower on an animacy hierarchy and yet more stable, not having to bear the same temporalities and decays of higher life. Of maybe "becoming cave," mingling intersubstantially with the mineral matter of the cave. This queer malingering timespace might offer respite, if an ambivalent one: Under the ruins of the convention center, it offers a kind of dysfunction, nonfunction that is generative in its proximities, its intimacies. A narrator speaks of being scared shitless as they attempt to enter, reminding of the queer stasis of Xombi, who marveled calmly that there is no waste. It leads directly to the reflection whether they are happier than we are, a question resonating from the ruins of modernity and of colonialism itself.

In 1981 the linguist Claudia Brugman wrote a dissertation titled "The Story of Over" as an attention to prepositions that have semantically evolved from motion verbs, such as *over*, and the conceptual nature of their polysemies.[18] "The bird flew 'over' the convention center" does not have the same "over" as in "the cloud is 'over' the convention center." Similarly, the "under" in "the river ran under the convention center" is not the same as in "the time capsule was under the convention center." One is a position, and one is a mental tracing of a path. And it turns out they are differently apprehended, differently processed, they are not equivalent abstractions. In work following this, cognitive linguists have come to realize that the uses of such mental tracing lexemes such as "over" the convention center actually requires different cognition than the positional "over," and indeed, according to measurements, takes more time to scan the path, to mentally animate that scan. There are other motion verbs used for spatial description, such as in "runs along," that also involve a mental scan. Linguist Teenie Matlock calls this "fictive motion."[19]

Returning to Perret's "underground," one can contrast its suggestion that its residents generally live in stasis and waiting punctuated by going to the other side, with the sense of scanned movement in the form of the Underground Railroad, a recognized route of fugitive movement from South to North away from slavery and its territorialities. That is, the "under" of the Underground Railroad was premised on movement, movement that also effected an emergence into freedom—rather, an expansion of a freedom that was already being theorized, practiced, and exercised.

The phrase "impressionable mind deranged by solitude and isolation" pings with questions about mental health or altered ways of being for those subject to quarantine in the pandemic, institutionalized, or incarcerated. A mind that went off the edge, perhaps in part because it could not perceive or benefit from the queer socialities and crip interdependencies that await in the underground. But also derangement as a reflex of the surround of disorder, disarrangement, a collapse of sensory or cognitive choreographies. Things have lost their function, and we feel everything and nothing and are not sure we are happy. Then again, what is happiness?

Here's queer disorientation, the blurring of percepts. Who can still go in a straight line? Certainly, some. I'm thinking of the uncanniness of the convention center that stands earthquake resilient and yet also in ruins, the streets and sidewalks that have been repurposed and are even less available to the unhoused, the questions of access come or gone; and the sudden ubiquitous overdeployment of the American Disabilities Act, an infrastructure good willed and yet legally somewhat toothless (because it says to institutions: yeah, definitely put in the ramp if you can afford it, don't worry about it if you can't), as the single exception to in-person teaching in order that we largely put to risk the ones we live with. As my colleague Susan Schweik noted to me in conversation, when Christchurch, New Zealand, underwent a major earthquake, the rush to recovery meant the abandonment of certain communitarian principles, including disability building laws. Any of us could name examples in the United States and around the world of the "rush to resume" that captures the years of the pandemic.

What to mourn of the choreographies of space that have previously lent themselves to inheritances of supremacy? Perhaps a bit, when we realize that hard-won racial and queer and crip publics and the things that are transmitted themselves, in a kind of lateral inheritance, have also been removed into the unmappable. But they have also always been underground; and for survival they must emerge, then remake certain structured publics, one of which goes by the name of mutual aid. Here is an opportunity.

Over the Edge, Again

And there is "over the edge." From a perch on the edge, "over" represents a precipice. The sense of precipice is so much greater because the ground has rearranged, and the mental scan of "over" can't trace a path. Like animacy, the grammatical nature, the underbedding, of the use of motion verbs as prepositions is a realm of activity that can get into trouble. Language works as a false or distortionary leader that mediates and constrains, but also offers reimagining. For many torn from the known social, imagination might become a richer kind of grounds. The ritual command of spatial language has to confront the disordering of space. Blurring away from ordered distinction, unmappable impropriety because the maps could not imagine.

And so, amid the chemical experiment of the world—some undesired—and its constant rearrangements, its endless confrontations of debility with disability that often transfer both the benefit of concreteness and entitlement to the latter, I continue to wonder about distinction as a model for theorizing, and particularly about the nondisability which academics are trained to rigorously maintain, since cognitive imprecision is an illegitimating dysfunction. Thirteen years ago, when I was describing an extended episode of brain fog and memory issues during a discussion with a top-level administrator to receive advice about my medical accommodations, she warned me to not declare it since the university might then consider my very employ in jeopardy.

This preference for cognitive clarity may seem self-evident, but I continue to ask to think otherwise, to think about the systemic, even contrastive, marking of incapacity in the academic institution, so defining that it's not perceived. I think here of Pierre Bourdieu's *Distinction*, which is about class and taste, and I feel it's not distinct from the classing of the academy: How do I demonstrate my acumen if not by exhibiting forms of distinction, segregation, selection?[20] I also think about the taxonomic distinctions of colonial science and the ways that eugenics depended in part on the characterization of sentience, including studies of "idiocy."

Agitations are about forms of improper or proper being in space that then, at least for some, must be governed. So what to make of undirected agitations? Where to direct them, if one can? What if one cannot? How to find respite, local stabilities, on the edge? Which of us will together go over the edge into the underground, to places, temporalities, and gravities unknown? Or will we choose to commune there, in the nooks we know well, having lost an original song? And if our training crucially rests on categorial or cognitive distinction, then when and how to give way to the unlearning that a blur offers, to the seemingly frightening but perhaps also happy indistinctions, or paradistinctions, of the underground, where "like a bat" is even perhaps, in its relation, freed of the asymmetric weight of a simile? In light of the chemical reorderings of cities and noncities alike and our porosity as beings to them, how to gauge between drives toward the recovery or security of purity, or repurification as detoxification, and the embrace of exogenous substances that now press into the lungs, into the skin, an infrastructural giving-way? And how can you say this during COVID—wherein the virus itself is one of those exogenous substances that now presses into the lungs? One that may have lasting, perhaps permanent, alteration that may involve the distinct loss of the pleasures of smell and taste? I am thinking of many things here. We go off the edge together. We are bound in illness. We have a chance to go, or go further, underground, to relax into a form of multispecies being/multibeing whose temporalities do not compel in the urgencies of the rebuilt convention center, but go by different rules—not even gravity as we know it.

Again and again I catch a glimpse of the ruins of the convention center, the ruins of the domain of the reputable source, the building of indigestion. *That* convention, the one I'd never quite found true gustatory conditions to enter. Going off the edge together is not the same as being thrown off the edge together, in inadvertent pedagogies and worldings that depopulate the edge, purport it doesn't exist. I think back to a book I ultimately withdrew mention of in the introduction, a book that believed it had wandered fairly into the underground but ultimately could not appreciate its own gendered investments, its hasty consumptions. That book throws so much off the edge, and it sits alone on a crumbling table deep in the edifice. Instead, I hold the hand of one of my fictional characters, Moxie, as we wing off together. In the midst of these decades of badly ingested literature and the force behind them, I've experienced a fairly consistent, imperturbable river of meaning in an otherwise confounding, violent, nonsensical world; fellow travelers on this river are essential collaborators in the constant worldmaking that is our daily labor, our daily distress, and our daily succor. I can imagine no better project. These are queer, crip, and racialized undergrounds/undergrowths, some of which are part of my world, and so many of us, I think, have gotten in the business of translating them to the overground, but with leaving some energies untranslatable, inexpropriable.

In writing on agitation I described the crip, the queer, and the raced as losing "diagnostic clarity"—so, distinction, short of identity, losing to the blur. If the assemblies of space and sociality are so profoundly altered, and mean not just the CDC rules for social distancing but the alteration of what is known in space as a response to the coterminous pandemic and ongoing climate dysregulation, the ruins of the convention center worldwide, each sociopolitical space in its own genre—it is "like" an experience of disoriented gravity, the experiential ground having gone from under. Under ground. What elites in the COVID-19 pandemic intuitively knew, of course, in the escape to segregated leisure colonies like Hawaii (their version anyway) and otherwise styled white supremacist spaces in Idaho and Montana, was that further away from the convention center, from heavily settled land, this underground might not be palpable enough to bother them. But they may not be right.

When disabled people are soundly ejected from the space of collective and collaboratively-made safety, there is particularly good reason to invoke disability in a broader form. Not just in the nomination of "long COVID," the pandemic-slash-climate space of the present and its economies and infrastructures that encompass disability language. Not just the broken convention center that represents a medicalized danger, but also the pipes that fail under temperature patterns they weren't built for, flaking rock, drying streams. If our bodies, like theirs, are also subject to giving way to the literal and metaphorical pressures of climate change, is it wrong to feel kin to, or even identify as, these bodies, given that animacy hierarchies have been administered as a means of betrayal?

In other words, I am pointing to inanimate identification, as part of the shifting address in Mai-Thu Perret's underground. Recently I've written of my use of the third-person pronominal *it* in relation to a lifelong hesitancy around humanness that is also surely borne of racisms, and pollutions, also a kind of trans ecological being; that is also a linguistic opportunity, or even a demand.[21] There is a "nothing" in its binding to a transnational perspective: English is a structural minority in the sense that in most languages of the world *it* and *they* don't distinguish human species in referring to a third party. My itness is a form of embrace of empire's underground. I am "it," Chinese "ta," a dynamic and shifting ensemble—also a chemical alterlife—in which my agitation as a spatiotemporal vibration that is both natural to me and a necessity for the politics I cannot help but embrace, that I embody, and that constitutes the complex shared wish of this interlaced, intimate, and transindividual embodiment.[22] I hope that sometimes you might come with me. I hope someday to join you. Again.

NOTES

INTRODUCTION

1. I'm thinking here of the jumble of associations with second books in the mythography of tenured academics, often (1) an emotional complex of "second book jitters" that sometimes leads to extended nonarrival of the book, or (2) a relaxed act of self-expression, "letting it out" as a follow-through of built confidence or a sense of explosive release along the lines of unbounded gestures, or (3) a result of further entrainment, having "learned one's lesson," or "gained bibliographic authority." All of these imaginations bump up against the reality of something otherwise, a gained humility and the embarrassment of having proffered declarative words at all in print form, and that friction can result in an emotionally confused manuscript or a nonarrival: "a failure to thrive or to publish." Frankly, I feel that second books, privilege or not, are a miracle if they happen at all.
2. Erevelles and Minear, "Unspeakable Offenses."
3. Chuh, "It's Not about Anything," 121. Also see my work on cognitive partiality: Chen, "Brain Fog," which appears here in revised form in chapter 3.
4. McKittrick, "Footnotes (Books and Papers Scattered Throughout the Floor)," 28–29. McKittrick was commenting on Ahmed's "White Men."
5. See the related volume published in 2023, *Crip Authorship: Disability as Method*.
6. Murphy, *Sick Building Syndrome*.
7. Puar, "Prognosis Time."
8. Chen, *Animacies*.
9. See Colin Dayan, *The Law Is a White Dog*.
10. Berg and Seeber, *Slow Professor*. For two years at the Association for Asian American Studies conferences, my colleagues Mimi Khúc, Mana Hayakawa, and most recently Sanzari Aranyak and I have led workshops called "Sloth Professor"—open to staff, students, untenured lecturers, and professors in the academy—that help to move conversations beyond management or compliance and toward rethinking care, anticapitalist practice, and academic ableism.
11. Murphy, "Alterlife," paragraph 10.

12 Chuh, *The Difference Aesthetics Makes*, 3.
13 Thank you to Julia Bryan-Wilson, whose work on craft I have had the privilege of following and learning from.
14 Samuels, *Fantasies of Identification*, 6.
15 For more on racialized neurodivergence, see Brown, Ashkenazy, and Onaiwu, *All the Weight of Our Dreams*.
16 Bailey and Mobley, "Work in the Intersections."
17 Bell, *Blackness and Disability*; Samuels, *Fantasies of Identification*; Pickens, *Black Madness :: Mad Blackness*. The volume *Crip Genealogies* (Duke University Press, 2023), which I coedited with Alison Kafer, Eunjung Kim, and Julie Minich, was Alison's brainchild many years ago. It is a collection of works, along with an extensive introduction, that challenge a genealogy of white, imperial disability studies. The four of us are, in addition, co-writing a short monograph with further attention to possibilities for pedagogy.
18 Wu, "Disability," 56.
19 I gratefully acknowledge Moten and Harney for articulating many resonant unlearnings so powerfully, and will revisit their work in chapter 3; Moten and Harney, *The Undercommons*.

CHAPTER 1. SLOW CONSTITUTION

1 A note on terms: "Mongoloid," as a reference to Down syndrome, survives to this day as a lay term; it is largely no longer accepted as a clinical term, even though it is still occasionally used by doctors. Down syndrome itself is often referred to instead as trisomy 21, referring to the presence in most, but not all, people with Down syndrome of the particularizing characteristic of three copies of chromosome 21, signaling a shift toward genetic accounts of disabilities. I should note here, too, that the shift not only in naming, but also in description, from "Down syndrome" to the more recent "trisomy 21" is a shift from a syndromic, assemblage-like rendering (*syn-drome*) attributed to a researcher, to a more unitary, and monovalent, genetic one named by the gene; it is a radical displacement of the constitutional *and* attributive means of a wholly definitive disease description. In this chapter, I use the term *Down syndrome* unless I am specifically referring to Down's own terminological choices; I prefer to avoid the notion of scientific finality or purity involved in the genetic description, and my using *Down syndrome* is meant to reflect the way in which the term looks back to Down's legacy.
2 Note "Mongoloid" is not the same as "Mongolian blue spots," a fully accepted term used to refer to birthmarks that occur disproportionately in those of African and Asian descent. In terms of clinical practice's continuation of "Mongoloid," I recall watching a television interview (I regret that I can no longer locate the source) with a Black woman physician specializing in obstetrics and gynecology; she was describing the importance of having Black obstetricians, and relayed the shock she had felt when a teaching physician during her training a few years earlier had freely used the term "Mongoloid." My understanding of the connection she was making was that some forms of medical racism could be abated by race-aware physicians.

3   This possessive version of the spelling, "Down's," continues in the UK, but as far as I can tell, the UK is alone internationally in this practice.
4   I thank Dr. Mark Minch-de Leon for a timely conversation about California Indians' long attempts to procure various forms of access and repatriation from the Hearst Museum at the University of California, Berkeley.
5   Gristwood, "Puerperal Insanity."
6   Blumenbach, *Anthropological Treatises*.
7   John Langdon Down, *Observations on an Ethnic Classification of Idiots*, 3:259–62.
8   This 10 percent estimation is particularly fascinating in part because it operates effectively as an imaginary mechanism of scale. The idea that a difference occupies a one-tenth proportion of a relevant population—such as that said to be true for left-handed people, or those in the globe having been infected with coronavirus in 2020—also echoes the recent myth of the occurrence of homosexuality in the general population (which has been most recently fallen out of consideration, perhaps due to its relative indistinction amidst transformations of social and political life around gender movements).
9   Down, *Ethnic Classification of Idiots*, 260.
10 In her detailed study of the treatment of "puerperal insanity" in three English asylums beginning in 1870, Helen Gristwood finds that "case notes at Brookwood show that at least 60% of women admitted with puerperal insanity were treated with drugs, and at least 50% of those admitted to Knowle. It is not possible to form an accurate picture of the dispensing of drugs at Colney Hatch." Gristwood, "Puerperal Insanity," 68.
11 Borthwick, "Racism, IQ, and Down's Syndrome," 405–6.
12 Kevles, "Mongolian Imbecility," 127.
13 Borthwick, "Racism, IQ, and Down's Syndrome."
14 Borthwick, "Racism, IQ, and Down's Syndrome," 403; Herrnstein and Murray, *The Bell Curve*.
15 A 2013 Prague conference was where the materials for this chapter began. Its description was productively animated with provocative terms like *backward*, *stagnation*, and *chronicity*.
16 Minh-ha, "Difference," 11–38.
17 Fabian, *Time and the Other*, 35.
18 Harrison, *Climates and Constitutions*.
19 Down, *Ethnic Classification of Idiots*, 259.
20 da Silva, *Toward a Global Idea of Race*.
21 Borthwick, "Racism, IQ, and Down's Syndrome," 406.
22 Carlson, *Faces of Intellectual Disability*.
23 Estreich, *Shape of the Eye*.
24 I refuse, however, the simplistic temptation to lend other antecedent status to something like the trigger warning, except for its part in simply acknowledging that vulnerability to re-citation can be challenging to a traumatized student's ability to remain present for the pedagogical exercise. Acknowledging vulnerability should always be happening, including to the historic harms of colonialism and

its legacies. Vulnerability, however, is not equivalent to fragility, nor is fragility equivalent to snowflakiness.

25 Erika Lopez Prater was fired from her teaching position at Hamline University as a result of showing an ancient Islamic image of the Prophet Muhammad in class. Despite her warnings and invitations to students to discuss this choice, the more powerful opinion amidst a range of opinions among Muslims and art historians was that it was now anti-Islamic and harmful to show the image. As much as there is no right way to handle questions of representation and harm, such moments require some renewed consideration about the desired project of critical thinking in higher education and to what degree they are capacitated to address histories of harm.

26 See my discussion of "goofiness" in *Animacies*.
27 Long and Lorenz, "Genetic Polymorphism."
28 TallBear, *Native American DNA*.
29 Kafer, *Feminist, Queer, Crip*.
30 "Blood Test Provides More Accurate Prenatal Testing for Down Syndrome," Shots: Health News from NPR, February 26, 2014, http://www.npr.org/blogs/health/2014/02/26/282095202/blood-test-provides-more-accurate-prenatal-testing-for-down-syndrome.
31 Kirksey, *Mutant Project*, 140–41.
32 Down, *Ethnic Classification of Idiots*, 259.
33 Down, *Ethnic Classification of Idiots*, 259.
34 Teng and Fairbank, eds., *China's Response to the West*, 24–27, translations by the editors.
35 Freeman, *Time Binds*.
36 Zheng, *Social Life of Opium in China*, 100.
37 Hartman, *Scenes of Subjection*, 19.
38 Tuck, "Suspending Damage."
39 Tuck, "An Indigenous Feminist's Take."
40 Puar, *The Right to Maim*. For an early reference, see Puar, "Prognosis Time."
41 Kang, "The Uses of Asianization," 441.
42 Sills and Ross-Thomas, "Toxic Assets," paragraph 2.
43 A few examples from this recent wave include Colson Whitehead's novel *Zone One*, Max Brooks's fictional "oral history" *World War Z*, and the films *28 Days Later*, *Zombieland*, *I Am Legend*, and *Warm Bodies*.
44 Nyong'o, "The Scene of Occupation"; Schneider, "It Seems as if. . . ."
45 Such genealogical work has been done elsewhere—for instance, by political scientist David McNally, who identifies the compelling nature of the Haitian Vodou zombi as a founding figure for the rapaciousness of Western capitalism. Film and performance scholars have also assessed the imagistic and discursive wake of early popular monster films. See McNally, *Monsters of the Market*.
46 See, for example, Cvetkovich, *Depression*.
47 *The Walking Dead* (comic book series). Created by Robert Kirkman and Tony Moore, first published in 2003 by Image Comics. *The Walking Dead* (TV show) is also a running TV show based on the comic, produced on AMC since 2010.

48 See the website for the disability rights group Not Dead Yet, www.notdeadyet.org.
49 Probyn, *Carnal Appetites*, 14.
50 See, for example, Hines, "Follow-Up."
51 Berlant, *Cruel Optimism*.
52 Graeber, *Debt*.
53 da Silva, *Unpayable Debt*.
54 Puar, "Coda," 151.
55 Brooks, *Zombie Survival Guide*.
56 Stein, "A Disability Story."
57 DeadRising Wiki's Citizensfortheundead.com About page, at http://deadrising.fandom.com/wiki/Citizensfortheundead.com/about.
58 Kim, *Curative Violence*, 8.
59 Halberstam, *Queer Art of Failure*.
60 Talk at University of California at Davis, April 2013.
61 *Xombi* #1 (2004), DC Comics.
62 See, for example, Jina Kim's work on *Animal's People*, a novel by Indra Sinha; Kim, "'People of the Apokalis': Spatial Disability and the Bhopal Disaster," a talk delivered at "Dis/Color," February 7, 2013, at the University of Michigan; and a slightly different published version, Kim, "Spatial Disability and the Bhopal Disaster."
63 Down, *Ethnic Classification of Idiots*, 259.
64 Alexander, *Pedagogies of Crossing*.

CHAPTER 2. AGITATION AS A CHEMICAL WAY OF BEING

1 For considerations of disability in relation to capitalism, see, for example, Erevelles, *Disability and Difference in Global Contexts*; and McRuer, *Crip Theory*. Samuels and Freeman, "Crip Temporalities," also points to the relationships between time, capitalism, and disability, particularly by flagging "waiting" and productivity.
2 Yergeau, *Authoring Autism*, has an excellent critique of rhetorical presumptions in relation to autistic intent (voluntary) and authorship.
3 Bergson, *Laughter*.
4 For a take on the question of agency that is particularly relevant to this book, see Chen, *Animacies*.
5 Bergson, *Laughter*, 12.
6 A shorter, different version of this chapter can be found in Chen, "Agitation."
7 American Psychiatric Association, DSM-5, "Agitation," 827.
8 Hatch, *Silent Cells*, 17.
9 Fabris, *Tranquil Prisons*, 40. For more essential consideration of the uneven connections between carcerality and disability and their relations to abolition, see Ben-Moshe, *Decarcerating Disability*.
10 Bierria, "Racial Conflation," 579.
11 Cavarero, *Horrorism*.
12 Cavarero, *Horrorism*, 5.
13 Schneider and Ruprecht, "In Our Hands," 114.

14 Bergson, *Laughter*, 13, 33.
15 I am thinking here of the work of, variously, Saidiya Hartman, Tavia Nyong'o, Uri McMillan, Zakiyyah Iman Jackson, Jian Chen, Juana María Rodríguez, and Eunjung Kim.
16 McMillan, *Embodied Avatars*.
17 Siebers, *Disability Theory*, 96–116.
18 Williams, *Keywords*, 49–54.
19 Schneider, *Performing Remains*, 90.
20 Persky quoted in Sam Levin, "Stanford Sexual Assault," paragraph 22.
21 Linderman, "Korryn Gaines."
22 Bruce, *How to Go Mad*, 81.
23 With thanks to Vivian Fumiko Chin for sharing the image of the cultural production of Asian American "sleepiness" with me so many years ago.
24 Metzl, *The Protest Psychosis*, 103.
25 Nelson, *Body and Soul*; see particularly chap. 5.
26 Scott, *Extravagant Abjection*, 64.
27 Scott, *Extravagant Abjection*, 64–66.
28 In addition, the originary histories of police forces as slave patrols, in the Carolinas, suggest a chilling legacy.
29 *CBS News*, October 13, 2016.
30 Brooks, *Bodies in Dissent*.
31 Brooks, *Bodies in Dissent*, 8.
32 Oxford English Dictionary online, v. *stunt*, n.2 (entry 192178). Accessed June 9, 2022. Noted to have obscure origin and to be earliest evidenced only within the domain of education, used by college students and schoolchildren.
33 For the inciting invitation to think along the lines of watchability, I am grateful to the coeditors of the published volume *Unwatchable*. This section is a further development of that initial investigation.
34 The subreddit "whatcouldgowrong," was created by reddit user peanutbuttered on April 27, 2013. It has split into a text-only subreddit, /wcgw, and a video subreddit, /whatcouldgowrong. My discussion pertains to the latter subreddit.
35 Hess, "The Silent Film Returns."
36 Bukatman, *The Poetics of Slumberland*.
37 "Two Tables and a Ladder: What Could Go Wrong?," Reddit, https://www.reddit.com/r/Whatcouldgowrong/comments/76v85p/two_tables_and_a_ladder_what_could_go_wrong/. The original post was deleted in 2017, but other versions exist.
38 This may recall a distinct but perhaps related gesture of filmic "temporality of rehearsal," the Lumière 1896 film *Demolition d'un mur*, which shows a sequence of demolition in its first half, then reverses it for the second: https://www.youtube.com/watch?v=9p0HI9t5IB0.
39 Halberstam, "Dude Where's My Gender?," 308.
40 Herring, *Another Country*. In line with Herring's relating of form to spatial politics, many of the WCGW videos are set in rural locations and seem to emulate, for commenters, "hillbilly" stereotypes.

41 Two abbreviations assist with the curation of different kinds of propriety: NSFW and NSFL, "not safe for work" and "not safe for life," respectively. The latter signals videos that represent a moment that is likely to have represented an actual death.
42 See Puar, *The Right to Maim*.
43 *Laughing Gas*, dir. Edwin S. Porter, 9 minutes, 1907, Edison Studios.
44 Hennefeld, *Specters of Slapstick*, 75.
45 Stewart, "What Happened in the Transition?," 120.
46 Barnes, "Everybody Wants to Pioneer."
47 See Brennan, *The Transmission of Affect*.
48 For an excellent study—and a critical method—of considering the raciality (including the visual culture) of eating in the nineteenth century, see Tompkins, *Racial Indigestion*.
49 Thanks particularly to Annalee Tai for being an irreplaceable part of these discussions.
50 De Kosnik, "Piracy Is the Future," 64.
51 Berlant, "The Commons."
52 Choy, *Ecologies of Comparison*, 142, 145.
53 K'gari is the Badtjala name for the place that is known by the settler state as Fraser Island. (K'gari is also the name of the national park that occupies part of the island.) I have chosen to exclusively refer to it as K'gari. The story of its naming after Eliza Fraser is a violent one: She was the Scottish wife of Captain James Fraser, and their ship wrecked on the island. Despite a known history of Badtjala hospitality and the explicit rejection of her story by other shipwreck survivors, she claimed she had been abducted and maltreated by them. Her actions played a significant role in the attacks on Badtjala people and sovereignty.
54 Foley, *Witnessing to Silence*.
55 Foley, *Biting the Clouds*, 62.
56 Foley, *Biting the Clouds*, 53–58.
57 Halberstam, *Wild Things*, 66.
58 TallBear, "Tell Me a Story," 11.

CHAPTER 3. UNLEARNING

Epigraph 1: Fabian, *Time and the Other*, 35.
Epigraph 2: Crayon, *All about Earlswood*, 21. This is a pamphlet given to those in a position to possibly donate to the asylum. Even so, the language betrays the arrangements that make such benevolence productive.

1 Ahmed, *What's the Use?*
2 With Dana Luciano I discuss "inhuman" in relation to a wide map of previous critical work engaging the human, in Luciano and Chen, "Has the Queer Ever Been Human?" The discussion is extensive and points to dehumanization and precarity, but in the interest of affect I quote here: "The slash through non/human, then, attempts to recollect and foreground the very histories of dehumanization too often overlooked in celebratory posthumanisms. 'Inhumanisms,' in

our view, performs a similar kind of work through its homonymic echo. Resonating against 'inhumane,' inhuman points to the violence that the category of the human contains within itself. Yet it also carries a sense of generativity—inhuman not simply as category, as a spatial designator or the name of a 'kind' of being, but as a process, an unfolding."

3   See Snaza and Singh, "Introduction: Dehumanist Education," 8.
4   Moten and Harney, *The Undercommons*.
5   See the archive at https://www.nytimes.com/column/disability. While many of my cherished colleagues are published there, the column has tended so far to favor white representation disproportionate to their proportion among disabled people.
6   Choy and Zee, "Condition—Suspension."
7   Glissant, *Poetics of Relation*, 189–94. I thank the organizers of the workshop "Thresholdings: Intimacies, Opacities, Embodiments," Alanna Thain and Megan Fernandes, and all the interlocutors at McGill University on March 25, 2019, for a stunning collective consideration, throughout our day together, of Glissant's notion of opacity. See also the performance of obscurity and the objectification of the possessive desire of Western knowledge in Santiago, "The Wily Homosexual," 13–19. I think here, too, of Kadji Amin, Amber Jamilla Musser, and Roy Pérez's description of "queer form," "a name for the range of formal, aesthetic, and sensuous strategies that make difference a little less knowable, visible, and digestible"; Amin, Musser, and Pérez, "Queer Form."
8   There are innumerable examples of the criminalization or dismissal of unrest, as well as the defanging of dangerous subjects by alleging that they are not capable subjects. I am thinking here of Colin Dayan's argument about the law and its ability to hold slaves criminally *liable*, while at the same moment considering them mentally *incapable*; Dayan, *The Law Is a White Dog*.
9   For neoliberal devisings tuned to extreme measures, the fictional BBC sitcom *W1A*, which aired in 2004, does an excellent job of panning the cultures that result from the mandate of "doing more with less."
10 For a catalog accompanying the Aboriginal-led exhibition on the campus of the University of Queensland that focuses on the sandstone universities, see Foley, Martin-Chew, and Nicoll, *Courting Blakness*.
11 Foley, *Black Opium*.
12 Foley, *Biting the Clouds*, 139.
13 Gillett, "Opium and Race Relations," 24.
14 Nicoll, "No Substitute."
15 Gillett, "Opium and Race Relations," 23.
16 Helen Meekosha, in "What the Hell Are You?," writes that in postwar Australia "the labour market was structured to exclude Indigenous and disabled people, focusing on healthy Caucasian and Asian locally born and immigrants," p. 171.
17 Andrew Gillett suggests a more politically local possible history. He points to the use of pituri, a native derivative from a native shrub, used as a stimulant and anesthetic, whose strict community controls on usage may have been declining

as the use of opium for payment was rising among employers. "Opium and Race Relations," 24–25.
18 Fiona Foley, personal conversation at the artist's home, May 22–23, 2017.
19 Foley, *Biting the Clouds*, 16.
20 State of Queensland Department of Environment and Science, "About Fraser Island Dingoes."
21 "Aboriginal Elders Say Fraser Island Dingo Attacks 'Could Have Been Avoided,'" NITV, 22 April 2019, https://www.sbs.com.au/nitv/nitv-news/article/2019/04/22/aboriginal-elders-say-fraser-island-dingo-attacks-could-have-been-avoided. The article uses the spelling "Butchulla."
22 Goldberg-Hiller and Silva, "Sharks and Pigs," 431.
23 See, for its application in educational theory, Murphy, "Active Learning as Destituent Potential."
24 In Foley's account, Bliss was actually the first room to be devised and constructed ("the most difficult one first"); my reading of "Bliss" as a possibly final room depends on one reaching it last, rather than first, in the approach, and also a bit in its physical uniqueness in relation to the other rooms, set off disproportionately. *Biting the Clouds*, 122.
25 With many thanks to Abigail De Kosnik for her work on transmedia storytelling and for conversations about its more atypical domains of application.
26 With many thanks to Mark Cladis for this observation.
27 Foley, *Biting the Clouds*.
28 Foley curated an exhibition featuring Aboriginal artists at Queensland University, one of the "sandstone universities," in 2014; an associated website and book followed on the exhibition. See Foley, Martin-Chew, and Nicoll, *Courting Blakness*.
29 King, *The Black Shoals*, 31.
30 Wolfe, *Traces of History*, 59.
31 Foley, "Black Power." See also Lothian, "Seizing the Time," on the uptake of the US Black Panthers' community support projects, and Trometter, *Aboriginal Black Power*.
32 Fiona Nicoll argues that the sexual politics of the racializing script of the opium den—particularly worries about miscegenation and other forms of mixing—are sent up in a series photograph depicting "a racially diverse group of men and women, in the style of a family photograph outside a house on the site of a Chinese opium den." See Nicoll, "No Substitute," 62.
33 Kirksey, "Chemosociality in Multispecies Worlds," 24.
34 Rowe, "Transpacific Studies," 146–7.
35 Rosalind Kidd's *The Way We Civilise* is an essential study of the settler state's twentieth-century treatment of Aboriginal peoples.
36 The Aborigines Regulations of 1972, quoted in Thornton and Luker, "The Wages of Sin," 649–50.
37 Re Cattle Station Industry (1966) 133 Commonwealth Arbitration Reports, quoted in Thornton and Luker, "The Wages of Sin," 653.
38 Clark, *Labor Conditions*, 65.
39 Clark, *Labor Conditions*, 47.

40 Miller, *Dying Days of Segregation*, 87–88. Miller's study of the case of the Yarrabah people near Cairns in North Queensland makes this diagnosis and blames the DAIA, the Queensland Department of Aboriginal and Islander Affairs, for a legacy of regressive anti-Aboriginal and anti-Islander policy.
41 Johnson and McRuer, "Cripistemologies: Introduction."
42 Haraway, "Situated Knowledges."
43 Gill, "Breaking the Silence."
44 World Bank memo dated December 12, 1991, unpublished (leaked).
45 Terry, *Attachments to War*.
46 Price, *Mad at School*.
47 Erevelles, *Disability and Difference in Global Contexts*.
48 Bey, *Cistem Failure*.
49 Hayward, "When Fish and Frogs Change Gender," 13.
50 Hutchins, *Cognition in the Wild*.
51 Chen, "Broadband Epistemologies."
52 Christian, "The Race for Theory."
53 McRuer, Johnson, et al., "Proliferating Cripistemologies," 163–64.
54 Kidd, *The Way We Civilise*.
55 Foley, *Biting the Clouds*, 124.
56 Chuh, The Difference Aesthetics Makes, 95.
57 Wynter, "Unsettling the Coloniality of Being/Power/Truth/Freedom."

AFTERWARDS

1 Koch and Hercus, *Aboriginal Placenames*, 42.
2 Wolfe, *Traces of History*, 52 and passim.
3 I thank Natalia Duong for the privilege of my encountering her research as a committee member; one thing we briefly discussed, and that may have set the pattern for my perspective on the chemical intimacy that binds those GIs and my mother, was the tentative and complicated relationship between Vietnamese descendants of those who experienced harm by Agent Orange, and members of the US military who were on the side of administration of the toxin.
4 Sorry Day was initiated as a national holiday in 1998, a century after the Aboriginals Protection and Restriction of the Sale of Opium Act in Queensland, after a suggestion by a different organization concerned with the Stolen Generations, called Bringing Them Home. Places around Australia that serve as sites for Aboriginal commemoration are called "sorry sites." Cranbrook Place is one of these sites.
5 Chen and Choy, "Corresponding in Time."
6 It has been commonly observed that the use of phrases such as "in these times," "in these troubled times," and "in these uncertain times" as a preface to emails swelled during the pandemic.
7 This phrase emerged in my conversation with philosopher and activist Alisa Bierria on 10/17/2020, about melancholies that do not end in what can be a strangely idealistic form of lossful nihilism, or that are perpetually delayed or

denied, but are permitted to exist, registering layers of complexity and acceptance of inevitable complicity and incompletion. Bierria is working on a project about melancholy.

8   In part, a good bit of the pressure of "figuring it out" has less to do with the idea of saving lives, or righting an inequity, than with knowing sooner rather than later, given the pace of content generation in the academy, which seems to have accelerated rather than let up—as if it had to make up for "lost" time. I write this while also acknowledging the incredible expository work of thinkers and activists who precisely have been figuring it out and spreading the word, because there is no time to lose. This is part of the contradiction that Tim and I were exploring together.

9   With thanks for Tim Choy's wonderful nomination. The word is an occasion for reflection.

10 Xiaodan Zhou, Kevin Josey, Leila Kamareddine, et al., "Excess of COVID-19 Cases and Deaths due to Fine Particulate Matter Exposure during the 2020 Wildfires in the United States," Science Advances, online, August 13, 2021, doi: 10.1126/sciadv.abi8789.

11 Wynter, "Unsettling the Coloniality of Being/Power/Truth/Freedom."

12 See particularly chap. 6 of Chen, *Animacies,* "Following Mercurial Affect."

13 For all of Donna Haraway's work on naturecultures, and anthropological and postcolonial feminisms' reimagining of these dualities, I feel that the divide persists when urbane intellectuals who live in/primarily by institutional conditions encounter what are presented as novel circumstances that involve some form of "nature" or "wildlife."

14 Mask Oakland volunteer signup page, maskoakland.org/volunteer. Accessed 10/17/2020.

15 Shah, *Contagious Divides.*

16 Fuss, introduction to *Inside/Out,* 1.

17 "Pandemic Time," a conversation with Judith Butler on pandemic time, gender, and art, Berkeley Art Museum, September 20, 2021.

18 Brugman, "The Story of Over."

19 Matlock, "Fictive Motion as Cognitive Stimulation."

20 Bourdieu, *Distinction.*

21 Chen, "Animacy as a Sexual Device."

22 Murphy, "Alterlife and Decolonial Chemical Relations."

BIBLIOGRAPHY

Ahmed, Sara. *What's the Use? On the Uses of Use.* Durham, NC: Duke University Press, 2019.

Ahmed, Sara. "White Men," *Feminist Killjoys* (blog), November 2, 2014.

Alexander, M. Jacqui. *Pedagogies of Crossing: Meditations on Feminism, Sexual Politics, Memory, and the Sacred.* Durham, NC: Duke University Press, Combined Academic, 2006.

American Psychiatric Association. *Diagnostic and Statistical Manual of Mental Disorders: DSM-5.* 5th ed. Arlington, VA: American Psychiatric Association, 2013.

Amin, Kadji, Amber Jamilla Musser, and Roy Pérez. "Queer Form: Aesthetics, Race, and the Violences of the Social." *ASAP/Journal* 2, no. 2 (May 2017): 227–39.

Bailey, Moya, and Izetta Autumn Mobley. "Work in the Intersections: A Black Feminist Disability Framework." *Gender & Society* 33, no. 1 (2019): 19–40.

Barnes, Barbara. "Everybody Wants to Pioneer Something Out Here: Landscape, Adventure, and Biopolitics in the American Southwest." *Journal of Sport and Social Issues* 33, no. 3 (2019): 172–85.

Bell, Chris. *Blackness and Disability: Critical Examinations and Cultural Interventions.* East Lansing: Michigan State University Press, 2011.

Ben-Moshe, Liat. *Decarcerating Disability: Deinstitutionalization and Prison Abolition.* Minneapolis: University of Minnesota Press, 2020.

Berg, Maggie, and Barbara K. Seeber. *Slow Professor: Challenging the Culture of Speed in the Academy.* Toronto: University of Toronto Press, 2016.

Bergson, Henri. *Laughter: An Essay on the Meaning of the Comic.* Translated by Cloudesley Brereton and Fred Rothwell. New York: Macmillan, [1899] 1911.

Berlant, Lauren. "The Commons: Infrastructures for Troubling Times." *Environment and Planning D: Society and Space* 34, no. 3 (2016): 393–419.

Berlant, Lauren. *Cruel Optimism.* Durham, NC: Duke University Press, 2011.

Bey, Marquis. *Cistem Failure: Essays on Blackness and Cisgender.* Durham, NC: Duke University Press, 2022.

Bierria, Alisa. "Racial Conflation: Rethinking Agency, Black Action, and Criminal Intent." *Journal of Social Philosophy* 53, no. 4 (Spring 2020): 1–20.

Blumenbach, Johann Friedrich. *The Anthropological Treatises of Johann Friedrich Blumenbach*. London: Longman, Roberts, and Green, 1865.

Borthwick, Chris. "Racism, IQ, and Down's Syndrome." *Disability and Society* 11 (1996): 403–10.

Bourdieu, Pierre. *Distinction: A Social Critique of the Judgement of Taste*. Cambridge, MA: Harvard University Press, 1984.

Brennan, Teresa. *The Transmission of Affect*. Ithaca, NY: Cornell University Press, 2004.

Brooks, Daphne. *Bodies in Dissent: Spectacular Performances of Race and Freedom, 1850–1910*. Durham, NC: Duke University Press, 2006.

Brooks, Max. *Zombie Survival Guide*. New York: Random House, 2003.

Brown, Lydia X. Z., E. Ashkenazy, and Morénike Giwa Onaiwu. *All the Weight of Our Dreams: On Living Racialized Autism*. Lincoln, NE: DragonBee Press, 2017.

Bruce, LaMarr Jurelle. *How to Go Mad without Losing Your Mind: Madness and Black Radical Creativity*. Durham, NC: Duke University Press, 2021.

Brugman, Claudia. "The Story of Over." PhD diss., University of California, Berkeley, 1981.

Bukatman, Scott. *The Poetics of Slumberland*. Berkeley: University of California Press, 2012.

Carlson, Licia. *The Faces of Intellectual Disability: Philosophical Reflections*. Bloomington: Indiana University Press, 2010.

Cavarero, Adriana. *Horrorism: Naming Contemporary Violence*. New York: Columbia University Press, 2008.

CBS News. "Wife of Man Killed by Charlotte Police Disputes Who Pulled the Trigger." CBSnews.com, October 13, 2016. cbsnews.com/news/keith-lamont-scott-charlotte-polic-shooting-wife-rakeyia-scott-speaks-out/.

Chen, Mel Y. "Agitation." In *Wildness*, ed. Jack Halberstam and Tavia Nyong'o', special issue, *South Atlantic Quarterly* 117, no. 3 (2018): 551–66.

Chen, Mel Y. *Animacies: Biopolitics, Racial Mattering, and Queer Affect*. Durham, NC: Duke University Press, 2012.

Chen, Mel Y. "Animacy as a Sexual Device." In *Language and Sexuality: A Handbook*, edited by Rusty Barrett and Kira Hall. Oxford: Oxford University Press, 2021.

Chen, Mel Y. "Brain Fog: The Race for Cripistemology." *Journal of Literary and Cultural Disability Studies* 8, no. 2 (2014): 171–84.

Chen, Mel Y. "Broadband Epistemologies." In *30-Year Retrospective on Language, Gender and Sexuality* (special issue), edited by Kira Hall, Rodrigo Borba, and Mie Hiramoto. *Journal of Gender and Language* 15, no. 3 (2021): 396–402.

Chen, Mel Y. "Lurching for the Cure? On Zombies and the Reproduction of Disability." *GLQ: A Journal of Lesbian and Gay Studies* 21, no. 1 (2015): 24–31.

Chen, Mel Y. "Toxic Animacies, Inanimate Affections." *GLQ: A Journal of Lesbian and Gay Studies* 17, no. 2–3 (2011): 265–86.

Chen, Mel Y., and Tim K. Choy. "Corresponding in Time." *ISLE: Interdisciplinary Studies of Literature and Environment* 27, no. 4 (Autumn 2020): 795–808.

Chen, Mel Y., Alison Kafer, Eunjung Kim, and Julie Minich, eds. *Crip Genealogies*. Durham, NC: Duke University Press, 2023.

Choy, Tim. *Ecologies of Comparison: An Ethnography of Endangerment in Hong Kong.* Durham, NC: Duke University Press, 2011.
Choy, Timothy, and Jerry Zee. "Condition—Suspension." *Cultural Anthropology* 30, no. 2 (2017): 210–23.
Christian, Barbara. "The Race for Theory." *Cultural Critique,* no. 6 (Spring 1987): 51–63.
Chuh, Kandice. *The Difference Aesthetics Makes.* Durham, NC: Duke University Press, 2019.
Chuh, Kandice. "It's Not about Anything." *Social Text* 32, no. 4 (2014): 121.
Clark, Victor Selden. *Labor Conditions in Australia.* Washington, DC: Government Printing Office, 1905.
Crayon, Christopher. *All about Earlswood: The Asylum for Idiots.* Red Hill, Surrey: Earlswood Institution, 1887.
Cvetkovich, Ann. *Depression: A Public Feeling.* Durham, NC: Duke University Press, 2012.
da Silva, Denise Ferreira. *Toward a Global Idea of Race.* Minneapolis: University of Minnesota Press, 2007.
da Silva, Denise Ferreira. *Unpayable Debt.* Sternberg Press, 2022.
Dayan, Colin. *The Law Is a White Dog: How Legal Rituals Make and Unmake Persons.* Princeton, NJ: Princeton University Press, 2011.
De Kosnik, Abigail. "Piracy Is the Future of Culture." *Third Text* 34, no. 1 (2020): 62–70.
Démolition d'un mur. Lumière film, 1896. https://www.youtube.com/watch?v=9poHI9t5IB0.
Down, John Langdon H. *Observations on an Ethnic Classification of Idiots.* London Hospital Reports, 1866, 3:259–62.
Edelman, P. D., D. C. McFarland, V. A. Mironov, and J. G. Matheny. "Commentary: In Vitro-Cultured Meat Production." *Tissue Engineering* 11, no. 5–6 (2005): 659–62.
Erevelles, Nirmala. "Crippin' Jim Crow: Disability, Dis-Location, and the School-to-Prison Pipeline." In *Disability Incarcerated: Imprisonment and Disability in the United States and Canada,* edited by Liat Ben-Moshe, Chris Chapman, and Allison C. Carey, 81–100. New York: Palgrave Macmillan, 2014.
Erevelles, Nirmala. *Disability and Difference in Global Contexts: Enabling a Transformative Bodily Politic.* Basingstoke: Palgrave Macmillan, 2016.
Erevelles, Nirmala, and Andrea Minear. "Unspeakable Offenses: Untangling Race and Disability in Discourses of Intersectionality." *Journal of Literary and Cultural Disability Studies* 4, no. 2 (2010): 127–45.
Estreich, George. *The Shape of the Eye: Down Syndrome, Family, and the Stories We Inherit.* Dallas: Southern Methodist University Press, 2011.
Evans, Raymond. *A History of Queensland.* Cambridge: Cambridge University Press, 2007.
Fabian, Johannes. *Time and the Other: How Anthropology Makes Its Object.* New York: Columbia University Press, 1983.
Fabris, Erick. *Tranquil Prisons: Chemical Incarceration under Community Treatment Orders.* Toronto: University of Toronto Press, 2011.
Fanon, Frantz. *The Wretched of the Earth.* Translated by Richard Philcox. New York: Grove, [1961] 2004.
Foley, Fiona. *Biting the Clouds.* St. Lucia: University of Queensland Press, 2020.

Foley, Fiona. *Black Opium*. Brisbane: State Library of Queensland, 2010. Exhibition catalog.

Foley, Fiona. *Black Opium*. 2006. Permanent installation, Queensland State Library, Brisbane, Australia.

Foley, Fiona. *Witnessing to Silence*. 2004. Art installation, Brisbane Magistrates Court, Brisbane, Australia.

Foley, Fiona, Michele Helmrich, Christine Morrow, and Rachel Kent. *Fiona Foley: Forbidden*. Sydney: Museum of Contemporary Art, 2009.

Foley, Fiona, Louise Martin-Chew, and Fiona Nicoll, eds. *Courting Blakness: Recalibrating Knowledge in the Sandstone University*. St. Lucia: University of Queensland Press, 2016.

Foley, Gary. "Black Power in Redfern 1968-1972." October 5, 2001. https://vuir.vu.edu.au/27009/1/Black%20power%20in%20Redfern%201968-1972.pdf.

Freeman, Elizabeth. *Time Binds: Queer Temporalities, Queer Histories*. Durham, NC: Duke University Press, 2011.

Fuss, Diana. Introduction to *Inside/Out: Lesbian Theories, Gay Theories*, edited by Diana Fuss. London: Routledge, 1991.

Gill, Rosalind. "Breaking the Silence: The Hidden Injuries of Neoliberal Academia." In *Secrecy and Silence in the Research Process: Feminist Reflections*, edited by Roisin Ryan-Flood and Rosalind Gill. London: Routledge, 2009.

Gillett, Andrew. "Opium and Race Relations in Queensland." In Foley, *Black Opium* (2010), 15-25.

Glissant, Édouard. *Poetics of Relation*. Translated by Betsy Wing. Ann Arbor: University of Michigan Press, 1997.

Goldberg-Hiller, Jonathan, and Noenoe K. Silva. "Sharks and Pigs: Animating Hawaiian Sovereignty against the Anthropological Machine." *South Atlantic Quarterly* 110, no. 2 (2011): 429-46.

Graeber, David. *Debt: The First 5,000 Years*. Brooklyn: Melville House, 2012.

Gristwood, Helen. "Puerperal Insanity: A Study of Women Admitted to the County Asylums at Brookwood in Surrey, Colney Hatch in Middlesex and Knowle in Hampshire between the Years 1870-1908." MA in English Local History, University of Leicester, 2012.

Halberstam, Jack. *Queer Art of Failure*. Durham, NC: Duke University Press, 2011.

Halberstam, Jack. *Wild Things: The Disorder of Desire*. Durham, NC: Duke University Press, 2020.

Halberstam, Judith. "Dude, Where's My Gender? Or, Is There Life on Uranus?" *GLQ: A Journal of Lesbian and Gay Studies* 10, no. 2 (2004): 308-12.

Haraway, Donna. "Situated Knowledges: The Science Question in Feminism and the Privilege of Partial Perspective." *Feminist Studies* 14, no. 3 (1988): 575-99.

Harris, Cheryl L. "Whiteness as Property." *Harvard Law Review* 106 (1993): 1709-1791, 1724-1737.

Harrison, Mark. *Climates and Constitutions: Health, Race, Environment and British Imperialism in India*. New Delhi: Oxford University Press, 2002.

Hartman, Saidiya. *Scenes of Subjection: Terror, Slavery, and Self-Making in Nineteenth Century America*. Oxford: Oxford University Press, 1997.

Hatch, Anthony Ryan. *Silent Cells*. Minneapolis: University of Minnesota Press, 2019.

Hayward, Eva. "When Fish and Frogs Change Gender." *IndyWeek.com*, August 3, 2011. https://indyweek.com/news/fish-frogs-change-gender/.

Herring, Scott. *Another Country: Queer Anti-Urbanism*. New York: NYU Press, 2010.

Hennefeld, Maggie. *Specters of Slapstick and Silent Film Comediennes*. New York: Columbia University Press, 2018.

Hernnstein, Richard R., and Charles Murray. *The Bell Curve: Intelligence and Class Structure in American Life*. New York: Free Press, 1994.

Hess, Amanda. "The Silent Film Returns—On Social Media." *New York Times*, September 13, 2017. https://www.nytimes.com/2017/09/13/movies/silent-film-youtube-videos.html.

Hines, Terence. "Follow-Up: Zombies and Tetrodotoxin." *Skeptical Inquirer,* May/June 2008.

Ho, Jennifer, and James Kyung-Jin Lee, eds. "The State of Illness and Disability in Asian America." *Amerasia Journal* 39, no. 1 (2013).

Huan, Yanzhong. *Toxic Politics: China's Environmental Health Crisis and Its Challenge to the Chinese State*. Cambridge: Cambridge University Press, 2020.

Hutchins, Edward. *Cognition in the Wild*. Cambridge, MA: MIT Press, 1996.

Iverson, Gunnar, Laura Horak, Maggie Hennefeld, and Nicholas Baer, eds. *Unwatchable*. New Brunswick, NJ: Rutgers University Press, 2019.

Jain, S. Lochlann. *Injury: The Politics of Product Design and Safety Law in the United States*. Princeton, NJ: Princeton University Press, 2006.

Johnson, Merri Lisa, and Robert McRuer. "Cripistemologies: Introduction." *Journal of Literary and Cultural Disability Studies* 8, no. 2 (January 2014): 127–47.

Kafer, Alison. *Feminist, Queer, Crip*. Bloomington: Indiana University Press, 2013.

Kang, Laura Hyun Yi. "The Uses of Asianization: Figuring Crises, 1997–98 and 2007–?" *American Quarterly* 64, no. 3 (2012): 411–36.

Kevles, Daniel. "Mongolian Imbecility: Race and Its Rejection in the Understanding of a Mental Disease." In *Mental Retardation in America: A Historical Reader*, edited by S. Noll and J. Trent, 120–29. New York: NYU Press, 2004.

Kidd, Rosalind. *The Way We Civilise: Aboriginal Affairs—The Untold Story*. St. Lucia: University of Queensland Press, 2005.

Kim, Eunjung. *Curative Violence: Rehabilitating Disability, Gender, and Sexuality in Modern Korea*. Durham, NC: Duke University Press, 2017.

Kim, Jina. "Spatial Disability and the Bhopal Disaster." *Disability Studies Quarterly* 34, no. 3 (2014). https://dsq-sds.org/article/view/3795/3271.

King, Tiffany Lethabo. *The Black Shoals: Offshore Formations of Black and Native Studies*. Durham, NC: Duke University Press, 2019.

Kirksey, Eben. "Chemosociality in Multispecies Worlds: Endangered Frogs and Toxic Possibilities in Sydney." *Environmental Humanities* 12, no. 1 (2020): 23–50.

Kirksey, Eben. *Mutant Project: Inside the Global Race to Genetically Modify Humans*. New York: St. Martin's Press, 2020.

Koch, Harold, and Luise Hercus, eds. *Aboriginal Placenames: Naming and Re-naming the Australian Landscape*. Australian National University E-Press and Aboriginal History Incorporated, 2009.

Koller, Dov. *The Restless Plant*. Cambridge, MA: Harvard University Press, 2011.

Kubler, Alison. "Fiona Foley and Her Fearful Asymmetry." In Foley, *Black Opium* (2010), 31–33.

Kumar, Amitava. "What's Behind India's Beef Lynchings?" *The Nation*, October 13, 2017.

Lee, James Kyung-Jin. *Pedagogies of Woundedness: Illness, Memoir, and the Ends of the Model Minority*. Philadelphia: Temple University Press, 2022.

Leonardo, Zeus, and Alicia Broderick. "Smartness as Property: A Critical Exploration of the Intersections between Whiteness and Disability." *Teachers College Record* 113, no. 10 (2011): 2206–32.

Levin, Sam. "Stanford Sexual Assault: Read the Full Text of the Judge's Controversial Decision." *Guardian*, June 14, 2016. theguardian.com/us-news/2016/jun/14/stanford-sexual-assault-read-sentence-judge-aaron-persky.

Levy, Sharon. "Rekindling Native Fires." *BioScience* 55, no. 4 (2005): 303–8.

Li, Yifei, and Judith Shapiro. *China Goes Green: Coercive Environmentalism for a Troubled Planet*. Cambridge: Polity Press, 2020.

Linderman, Juliet. "Korryn Gaines: Twenty-Three-Year-Old Mother Killed by Police, Posted Parts of Standoff on Facebook." *GlobalNews* August 2, 2016. globalnews.ca/news/2861722/facebook-deactivates-shotgun-wielding-womans-accounts-in-midst-of-standoff-with-police/.

Long, Jeffrey C., and Joseph G. Lorenz. "Genetic Polymorphism and American Indian Health." *Western Journal of Medicine* 176, no. 3 (May 2002): 203–5.

Lothian, Kathy. "Seizing the Time: Australian Aborigines and the Influence of the Black Panther Party, 1969-1972." *Journal of Black Studies* 35, no. 4 (March 2005): 179–200.

Luciano, Dana, and Mel Y. Chen, "Has the Queer Ever Been Human?," *GLQ: A Journal of Lesbian and Gay Studies* 21, no. 2–3 (2015): 182–207.

Matlock, Teenie. "Fictive Motion as Cognitive Stimulation." *Memory and Cognition* 32 (2004): 1389–1400.

Martin-Chew, Louise. "Under the Act: A Poisoned Chalice." In Foley, *Black Opium* (2010), 37–40.

Maude, Ulrika. "Chronic Conditions: Beckett, Bergson, and Samuel Johnson." *Journal of Medical Humanities* 37, no. 2 (2016): 193–204.

McKittrick, Katherine. "Footnotes (Books and Papers Scattered about the Floor)." In *Dear Science: And Other Stories*, 14–34. Durham, NC: Duke University Press, 2021.

McMillan, Uri. *Embodied Avatars: Genealogies of Black Feminist Art and Performance*. New York: NYU Press, 2016.

McNally, David. *Monsters of the Market: Zombies, Vampires, and Global Capitalism*. Boston: Leiden, 2011.

McRuer, Robert. *Crip Theory: Cultural Signs of Queerness and Disability*. New York: NYU Press, 2006.

McRuer, Robert. "The Crip's Speech; or, Benefit-Scrounging Scum." Paper presented at the American Studies Association Meeting, Baltimore, Maryland, October 21, 2011.

McRuer, Robert, Merri Lisa Johnson, et al. "Proliferating Cripistemologies": A Virtual Roundtable." *Journal of Literary and Cultural Disability Studies* 8, no. 2 (2014): 149–69.

Meekosha, Helen, "What the Hell Are You? An Intercategorial Analysis of Race, Ethnicity, Gender, and Disability in the Australian Body Politic," *Scandinavian Journal of Disability Research* 8, no. 2-3 (2006): 161-76.

Metzl, Jonathan. *The Protest Psychosis: How Schizophrenia Became a Black Disease*. Boston: Beacon Press, 2010.

Miller, Barbara. *Dying Days of Segregation: Case Study Yarrabah*. Cairns: Barbara Miller, 2018.

Mills, Mara, and Rebecca Sanchez, eds. *Crip Authorship: Disability as Method*. New York: NYU Press, 2023.

Minh-ha, Trinh T. "Difference: A Special Third World Women Issue." *Discourse* 8 (Fall 1986-Winter 1987): 11-38.

Moten, Fred. *Black and Blur*. Durham, NC: Duke University Press, 2017.

Moten, Fred, and Stefano Harney. *The Undercommons: Fugitive Planning and Black Study*. London: Minor Compositions, 2013.

Murphy, Michael P. A. "Active Learning as Destituent Potential: Agambenian Philosophy of Education and Moderate Steps towards the Coming Politics." *Educational Philosophy and Theory* 52, no. 1 (2020): 66-78.

Murphy, Michelle. "Alterlife and Decolonial Chemical Relations." *Cultural Anthropology* 32, no. 4 (November 2017): 494-502.

Murphy, Michelle. *Sick Building Syndrome and the Problem of Uncertainty: Environmental Politics, Technoscience, and Women Workers*. Durham, NC: Duke University Press, 2006.

Nelson, Alondra. *Body and Soul: The Black Panther Party and the Fight against Medical Discrimination*. Minneapolis: University of Minnesota Press, 2013.

Nicoll, Fiona. "No Substitute: Political Art against the Opiate of the Colonising Euphemism." In Michele Helmrich and Christine Morrow, *Fiona Foley: Forbidden*, 60-63. Sydney: Museum of Contemporary Art, 2009. Exhibition catalog.

Nyong'o, Tavia. "The Scene of Occupation." *TDR: The Drama Review* 56, no. 4 (2012): 138-51.

Perret, Mai-Thu. *Underground*. 2007. Screen print. 33 × 22½ in. San Francisco Museum of Modern Art.

Pickens, Therí Alyce. *Black Madness: Mad Blackness*. Durham, NC: Duke University Press, 2019.

Porter, Edwin. *Laughing Gas*. 1907. Short film.

Price, Margaret. *Mad at School: Rhetorics of Mental Disability and Academic Life*. Ann Arbor: University of Michigan Press, 2011.

Probyn, Elspeth. *Carnal Appetites: FoodSexIdentities*. New York: Routledge, 2000.

Puar, Jasbir. "Prognosis Time: Towards a Geopolitics of Affect, Debility, and Capacity." *Women and Performance: A Journal of Feminist Theory* 19, no. 2 (2009): 161-72.

Puar, Jasbir K. "Coda: The Cost of Getting Better; Suicide, Sensation, Switchpoints." *GLQ: A Journal of Lesbian and Gay Studies* 18, no. 1 (2012): 149-58.

Puar, Jasbir. *The Right to Maim: Debility, Capacity, Disability*. Durham, NC: Duke University Press, 2017.

Rifkin, Mark. *Fictions of Land and Flesh: Blackness, Indigeneity, Speculation*. Durham, NC: Duke University Press, 2019.

Rowe, John Carlos. "Transpacific Studies and the Cultures of U.S. Imperialism." In *Transpacific Studies: Framing an Emerging Field*, edited by Janet Hoskins and Viet Thanh Nguyen, 134–50. Honolulu: University of Hawaii Press, 2014.

Samuels, Ellen. *Fantasies of Identification: Disability, Gender, Race*. New York: NYU Press, 2014.

Samuels, Ellen, and Elizabeth Freeman, eds. "Crip Temporalities." *South Atlantic Quarterly* 120, no. 2 (2021): 245–54.

Santiago, Silviano. "The Wily Homosexual (First—and Necessarily Hasty—Notes)." In *Queer Globalizations: Citizenship and the Afterlife of Colonialism*, edited by Arnaldo Cruz-Malave and Martin Manalansan. New York: NYU Press, 2002.

Schiebinger, Londa. *Nature's Body: Gender in the Making of Modern Science*. New Brunswick, NJ: Rutgers University Press, 1993.

Schneider, Rebecca. *Performing Remains: Art and War in Times of Theatrical Reenactment*. New York: Routledge, 2011.

Schneider, Rebecca. "It Seems as if . . . I Am Dead: Zombie Capitalism and Theatrical Labor." *TDR: The Drama Review* 56, no. 4 (2012): 150–62.

Schneider, Rebecca, and Lucia Ruprecht. "In Our Hands: An Ethics of Gestural Response-ability." *Performance Philosophy* 3, no. 1 (2017): 108–25.

Scott, Darieck. *Extravagant Abjection: Blackness, Power, and Sexuality in the African American Literary Imagination*. New York: NYU Press, 2010.

Shah, Nayan. *Contagious Divides: Epidemics and Race in San Francisco's Chinatown*. Berkeley: University of California Press, 2001.

Shotwell, A. *Against Purity: Living Ethically in Compromised Times*. Minneapolis: University of Minnesota Press, 2016.

Siebers, Tobin. *Disability Theory*. Ann Arbor: University of Michigan Press, 2008.

Sills, Ben, and Emma Ross-Thomas. "Spain Should Take Toxic Assets off Banks' Books, Montoro Says." Bloomberg, July 9, 2012. http://www.bloomberg.com/news/2012-07-09/spain-should-take-toxic-assets-off-banks-books-montoro-says.html.

Smout, Chris T. "The Alien Species in 20th-Century Britain: Constructing a New Vermin." *Landscape Research* 29, no. 1 (2003): 11–20.

Snaza, Nathan, and Julietta Singh, eds. "Introduction: Dehumanist Education and the Colonial University." In *Educational Undergrowth* (special issue), edited by Nathan Snaza and Julietta Singh. *Social Text* 39, no. 1 (2021): 1–19.

State of Queensland Department of Environment and Science. "About Fraser Island Dingoes." https://parks.des.qld.gov.au/parks/fraser/fraser-island-dingoes.html.

Stein, Isaac. "A Disability Story." *Disability Studies Quarterly* 30, no. 2 (2010).

Stewart, Jacqueline Najuma. "What Happened in the Transition? Reading Race, Gender and Labor between the Shots." In *American Cinema's Transitional Era: Audiences, Institutions, Practices*, edited by Charles Keil and Shelley Stamp. Los Angeles: University of California Press, 2004.

Subramaniam, Banu. "The Aliens Have Landed! Reflections on the Rhetoric of Biological Invasions." *Meridians: Feminism, Race, Transnationalism* 2, no. 1 (2001): 26–40.

Subramaniam, Banu. *Ghost Stories for Darwin: The Science of Variation and the Politics of Diversity*. Urbana: University of Illinois Press, 2014.

TallBear, Kim. "Genomic Articulations of Indigeneity." *Social Studies of Science* 43, no. 4 (August 2013): 509–33.

TallBear, Kim. *Native American DNA: Tribal Belonging and the False Promise of Genetic Science*. Minneapolis: University of Minnesota, 2013.

TallBear, Kim. "Tell Me a Story: Genomics vs. Indigenous Origin Narratives." *GeneWatch* 26, no. 4 (August/October 2013); reprinted at https://kimtallbear.substack.com/p/tell-me-a-story-genomics-vs-indigenous.

Teng, Ssu-yü, and John Fairbank, eds. *China's Response to the West: A Documentary Survey, 1839–1923*. Cambridge, MA: Harvard University Press, 1954–1979.

Terry, Jennifer. *Attachments to War: Biomedical Logics and Violence in Twenty-First-Century America*. Durham, NC: Duke University Press, 2017.

Terry, Jennifer. "Woundscapes of War in the 21st Century." Paper presented at the University of California, Berkeley, Department of Geography Colloquium Series, November 13, 2012.

Thornton, Margaret, and Trish Luker. "The Wages of Sin: Compensation for Indigenous Workers." *University of New South Wales Law Journal* 32, no. 3 (2009): 647–73.

Tompkins, Kyla Wazana. *Racial Indigestion: Eating Bodies in the 19th Century*. Durham, NC: Duke University Press, 2012.

Trometter, Alyssa. *Aboriginal Black Power and the Rise of the Australian Black Panther Party, 1967–1972*. Cham: Palgrave Macmillan, 2022.

Tuck, Eve. "An Indigenous Feminist's Take on the Ontological Turn: 'Ontology' Is Just Another Word for Colonialism." *Journal of Historical Sociology* 29, no. 1 (2016): 4–22.

Tuck, Eve. "Suspending Damage: A Letter to Communities." *Harvard Educational Review* 79, no. 3 (2009): 409–28.

"Two Tables and a Ladder: What Could Go Wrong?" Reddit. https://www.reddit.com/r/Whatcouldgowrong/comments/76v85p/two_tables_and_a_ladder_what_could_go_wrong/.

Williams, Raymond. *Keywords: A Vocabulary of Culture and Society*. Oxford: Oxford University Press, 1976.

Wolfe, Patrick, ed. *The Settler Complex: Recuperating Binarism in Colonial Studies*. Los Angeles: UCLA American Indian Studies Center, 2016.

Wolfe, Patrick. *Traces of History: Elementary Structures of Race*. London: Verso, 2016.

Wu, Cynthia. *Chang and Eng Reconnected: The Original Siamese Twins in American Culture*. Philadelphia: Temple University Press, 2012.

Wu, Cynthia. "Disability." In *Keywords for Asian American Studies*, edited by Cathy J. Schlund-Vials, Linda Trinh Võ, and Kevin Scott Wong. New York: NYU Press, 2015.

Wynter, Sylvia. "Unsettling the Coloniality of Being/Power/Truth/Freedom: Towards the Human, after Man, Its Overrepresentation—An Argument." *CR: The New Centennial Review* 3, no. 3 (Fall 2003): 257–337.

Yergeau, M. Remi. *Authoring Autism: On Rhetoric and Neurological Queerness*. Durham, NC: Duke University Press, 2018.

Zheng, Yangwen. *The Social Life of Opium in China*. Cambridge: Cambridge University Press, 2005.

INDEX

Aboriginal people, 2, 93-94, 144, 145, 172n10, 173n28, 173n35; and Blackness, 117-18; considered in and around Foley's *Black Opium*, 106-24, 136-38; racialization, 2, 117
Aboriginals Protection and Restriction of the Sale of Opium Act, 2, 107, 116, 124
access, 15, 21, 43-44, 79, 148, 160, 167n4
affect, 5, 6, 7, 14, 29, 65-66, 74, 85, 90, 100, 103, 155, 171n2, 175n12
agitation, 10, 12, 13, 22, 63-124, 136-41; animacy, 43; in context of Blackness and agency, 69-70; emergent, 105; gesture, 70-72; intention, 70, 72; queer life and, 99; terminological use, 68-71; in university, 104-5; whiteness, 82-88
Ah Chie, 119-20
air, 86, 88, 91-98, 103, 148-54; and ash, 92-93
Alexander, M. Jacqui, 60
alterlife, 10, 163
American Disabilities Act, 7, 14, 54, 160
American Disabled for Attendant Programs (ADAPT), 88
argument, 15-16, 63-64, 91
ash, 92-99, 107-8, 115, 124, 138, 143, 144, 151
Asianness, 2, 10, 13-14; in context of Down, 19, 21, 22, 31, 33-34, 38-42, 61, 76-77, 83, 87, 106, 137-38, 148, 150-54, 166n2, 172n16

Badtjala, 111, 112, 171
Bailey, Moya, 13
Bell, Chris, 13
Bergson, Henri, 63-64, 66, 72, 73-75, 82

Berlant, Lauren, 53, 90
Bey, Marquis, 121
Bierria, Alisa, 69-71, 174-75n7
biochemical process, 28, 34-35, 52, 58, 73, 78, 81, 150
Black Opium (Foley), 10, 101, 106-18, 136-39
Black study, 117-18
Blumenbach, Johann F., 23, 60
blur, 19, 39, 48, 49, 116, 118, 139, 158, 161. *See also* indistinction
bodily insurgency, 78, 81
Borthwick, Chris, 26
Bow, Leslie, 14
brain fog, 124-31, 161
Brisbane Magistrates Court, 93, 97, 109
Brooks, Daphne, 81
Brooks, Max, 54
Brown, Lydia, 14
Bruce, LaMarr Jurelle, 76
Brugman, Claudia, 159

capacity, 4, 8, 28, 29, 30, 56, 57, 80, 86, 114, 122, 127, 133, 134; and Asianness, 31; and capital, 45, 47, 49
Carlson, Licia, 30
Cavarero, Adriana, 71
chemical intimacy, 2, 5, 12, 151, 174n3
chemicality, 5, 6, 7, 30, 66, 76, 80, 86, 87, 88, 101, 102
chemical restraint, 24, 41, 68
chemosociality, 118, 130-31
Chinatown, 9, 39, 60, 134, 144, 154

Chinese, 2, 6, 39–42, 60, 107–9, 115, 118–21, 123, 136–38, 144, 146
Chinese language, 143, 163
Choy, Tim, 91, 147, 175n9
Christian, Barbara, 135
chronicity, 41, 61, 127, 133, 134, 167n15
Chuh, Kandice, 11, 139
ciscognators, 131
climate change, 11, 149, 156, 163
coevalness, 28; and Asianness, 22
Collapse theory, 90
colonialism, 25, 44, 52, 82, 97, 113, 117, 137, 138, 150, 159, 167–68n24
comedy, 66–68, 73–75, 78, 81, 82–87
compassion, 21–22, 55, 63, 85, 109, 148
constitution, 8, 9, 12, 34–35, 37, 58, 62, 80, 88, 91, 126, 133, 138; by policy, 42–44; scope of, 28–31; slow constitution, 60
Courting Blakness, 172n10
COVID-19, 6, 14, 47, 85–86, 92, 103, 124, 147–53, 158, 162

damage-based research, 10, 44
da Silva, Denise Ferreira, 30, 53
Dayan, Colin, 172n8
debility, 6–7, 11, 22, 72, 73, 74, 76, 116, 133, 136, 161; agitative, 81; and chronicity, 41; conditioning muscularity, 77–78; vs. disability, 6, 45–46; and finance capital, 45–48; and zombie life, 48–56
De Kosnik, Abigail, 90, 173n25
delay, 9, 25, 27, 30, 33, 37–38, 58, 60, 102
Deleuze and Guattari, 99
Demolition d'un mur, 170n38
development, 10, 26–30, 35, 102, 120, 140, 159; and education, 102; and narrative logic, 61; and sexuality, 27, 131
differential being, 101–2, 129, 140, 149
dingoes, 112–13
disability: vs. debility, 6, 45–46; selective entitlement of, 103; and undergrowth, 102
distributed cognition, 121–22
Down, John Langdon, 4, 18, 20, 25, 30, 145
Down syndrome, 9, 18–19, 24–27, 30–31, 34, 36, 37, 59, 60, 166n1. *See also* mongoloid idiocy
Duong, Natalia, 14, 174n3

Earlswood Asylum, 143; as Royal Earlswood Park, 145
eating: reflections on the scene and materiality of, 88; and zombies, 49–51
edge, 155–56
end times, 101, 147, 155
environmentalization, 48, 63, 66, 80, 87
epistemology, 124, 126, 131, 135–38
Erevelles, Nirmala, 13, 169n1
Estreich, George, 31, 60, 61

Fabian, Johannes, 28, 100
Fabris, Erick, 68
Fanon, Frantz, 72, 77
Flint, Michigan, 43, 80
Foley, Fiona, 10, 13, 66, 88, 93–97, 107–19, 137–38
Foley, Gary, 117
Freeman, Elizabeth, 41, 169n1
Fuss, Diana, 154

gesture, 66, 68, 70–81, 104; and intentionality, 72
Glissant, Édouard, 172n7
Goldberg-Hiller, Jonathan, 113
Graeber, David, 53
Gristwood, Helen, 23, 167n10

Halberstam, Jack, 67, 85, 95
Haraway, Donna, 135
Harrison, Mark, 29
Hartman, Saidiya, 43
Hatch, Anthony Ryan, 68
Hayward, Eva, 131
health, and economy, 45, 47
Hennefeld, Maggie, 86
Herring, Scott, 85, 170n40
Huang, Michelle, 14
Hutchins, Edward, 132

inanimate identification, 163
indistinction, 6, 136–37, 139; vs. distinction, 161. *See also* blur
inhumanism, 78, 131–32; and agitation, 102
inside/outside, 154–55
interconnectedness, 89–91; and unlearning, 90
intoxicated method, 64, 132–36, 138–40

Johnson, Merri, 126

Kafer, Alison, 36, 167n17
Kang, Laura Hyun Yi, 47
Kevles, Daniel, 26, 30
K'gari (Fraser Island), 93, 111, 112, 171n53
Khúc, Mimi, 14
Kidd, Rosalind, 137
Kim, Eunjung, 14, 55, 166n17
Kim, Jina, 14, 169n61
King, Tiffany Lethabo, 117
Kinsey, Charles, 79–80
Kirksey, Eben, 36, 118–19

Langdon Down Centre, 20, 25
Laughing Gas, 86–87
Lee, James Kyung-jin, 14
Letter of Advice to Queen Victoria, 39–41
Link-Up, 114, 145–46
Lin Tse-Hsu, 39, 41–42, 138, 143
London, 9, 20, 23, 39, 40, 60
Luciano, Dana, 171n2
Lunacy Acts of 1845, 142

Mabo, Eddie Koiki, 121
Martin-Chew, Louise, 172n10
Mask Oakland, 153
Matlock, Teenie, 159
McKittrick, Katherine, 3
McMillan, Uri, 73
McRuer, Robert, 56, 126
Meekosha, Helen, 172n16
method, 3, 11, 15–16, 21, 22, 29, 38, 43, 60, 64, 90. *See also* intoxicated method
metonymies. *See* subordinated metonymies
Metzl, Jonathan, 77
Minh-ha, Trinh T., 28
Mobley, Izetta Autumn, 13
molarity, 99
molecularity, 37, 38, 98
Mongoloid, 24, 29, 34, 42; terminology, 20, 26, 166nn1–2
mongoloid idiocy, 2, 9, 18, 37, 58
Montoro, Cristobal, 47
Moore, Leroy, 13

Moten, Fred, 117, 166n19
Murphy, Michelle, 5, 10

Narveah, 119–20
Nelson, Alondra, 13, 77
neurodiversity, 65; and learning, 64; and reading, 65
Nicoll, Fiona, 118, 172n10, 173n32
Normansfield Asylum, 20–21
nothing, 15–16, 149, 163
nothingness, 91
notion, 11, 22, 28–29, 43, 103
Nyong'o, Tavia, 49

opium: Down syndrome diagnostic, 37; institutional use, 43; likeness to slowness, 37; use in China, 42; wars, 39, 41, 42, 138, 143–44

Perret, Mai-Thu, 156–57
Pickens, Therí Alyce, 13
Price, Margaret, 129
Probyn, Elspeth, 51
pronouns, 16, 163
Puar, Jasbir, 6, 13, 46, 53, 56, 135

Queensland, Australia, 124, 138, 144, 174n40
Queensland State Library, 106–7
Queen Victoria, 39, 133, 143, 144
queerness, 16, 32, 46, 57; and Asianness, 33; and blurring, 160
queer reproductivity, and linear transgenerational heredity, 25; queer density, 58–59; and sterilization, 35; and toxic assets, 46

racialization of Aboriginal people, 2, 117
racial tuning, 9, 35; within constitution, 60
Regustus, Bertha, 86–88
Rios, Arnaldo, 79–80

Samuels, Ellen, 12, 13, 166n17
Schalk, Sami, 13
Schneider, Rebecca, 71–72, 74
Schweik, Susan, 160
Scott, Darieck, 77
Scott, Keith Lamont, 78–79

security, 68–82; and chemical restraint, 68; and inhumanism, 78; and schooling, 69
Shah, Nayan, 154
Shomura, Chad, 14
Siebers, Tobin, 73
Silva, Noenoe K., 113
Singh, Julietta, 102, 103, 140
slowness, 9–10, 12, 19, 37, 48, 61, 62, 65, 66, 99, 101, 103, 136; approach to, 27–31; materiality, 80; opiate affectivity, 37, 42, 58, 76, 118, 121; racial loading of, 70; in relation to speed, 63; in the university, 124, 139; zombies, 53–56
Slow Worker Clause, 121–23
Snaza, Nathan, 102, 103, 107
species, 57, 89, 101, 152, 155; animals and settler colonialism, 113–14; and constitution, 29–30; environment, 78, 131, 150; and inhumanity, 163; and primate impression, 82; and reproductivity, 7
speed, vs. slowness, 63
Stein, Isaac, 55
Stewart, Jacqueline Najuma, 86
subordinated metonymies, 5

TallBear, Kim, 36, 98
temporality, inhuman of opium, 34; of narrative, 60
Terry, Jennifer, 129
Tompkins, Kyla Wazana, 171n48
Torres Strait Islander, 2, 107, 108, 114, 116, 118, 119, 121, 136, 137, 138, 144, 145

toxic assets, 44–52; human stand-ins for, 47; as queer / racial, 46. *See also* toxicity
toxicity, 4–7, 11, 19, 20, 35, 37, 80, 128, 131, 132–33. *See also* toxic assets
trans, 16, 17, 70, 152, 153, 163; trans studies, 131
Tuck, Eve, 43–44
"Two Tables and a Ladder: What Could Go Wrong?," 83–84

underground, the, 156–60
undergrowth, 102–4
unlearning, 116–17
US Capitol, January 6, 2021 occupation of, 87–88

What Could Go Wrong videos, 83–86; and death, 85
white Mongol, 25, 59, 143
whiteness, 85–86, 135, 148
William Hung, 31–34
Williams, Raymond, 74
Witnessing to Silence, 93–98
Wolfe, Patrick, 117
Wu, Cynthia, 13, 14
Wynter, Sylvia, 139, 152

Xombi, 56–57, 159

Zhang, Yangwen, 42
zombies, 48–57; and eating, 49–51; and indebtedness to Vodou, 48–49